The Fundamentals of Customer Service

M L Rusciak

Trient Press
3375 S Rainbow Blvd
#81710, SMB 13135
Las Vegas,NV 89180

Ordering Information:
Quantity sales. Special discounts are available on quantity purchases by corporations, associations, and others. For details, contact the publisher at the address above.
Orders by U.S. trade bookstores and wholesalers. Please contact Trient Press: Tel: (775) 996-3844; or visit www.trientpress.com.

Printed in the United States of America

Publisher's Cataloging-in-Publication data
Ruscsak, M.L.
A title of a book : The Fundamentals of Customer Service
ISBN
Hard Cover   979-8-88990-001-6

Paper Back   979-8-88990-002-3

Ebook   979-8-88990-003-0

PART 1:
FOUNDATIONS OF
CUSTOMER SERVICE:

Customer service is a fundamental aspect of any successful business. It is the process of providing quality service and support to customers before, during, and after the purchase of a product or service. Customer service is not only about addressing customer concerns, but also about building relationships with them. This introduction to customer service will provide a thorough understanding of the fundamentals of customer service, its importance in business, and the basics of understanding customers.

The Importance of Customer Service in Business

In today's competitive business environment, providing exceptional customer service is more important than ever before. It has become a key differentiator that separates successful businesses from those that struggle. Customers expect more than just a quality product or service; they want an exceptional customer experience. Providing excellent customer service can result in customer loyalty, positive word-of-mouth advertising, and increased revenue.

For example, let's consider a small retail store that sells clothes. If the store provides excellent customer service, customers are more likely to return for future purchases and recommend the store to others. On the other hand, if the store provides poor customer service, customers are more likely to take their business elsewhere, resulting in lost revenue.

Understanding Your Customers

One of the keys to providing exceptional customer service is understanding your customers. This involves understanding their needs, wants, preferences, and expectations. Customers come from a wide range of backgrounds, with varying levels of knowledge and experience. It is important to approach each customer as an individual and tailor the service to their needs.

For example, let's consider a customer who has just purchased a new smartphone. The sales associate should take the time to understand the customer's level of knowledge about the device and provide them with appropriate support and guidance. If the customer is a tech-savvy individual, they may require less assistance than someone who is less familiar with technology.

Effective communication is also key in understanding customers. It involves not only listening to their needs and concerns but also conveying information clearly and effectively. Good communication helps to build trust and establish a positive relationship with customers.

Conclusion

In conclusion, providing excellent customer service is an essential aspect of running a successful business. It involves understanding the needs and preferences of customers, providing them with the appropriate support and guidance, and communicating effectively with them. Understanding the importance of customer service and how to provide exceptional service is crucial for any individual seeking a career in customer service. In the following chapters, we will dive deeper into the fundamental principles of customer service and explore various techniques and strategies to provide exceptional service to customers.

CHAPTER 1: INTRODUCTION TO CUSTOMER SERVICE

Customer service is a fundamental aspect of any successful business. In today's competitive marketplace, providing excellent customer service is essential to differentiate yourself from competitors and retain customers. This chapter will introduce the concept of customer service, define key terms, and explain why it is crucial for businesses of all types and sizes. Additionally, this chapter will discuss the benefits of providing exceptional customer service and explain how customer service impacts business performance.

What is Customer Service?

Customer service is a broad term that refers to any interaction between a customer and a business. It can take many forms, including face-to-face interactions, phone conversations, emails, and online chat sessions. In essence, customer service is about meeting the needs and expectations of customers and ensuring their satisfaction with a product or service.

Defining Key Terms:

Before diving deeper into the topic of customer service, it's important to define key terms that will be used throughout this chapter and the rest of the textbook. These terms include customer satisfaction, customer loyalty, customer experience, and customer engagement.

Customer Satisfaction: Customer satisfaction is the measure of how well a product or service meets the expectations of the customer. It is typically measured through surveys and other feedback mechanisms.

Customer Loyalty: Customer loyalty is the degree to which a customer repeatedly buys from a particular business or brand. Loyal customers are more likely to recommend a business to others, providing free advertising and referrals.

Customer Experience: Customer experience refers to the sum of all interactions between a customer and a business. It includes all aspects of a customer's journey, from the initial awareness of a brand to post-purchase follow-up.

Customer Engagement: Customer engagement is the degree to which a customer is invested in a particular brand or business. Engaged customers are more likely to be loyal and recommend a business to others.

Why is Customer Service Important?
Customer service is critical for business success for several reasons. Firstly, it can differentiate a business from its competitors. In today's competitive marketplace, providing excellent customer service can be the key factor that sets a business apart from its competitors. Secondly, it can lead to increased customer satisfaction and loyalty. Customers who have positive experiences with a business are more likely to continue doing business with them and recommend them to others. Finally, it can lead to increased revenue and profitability. Satisfied and loyal customers are more likely to spend more money and make repeat purchases, leading to increased revenue and profitability for the business.

Conclusion:
In conclusion, customer service is an essential aspect of any business. Providing excellent customer service can differentiate a business from its competitors, increase customer satisfaction and loyalty, and lead to increased revenue and profitability. As this textbook explores the principles and practices of customer service, it's important to keep these key concepts in mind.

Defining customer service

Customer service is a term that has been used in business for decades, and it is often used interchangeably with other terms such as customer support, customer experience, and customer satisfaction. However, customer service is a distinct concept that refers to the specific actions that a business takes to meet the needs of its customers. In this section, we will explore the definition of customer service and the key elements that make up this important aspect of business.

What is Customer Service?

At its core, customer service is the process of providing support, assistance, and guidance to customers before, during, and after a purchase. It encompasses everything that a business does to ensure that its customers are satisfied with their experience, including answering questions, resolving problems, and providing information about products or services.

While customer service is often associated with traditional customer-facing roles such as sales and support, it is important to note that customer service is relevant to every aspect of a business. From the production line to the executive suite, every employee has a role to play in delivering exceptional customer service.

Key Elements of Customer Service

To understand the key elements of customer service, it is helpful to break down the process into its component parts. These elements include:

Understanding Customer Needs: The first step in providing exceptional customer service is to understand the needs of your customers. This includes everything from understanding their preferences and purchasing habits to identifying their pain points and areas where your business can improve.

Clear Communication: Effective communication is critical in providing exceptional customer service. This includes clear and concise messaging, active listening, and the ability to provide accurate and helpful information.

Timely Response: Customers expect prompt and efficient service. This means responding to inquiries quickly and providing timely updates on the status of a request or order.

Problem Solving: Customers may encounter problems or issues with a product or service, and it is essential to have a process in place to address these concerns. This includes identifying the problem, developing a solution, and communicating the resolution to the customer.

Follow-up: Following up with customers is an important part of customer service. This includes checking in after a sale, soliciting feedback, and addressing any outstanding issues or concerns.

In conclusion, customer service is an essential component of any successful business. It involves understanding customer needs, clear communication, timely response, problem-solving, and follow-up. By focusing on these key elements, businesses can deliver exceptional customer service and build strong, lasting relationships with their customers.

Why customer service matters

Customer service is a critical component of any successful business, and it is an essential factor in retaining customers and maintaining customer loyalty. In today's increasingly competitive marketplace, businesses that fail to provide outstanding customer service will struggle to survive. This chapter will explore why customer service matters and how it can impact a business's success.

Customer Retention

One of the primary reasons why customer service is crucial to a business's success is that it plays a critical role in customer retention. Customers who receive excellent customer service are more likely to remain loyal to a business and continue to make purchases in the future. In contrast, customers who receive poor customer service are more likely to take their business elsewhere. Businesses that prioritize customer service and go above and beyond to ensure customer satisfaction are more likely to retain customers and benefit from their repeat business.

Word-of-Mouth Marketing

Another critical reason why customer service matters is that it can impact a business's reputation and lead to positive word-of-mouth marketing. Customers who receive exceptional customer service are more likely to recommend a business to their friends and family, which can lead to new customers and increased revenue. On the other hand, customers who receive poor customer service are likely to share their negative experiences with others, which can damage a business's reputation and lead to lost sales.

Competitive Advantage

Providing excellent customer service can also give a business a competitive advantage. In today's marketplace, where many businesses offer similar products and services, customer service can be the deciding factor that sets a business apart from its competitors. Businesses that prioritize customer service and provide outstanding experiences are more likely to win customers over and gain a competitive edge.

Customer Lifetime Value

Customer service can also impact a business's customer lifetime value, which is the total amount of money a customer is expected to spend on a business's products or services over the course of their lifetime. Customers who receive exceptional customer service are more likely to continue doing business with a company, which can lead to increased lifetime value. On the other hand, customers who receive poor customer service are likely to stop doing business with a company, which can result in lost revenue and decreased lifetime value.

Conclusion

In conclusion, customer service is critical to a business's success for many reasons. It impacts customer retention, word-of-mouth marketing, competitive advantage, and customer lifetime value. Businesses that prioritize customer service and go above and beyond to ensure customer satisfaction are more likely to succeed and thrive in today's competitive marketplace.

The benefits of providing excellent customer service

In today's competitive business world, companies that provide excellent customer service are more likely to succeed and grow than those that don't. This section will explore the benefits of providing excellent customer service and how it can improve a company's bottom line.

Increased Customer Loyalty

One of the biggest benefits of providing excellent customer service is increased customer loyalty. When customers receive excellent service, they are more likely to remain loyal to a company and continue to purchase its products or services. According to a study by the White House Office of Consumer Affairs, loyal customers are worth up to 10 times as much as their first purchase. This means that investing in excellent customer service can lead to increased revenue in the long term.

Word of Mouth Marketing

Another benefit of providing excellent customer service is the power of word-of-mouth marketing. Satisfied customers are more likely to tell their friends, family, and colleagues about their positive experience with a company. This can lead to new customers and increased revenue without additional marketing expenses. In fact, a study by the Temkin Group found that customers are 4 times more likely to refer a friend to a company if they have an excellent customer service experience.

Increased Sales and Revenue

Providing excellent customer service can also lead to increased sales and revenue. Customers who receive excellent service are more likely to make repeat purchases and spend more money on those purchases. They are also more likely to purchase additional products or services from the same company. According to a study by McKinsey, customers who are highly satisfied with their experience are 73% more likely to purchase again and 88% more likely to recommend the company to others.

Reduced Costs

Providing excellent customer service can also lead to reduced costs for a company. Happy customers are less likely to return products or complain about their experience, which can reduce the costs associated with returns and refunds. In addition, satisfied customers are less likely to require extensive support or assistance, which can reduce the costs associated with customer service operations.

Improved Employee Morale and Retention

Another benefit of providing excellent customer service is improved employee morale and retention. When employees are able to provide excellent service and make customers happy, they are more likely to feel a sense of pride in their work and job satisfaction. This can lead to reduced turnover rates and lower recruitment costs. In addition, happy employees are more likely to provide excellent service, leading to a positive feedback loop of satisfied customers and happy employees.

Conclusion

In conclusion, providing excellent customer service can have numerous benefits for a company. From increased customer loyalty and word-of-mouth marketing to increased sales and revenue, reduced costs, and improved employee morale and retention, excellent customer service is a crucial component of any successful business. Companies that invest in customer service are more likely to succeed in the long term, while those that neglect it are at risk of falling behind their competitors.

What makes a good customer service representative

Customer service representatives are the frontline employees who interact with customers, representing the face of the organization. They must have a range of skills, including the ability to listen, communicate effectively, and solve problems, all while projecting a positive image of the company. In this section, we will examine some of the key qualities and characteristics that make a good customer service representative.

Strong Communication Skills
Effective communication is essential in the customer service industry. Customer service representatives must be able to convey information clearly, actively listen to customers' needs, and respond to questions and concerns in a way that is easily understandable. They must also be able to communicate effectively across various mediums, including phone, email, chat, and in-person.

Empathy
Empathy is the ability to understand and share the feelings of others. In the context of customer service, this means the ability to put oneself in the customer's shoes and see things from their perspective. Good customer service representatives are empathetic and able to connect with customers on a personal level. They understand that customers are not just a number but real people with real problems.

11

Patience

Patience is a crucial skill for customer service representatives. They must be able to handle difficult situations, such as angry or upset customers, without losing their cool. They must be able to remain calm, composed, and professional, even in the face of challenging interactions.

Problem-solving skills

Customer service representatives must be able to think critically and solve problems quickly. They must be able to analyze a situation and come up with a solution that meets the customer's needs while still aligning with the organization's policies and procedures.

Time Management

Customer service representatives must be able to balance multiple tasks and prioritize their workload. They must be able to manage their time effectively to ensure that they can respond to customers' needs in a timely and efficient manner.

Product and Service Knowledge

To provide excellent customer service, representatives must have a deep understanding of the products and services offered by their organization. They must be able to answer questions accurately and provide helpful information to customers. It's important to note that knowledge can be gained through training and experience, so it's not necessarily a requirement for every new employee.

Positive Attitude

A positive attitude can go a long way in the customer service industry. Good customer service representatives are friendly, approachable, and enthusiastic about their job. They project a positive image of the company, and this can be infectious, making customers feel good about their interactions with the organization.

Adaptability

The ability to adapt to changing situations is crucial in the customer service industry. Good customer service representatives can adjust their approach based on the customer's needs and the situation at hand. They are flexible and able to handle unexpected changes in a professional and efficient manner.

Attention to Detail

Customer service representatives must pay attention to the details of each interaction. They must be able to accurately record information, follow up on promises, and ensure that the customer's needs are met. Good customer service representatives are detail-oriented, ensuring that nothing falls through the cracks.

In conclusion, providing excellent customer service requires a combination of skills, knowledge, and attitude. Good customer service representatives have strong communication skills, empathy, patience, problem-solving skills, time management skills, product and service knowledge, a positive attitude, adaptability, and attention to detail. By possessing these qualities, customer service representatives can deliver exceptional service that meets the needs of their customers and enhances the reputation of their organization.

CHAPTER 2: THE IMPORTANCE OF CUSTOMER SERVICE IN BUSINESS

In today's competitive business environment, providing exceptional customer service has become more critical than ever. Businesses that focus on delivering an outstanding customer experience have a competitive advantage over those that don't. Studies show that customers are more likely to do business with a company that provides excellent customer service, and they are also more likely to recommend that company to others.

This chapter will explore the importance of customer service in business. We will examine why customer service matters, the benefits of providing excellent customer service, and what makes a good customer service representative. By the end of this chapter, you will have a thorough understanding of why customer service is so crucial in today's business world.

Why Customer Service Matters

Customer service is the act of providing assistance and support to customers before, during, and after a purchase. It encompasses a range of activities, from answering questions about a product or service to handling complaints and resolving issues.

Customer service matters for several reasons. First, it is a crucial factor in customer satisfaction. When customers have a positive experience with a company's customer service team, they are more likely to be satisfied with their overall experience and more likely to become loyal customers. On the other hand, when customers have a negative experience with customer service, they are less likely to do business with that company in the future.

Second, customer service is essential for customer retention. Customers who have a positive experience with a company's customer service are more likely to continue doing business with that company. In contrast, customers who have a negative experience are more likely to switch to a competitor.

Third, customer service is critical for generating positive word-of-mouth. Customers who have a positive experience with customer service are more likely to recommend that company to others. This can result in new business and increased revenue.

Finally, customer service is essential for identifying and resolving issues. By listening to customer feedback and addressing concerns, companies can identify areas for improvement and make necessary changes to products, services, and processes.

The Benefits of Providing Excellent Customer Service

Providing excellent customer service has several benefits for businesses. First, it can lead to increased customer loyalty. When customers have a positive experience with a company's customer service team, they are more likely to become loyal customers. Loyal customers are more likely to do repeat business, and they are also more likely to recommend that company to others.

Second, providing excellent customer service can lead to increased revenue. Customers who have a positive experience with a company's customer service are more likely to spend more money with that company over time. Additionally, they are more likely to recommend that company to others, which can result in new business and increased revenue.

Third, providing excellent customer service can help businesses differentiate themselves from competitors. In today's crowded marketplace, businesses need to find ways to stand out. Providing exceptional customer service can help a company create a competitive advantage.

Fourth, providing excellent customer service can help businesses identify and resolve issues. By listening to customer feedback and addressing concerns, companies can identify areas for improvement and make necessary changes to products, services, and processes. This can lead to increased customer satisfaction and loyalty, as well as improved business operations.

What Makes a Good Customer Service Representative

A good customer service representative possesses several key qualities that enable them to provide exceptional service to customers. First, they must have excellent communication skills. This includes both verbal and written communication skills, as well as active listening skills. A good customer service representative should be able to clearly communicate information and ideas to customers, as well as listen actively to their concerns.

Second, a good customer service representative should be empathetic. They should be able to put themselves in the customer's shoes and understand their perspective. This enables them to provide more personalized and effective service to each customer.

Third, a good customer service representative should be patient and have a positive attitude. Customers may be frustrated or upset, and a good representative should be able to remain calm and maintain a positive demeanor in order to diffuse any tension or negative feelings.

Fourth, a good customer service representative should be knowledgeable about the products or services they are providing support for. They should be able to answer any questions or concerns a customer may have, and be able to provide clear and accurate information.

Fifth, a good customer service representative should be problem-solvers. They should be able to think critically and creatively to find solutions to customer issues and concerns, and be willing to go above and beyond to ensure customer satisfaction.

Sixth, a good customer service representative should be organized and efficient. They should be able to manage their time effectively in order to handle multiple tasks and inquiries from customers, while also maintaining accurate records and documentation of customer interactions.

Finally, a good customer service representative should be adaptable and flexible. They should be able to quickly adjust to changes in procedures or customer needs, and be open to learning new skills and techniques to improve their performance.

In order to select and train effective customer service representatives, businesses should develop clear job descriptions outlining the required skills and qualities, and conduct thorough interviews and assessments to evaluate candidates. Training programs should also focus on developing and honing these key skills, through a combination of classroom instruction, role-playing exercises, and on-the-job training.

In addition to the benefits of providing excellent customer service, there are also significant costs associated with poor customer service. Dissatisfied customers may share their negative experiences with others, resulting in lost sales and damaged reputation for the business. Furthermore, the cost of acquiring new customers is often significantly higher than retaining existing customers, making it crucial for businesses to prioritize customer service as a key component of their overall strategy.

In the next section, we will explore the various ways in which businesses can measure and assess customer satisfaction, and the importance of using this feedback to continually improve the customer experience.

The impact of customer service on customer loyalty and retention

The success of any business is dependent on customer loyalty and retention. It is crucial for businesses to understand the impact of customer service on customer loyalty and retention. In this section, we will explore the concept of customer loyalty and retention, and how customer service plays a vital role in it.

Customer Loyalty and Retention

Customer loyalty refers to the willingness of customers to repeatedly buy products or services from a particular company. It is the result of a positive customer experience, which leads to a relationship between the customer and the business. Loyalty is not only reflected in the frequency of purchases but also in the customer's willingness to recommend the business to others.

Customer retention refers to the ability of a company to retain its customers over a period of time. Retaining customers is important as it leads to long-term revenue and growth for the company. Studies have shown that it costs more to acquire a new customer than to retain an existing one. Therefore, companies that focus on customer retention are more likely to be successful in the long run.

The Role of Customer Service in Customer Loyalty and Retention

Customer service plays a vital role in customer loyalty and retention. Customers who have positive experiences with customer service are more likely to remain loyal to the company. A good customer service experience creates a positive emotional connection with the company, which in turn leads to customer loyalty.

On the other hand, a negative customer service experience can lead to customer dissatisfaction, and customers may switch to a competitor. Studies have shown that customers who have had a bad customer service experience are more likely to share their experience with others, which can have a negative impact on the company's reputation.

Examples of Customer Service Impact on Loyalty and Retention

Let's take a look at some examples of how customer service impacts customer loyalty and retention in various industries.

Retail Industry: A customer visits a retail store looking for a particular product. The sales associate takes the time to understand the customer's needs and recommends a product that fits their requirements. The customer has a positive experience and is more likely to return to the store for future purchases.

Hospitality Industry: A customer checks into a hotel and is greeted by the front desk staff with a warm smile and welcoming attitude. The customer is impressed with the level of service and is more likely to return to the hotel for future stays.

Banking Industry: A customer contacts the bank's customer service department to resolve an issue with their account. The customer service representative listens attentively and resolves the issue quickly and efficiently. The customer is satisfied with the level of service and is more likely to remain a customer of the bank.

Conclusion

In conclusion, customer service plays a critical role in customer loyalty and retention. A good customer service experience creates a positive emotional connection with the company, which leads to customer loyalty. Conversely, a negative customer service experience can lead to customer dissatisfaction and loss of business. Therefore, it is important for companies to invest in customer service training and ensure that their representatives have the necessary skills to provide exceptional service to customers. By doing so, they can build long-term relationships with customers, leading to increased revenue and growth for the company.

The link between customer service and revenue

The link between customer service and revenue is a crucial concept for any business owner or manager to understand. In short, providing excellent customer service can directly impact a company's revenue and overall success.

One study found that customers who had a positive experience with a company were more likely to make repeat purchases and spend more money than customers who had a negative experience. This is because satisfied customers are more likely to become loyal customers and recommend the company to others. In fact, the same study found that customers who had a positive experience were likely to tell nine other people about it, while those who had a negative experience were likely to tell sixteen other people. This means that providing excellent customer service not only helps retain existing customers, but can also lead to new business through word-of-mouth referrals.

On the other hand, poor customer service can have a detrimental effect on a company's revenue. A dissatisfied customer is likely to stop doing business with the company and may even write negative reviews or tell others about their negative experience, deterring potential customers from using the company's services or products. In fact, one study found that customers who had a negative experience were likely to tell twice as many people about it as customers who had a positive experience.

In addition to affecting revenue through customer retention and acquisition, customer service can also impact revenue by reducing costs. For example, a company that provides excellent customer service may have fewer returns or complaints, leading to lower costs associated with these issues. Additionally, satisfied customers are less likely to require costly marketing campaigns to attract new customers, as they are more likely to recommend the company to others.

It is important for companies to prioritize customer service in order to maximize revenue and success. This can be done by investing in training and resources for customer service representatives, regularly soliciting customer feedback and addressing any issues that arise, and implementing policies and procedures that prioritize the customer experience. By doing so, companies can reap the benefits of positive customer experiences and avoid the costs associated with negative experiences.

To reinforce this concept, students could participate in exercises that explore the impact of customer service on revenue, such as analyzing case studies of companies that have successfully leveraged customer service to increase revenue, or creating hypothetical scenarios where customer service plays a key role in business success. Additionally, students could be asked to develop strategies for improving customer service within a specific industry or company, taking into account the various factors that contribute to customer satisfaction and loyalty.

The role of customer service in brand reputation and marketing

In today's highly competitive business landscape, companies need to differentiate themselves from their competitors in order to succeed. One way they can do this is by providing excellent customer service. Not only does exceptional customer service lead to increased customer loyalty and retention, but it can also have a significant impact on a company's brand reputation and marketing efforts.

In this section, we will explore the role of customer service in brand reputation and marketing, and how businesses can leverage this to their advantage.

The Impact of Customer Service on Brand Reputation

A company's brand reputation is critical to its success. It can take years to build a positive reputation, but it can be quickly tarnished by a single negative experience. Customer service plays a critical role in shaping a company's brand reputation, as it is often the first point of contact between the customer and the company.

Excellent customer service can help to establish a positive brand reputation by creating a perception of the company as being customer-centric, responsive, and attentive to the needs of its customers. This can lead to increased brand loyalty, as customers are more likely to remain loyal to a company that they perceive as being customer-focused.

On the other hand, poor customer service can quickly damage a company's brand reputation. Negative customer experiences can lead to negative reviews, which can be shared on social media and other online platforms, potentially reaching millions of people. This can be particularly damaging in today's digital age, where negative reviews and comments can spread quickly and have a lasting impact on a company's brand reputation.

The Role of Customer Service in Marketing

Customer service can also play a critical role in a company's marketing efforts. A positive customer experience can lead to word-of-mouth referrals, which can be a powerful marketing tool. When customers are happy with a company's customer service, they are more likely to recommend that company to their friends and family.

In addition to word-of-mouth referrals, customer service can also play a role in online marketing efforts. Positive customer reviews can help to improve a company's online reputation, making it more attractive to potential customers who are researching the company online.

Furthermore, excellent customer service can help to build trust and credibility with potential customers, which can be particularly important in industries where there is a high degree of competition. When customers feel that they can trust a company, they are more likely to make a purchase or engage with that company in other ways.

Examples of the Impact of Customer Service on Brand Reputation and Marketing

To illustrate the impact of customer service on brand reputation and marketing, let's consider a few examples.

Example 1: Zappos

Zappos is an online shoe and clothing retailer that has built its reputation on providing exceptional customer service. The company is known for its free shipping and returns policy, as well as its 24/7 customer service hotline. Zappos' commitment to customer service has helped to establish the company as a leader in the online retail space, with a loyal customer base and a positive brand reputation.

Example 2: Nordstrom

Nordstrom is a high-end department store that has also built its reputation on exceptional customer service. The company's sales associates are trained to provide personalized service to each customer, and the company offers a generous return policy. Nordstrom's commitment to customer service has helped to establish it as a trusted and respected brand, with a loyal customer base and a strong reputation for quality.

Example 3: Apple

Apple is known for its sleek and innovative products, but the company's commitment to customer service has also played a role in its success. Apple's Genius Bar provides customers with technical support and assistance, and the company's customer service representatives are known for their knowledge and expertise. Apple's commitment to customer service has helped to establish the company as a leader in the technology industry, with a loyal customer base and a strong brand reputation.

Apple's customer service has also played a key role in the company's marketing strategy. The company's advertising campaigns often feature testimonials from satisfied customers, highlighting the quality of Apple's products as well as the company's commitment to customer service. These advertisements not only promote Apple's products but also reinforce the company's brand image as a customer-centric and innovative technology company.

In addition to traditional advertising, Apple also uses social media to connect with its customers and provide support. The company has a dedicated Twitter account for customer support, where customers can ask questions and receive assistance in real-time. This approach to customer service not only helps to resolve issues quickly but also demonstrates Apple's commitment to its customers and their satisfaction.

Apple's customer service also extends beyond its retail stores and technical support services. The company's website features a comprehensive support section that includes user manuals, troubleshooting guides, and a community forum where customers can connect with each other and share tips and advice. This approach to customer service helps to empower customers and foster a sense of community around Apple's products, which can in turn lead to increased brand loyalty and repeat business.

Overall, Apple's focus on customer service has helped to establish the company as a leader in the technology industry, with a strong brand reputation and a loyal customer base. By providing exceptional technical support and assistance, as well as empowering customers to troubleshoot and connect with each other, Apple has demonstrated a commitment to its customers that has helped to drive its success.

Examples of companies with exceptional customer service

Providing exceptional customer service can be a key differentiator for companies, helping to establish brand reputation, increase customer loyalty, and drive revenue. Many companies have recognized the importance of customer service and have implemented strategies to provide exceptional service to their customers. In this section, we will examine some examples of companies with exceptional customer service and analyze the strategies they use to achieve this.

Ritz-Carlton: A luxury hotel chain, Ritz-Carlton is known for its impeccable customer service. The company has a set of guiding principles, called the "Gold Standards," which outline the expectations for employees when it comes to customer service. These standards include anticipating the needs of guests, using guests' names whenever possible, and taking ownership of problems and finding solutions. The result is a high level of customer satisfaction and loyalty.

Chick-fil-A: A fast-food restaurant chain, Chick-fil-A is known for its friendly and efficient customer service. The company has a rigorous hiring process and trains its employees to focus on creating a positive experience for customers. Chick-fil-A has a reputation for going above and beyond for its customers, including opening on Sundays for special events and offering free food to customers in need during natural disasters.

Costco: A membership-based warehouse club, Costco is known for its customer-friendly policies and practices. The company offers a generous return policy, allowing customers to return most items at any time for a full refund. Costco also prioritizes employee satisfaction, with a focus on offering competitive wages and benefits. This results in a positive and helpful shopping experience for customers.

These companies demonstrate the importance of prioritizing customer service and creating a positive experience for customers. By focusing on the needs and expectations of customers, these companies have been able to create loyal customer bases and achieve long-term success.

Here are a few exercises to reinforce the concepts discussed in this section:

Pick a company that you believe provides exceptional customer service. Research the company and write a brief report outlining the company's customer service practices and policies.

Imagine that you are a customer service representative for a company. Write a script for how you would handle a difficult customer complaint, using the principles outlined in this section.

Think of a time when you had a negative customer service experience. Write a reflection on what went wrong and what the company could have done differently to improve the situation.

CHAPTER 3: UNDERSTANDING YOUR CUSTOMERS

Customer service is a vital aspect of any business. It is the primary means through which businesses interact with their customers, and it has a direct impact on a company's reputation, sales, and profits. In this chapter, we will discuss the importance of understanding your customers, and how it can help you provide exceptional customer service.

Understanding your customers is about knowing their needs, wants, and preferences. It involves understanding their buying behaviors, their motivations, and their pain points. By understanding your customers, you can tailor your products, services, and customer service to meet their specific needs, and provide them with a positive experience.

Importance of Understanding Your Customers:

There are several reasons why understanding your customers is essential. Firstly, it can help you improve your products and services. By understanding your customers' needs and preferences, you can tailor your products and services to meet their specific requirements, making them more attractive to your target audience.

Secondly, it can help you provide better customer service. By understanding your customers' pain points and motivations, you can provide them with more personalized and relevant customer service, which can help you build stronger relationships with your customers and improve their overall experience with your business.

Finally, understanding your customers can help you stand out from your competitors. By providing exceptional customer service that meets your customers' needs, you can differentiate your business from your competitors, making your business more attractive to potential customers.

Example of a Company with Exceptional Customer Service:

Southwest Airlines

Southwest Airlines is a low-cost airline that is known for its exceptional customer service. The company has built its reputation on its commitment to providing a positive and friendly travel experience to its customers.

Southwest Airlines empowers its employees to make decisions that will benefit the customer, and it encourages them to go above and beyond to provide exceptional service. The company also offers a no-fee policy for flight changes and cancellations, making it more convenient for its customers.

Conclusion:

Understanding your customers is essential for providing exceptional customer service. By knowing your customers' needs, wants, and preferences, you can tailor your products, services, and customer service to meet their specific requirements, improving their overall experience with your business. Companies like Zappos, Ritz-Carlton, and Southwest Airlines have built their reputation on their commitment to providing exceptional customer service, and they serve as excellent examples of companies that understand the importance of understanding their customers.

The importance of knowing your customers' needs and preferences

In order to provide exceptional customer service, it is essential to understand your customers' needs and preferences. This requires a deep understanding of their behavior, motivations, and expectations. In this chapter, we will explore the importance of knowing your customers' needs and preferences, and the various methods and tools that can be used to gain this understanding.

Section 1: Why Knowing Your Customers Is Important

Customers are the lifeblood of any business, and understanding their needs and preferences is crucial to the success of a company. By knowing your customers, you can tailor your products and services to meet their needs, create more effective marketing campaigns, and provide personalized customer service.

One of the main benefits of knowing your customers is the ability to tailor your products and services to their needs. By understanding what your customers want and need, you can create products and services that are more likely to meet their expectations. This can lead to increased customer satisfaction and loyalty.

In addition, knowing your customers can help you create more effective marketing campaigns. By understanding your customers' behavior and preferences, you can create targeted campaigns that are more likely to resonate with them. This can lead to increased engagement and conversions.

Finally, knowing your customers can help you provide personalized customer service. By understanding your customers' needs and preferences, you can provide tailored support that meets their specific requirements. This can lead to increased customer satisfaction and loyalty.

Section 2: Methods for Understanding Your Customers

There are several methods and tools that can be used to gain a deep understanding of your customers' needs and preferences.

Surveys: Surveys are a common method of collecting information from customers. They can be conducted online or in-person, and can provide valuable insights into customers' preferences and behavior.

Focus groups: Focus groups are small groups of customers who are brought together to discuss their experiences and opinions. This can provide a more in-depth understanding of customers' behavior and preferences.

Customer feedback: Customer feedback can be collected through various channels, such as social media, email, or phone. This can provide real-time feedback on customers' experiences with your products and services.

Sales data: Sales data can provide valuable insights into customers' behavior and preferences. By analyzing sales data, you can identify trends and patterns in customers' purchasing habits.

Customer personas: Customer personas are fictional representations of your ideal customers. They can help you understand your customers' needs and preferences, and create targeted marketing campaigns.

Section 3: Exercises and Questions

Think about a business that you frequent often. What do you like about their products or services? What could they improve upon?

Conduct a survey among your peers to understand their preferences and behavior when it comes to a particular product or service.

Create a customer persona for a business that you are interested in starting.

Analyze sales data for a business that you are familiar with. What trends or patterns do you notice?

In what ways can a business use customer feedback to improve their products and services?

How to gather customer feedback and insights

The Importance of Knowing Your Customers' Needs and Preferences

In today's business world, customer satisfaction is a critical factor in determining the success of a company. Companies that are committed to understanding and meeting their customers' needs and preferences have a distinct advantage over those that do not. In this chapter, we will explore the importance of knowing your customers' needs and preferences, and provide strategies for gathering customer feedback and insights.

The Benefits of Knowing Your Customers' Needs and Preferences

Knowing your customers' needs and preferences is essential for a variety of reasons. Firstly, it helps you create better products and services that are tailored to your customers' requirements. When you understand your customers' needs, you can design products that meet their specific needs and preferences, resulting in higher customer satisfaction and loyalty.

Secondly, understanding your customers' needs and preferences allows you to provide better customer service. When you know what your customers want, you can provide personalized and efficient service that meets their expectations. This can lead to increased customer satisfaction, loyalty, and positive word-of-mouth recommendations.

Finally, understanding your customers' needs and preferences can help you stay ahead of the competition. By continually gathering feedback and insights from your customers, you can identify areas where your competitors may be falling short and take steps to differentiate yourself from them.

Gathering Customer Feedback and Insights

To understand your customers' needs and preferences, you must gather feedback and insights from them. There are various methods for collecting customer feedback, and each has its advantages and disadvantages. Some common methods include:

Surveys

Surveys are an effective way to gather feedback from customers. They can be conducted online, by phone, or in person, and can be used to gather quantitative and qualitative data. Surveys can be used to collect information on customers' preferences, opinions, and experiences with your products or services.

One advantage of surveys is that they allow you to collect data from a large number of customers quickly and efficiently. However, one disadvantage is that customers may not always provide accurate or detailed feedback.

Interviews

Interviews are another way to gather feedback from customers. Unlike surveys, interviews provide the opportunity to ask follow-up questions and clarify responses. Interviews can be conducted in person, by phone, or through video conferencing.

One advantage of interviews is that they allow you to gather more detailed and nuanced feedback from customers. However, one disadvantage is that they are more time-consuming and may be more expensive than surveys.

Focus Groups

Focus groups are a form of group interview that involves bringing together a small group of customers to discuss a particular topic or issue. Focus groups can be used to gather detailed feedback on a particular product or service, as well as to identify areas for improvement.

One advantage of focus groups is that they allow you to gather feedback from a diverse group of customers with different perspectives and experiences. However, one disadvantage is that they can be expensive and time-consuming to conduct.

Social Media Listening

Social media platforms provide a wealth of information on customers' opinions, preferences, and experiences with your products or services. Social media listening involves monitoring and analyzing social media platforms for mentions of your brand, products, or services.

One advantage of social media listening is that it allows you to gather feedback in real-time and to respond quickly to customers' concerns or issues. However, one disadvantage is that it can be challenging to analyze large amounts of data and to separate relevant feedback from noise.

Customer Feedback Forms

Customer feedback forms can be used to gather feedback from customers at various touchpoints, such as after a purchase or after a customer service interaction. Feedback forms can be designed to gather both quantitative and qualitative data. Quantitative data refers to numerical data, such as ratings or the number of times a particular issue was mentioned, while qualitative data refers to non-numerical data, such as comments or feedback about a customer's experience.

When designing feedback forms, it is important to keep in mind the goal of the feedback and the type of information that will be most useful. For example, if the goal is to gather information on specific aspects of a product or service, the questions on the feedback form should be focused on those areas.

In addition to feedback forms, companies can also gather customer insights through social media listening and online reviews. Social media listening involves monitoring social media platforms for mentions of the company or its products, while online reviews are customer reviews and ratings posted on websites such as Yelp, TripAdvisor, or Amazon. Both social media listening and online reviews can provide valuable information about customers' experiences and opinions.

Another way to gather customer feedback is through focus groups or customer panels. Focus groups are small groups of customers who are brought together to discuss their experiences and opinions on a particular product or service. Customer panels are groups of customers who are regularly surveyed and asked to provide feedback on new products or services.

One common tool for gathering customer feedback is the Net Promoter Score (NPS). NPS is a metric that measures customer loyalty by asking customers to rate the likelihood that they would recommend a company to a friend or colleague on a scale of 0-10. Based on their responses, customers are grouped into three categories: detractors (those who give a score of 0-6), passives (those who give a score of 7-8), and promoters (those who give a score of 9-10). The NPS score is calculated by subtracting the percentage of detractors from the percentage of promoters.

Overall, gathering customer feedback and insights is crucial for companies to improve their products and services and enhance customer satisfaction. By using a combination of feedback forms, social media listening, online reviews, focus groups, and customer panels, companies can gain a deeper understanding of their customers and their needs, preferences, and expectations.

Segmentation and targeting in customer service

Segmentation and targeting are essential aspects of customer service that enable companies to understand their customers better and provide personalized experiences. Segmentation involves dividing customers into distinct groups based on shared characteristics such as demographics, behavior, and preferences. Targeting involves identifying the most profitable segments and designing customer service strategies that cater to their unique needs and preferences. This section will explore the importance of segmentation and targeting in customer service, how to segment and target customers, and the benefits and challenges of segmentation and targeting.

Importance of Segmentation and Targeting in Customer Service

Segmentation and targeting are crucial in customer service because they help companies provide personalized experiences that meet the unique needs and preferences of their customers. By segmenting customers into distinct groups, companies can understand their customers better, anticipate their needs, and provide tailored solutions that enhance the customer experience. Targeting the most profitable segments enables companies to optimize their resources and focus on the customers that generate the most value for their business. Additionally, segmentation and targeting can help companies differentiate themselves from their competitors and create a competitive advantage by providing superior customer service.

How to Segment and Target Customers

Segmentation and targeting involve a series of steps that companies can follow to identify the most valuable segments and design customer service strategies that cater to their needs. The following are the steps involved in segmentation and targeting:

Step 1: Identify relevant segmentation criteria

The first step in segmentation is to identify relevant criteria that will be used to divide customers into distinct groups. The criteria can include demographics such as age, gender, income, and education, behavior such as purchase history, frequency of visits, and loyalty, and preferences such as product preferences, communication preferences, and service expectations.

Step 2: Collect data

The next step is to collect data on customers based on the segmentation criteria identified in step 1. Companies can use various methods such as surveys, focus groups, and social media listening to collect data on their customers.

Step 3: Analyze data

The data collected in step 2 is analyzed to identify patterns and trends that can be used to segment customers into distinct groups. Companies can use various analytical techniques such as clustering, factor analysis, and regression analysis to identify customer segments.

Step 4: Select target segments

The next step is to select the most valuable segments based on various factors such as revenue potential, growth potential, and customer loyalty. Companies can use various methods such as customer lifetime value analysis and market attractiveness analysis to identify the most valuable segments.

Step 5: Develop customer service strategies

The final step is to develop customer service strategies that cater to the needs and preferences of the selected segments. Companies can use various tactics such as personalized communication, tailored products and services, and customized pricing to provide personalized experiences to their target segments.

Benefits and Challenges of Segmentation and Targeting

Segmentation and targeting offer various benefits to companies such as:

Improved customer satisfaction: By providing personalized experiences that meet the unique needs and preferences of customers, companies can improve customer satisfaction and loyalty.

Increased revenue: By targeting the most profitable segments, companies can increase their revenue and profitability.

Better resource allocation: By focusing on the most valuable segments, companies can optimize their resources and allocate them more effectively.

However, segmentation and targeting also pose various challenges such as:

Data collection and analysis: Collecting and analyzing data on customers can be time-consuming and expensive, especially for small businesses with limited resources.

Complexity: Segmentation and targeting involve a complex process that requires specialized skills and knowledge.

Limited resources: Small businesses may not have the resources to develop customized customer service strategies for multiple segments.

Conclusion

Segmentation and targeting are crucial aspects of customer service that enable companies to understand their customers better, provide personalized experiences, and optimize their resources. By following the steps outlined in this chapter, companies can segment their customer base effectively and target the right customers with the right message at the right time.

Effective segmentation and targeting require companies to gather data, analyze it, and use it to create actionable insights. It is essential to use a mix of quantitative and qualitative data to gain a comprehensive understanding of customers' needs, preferences, and behaviors.

Once a company has segmented its customer base, it can target specific groups with tailored marketing messages and customer service experiences. Targeted customer service experiences can lead to increased customer satisfaction and loyalty, which in turn can lead to increased revenue and profitability.

However, it is important to note that segmentation and targeting are not a one-time process. Customer needs and behaviors change over time, and companies must continually gather and analyze data to adjust their segmentation and targeting strategies accordingly.

In conclusion, segmentation and targeting are essential components of effective customer service. Companies must gather data, analyze it, and use it to create actionable insights that enable them to provide personalized experiences and optimize their resources. By doing so, companies can improve customer satisfaction, loyalty, and profitability over time.

Developing buyer personas

Developing buyer personas is an essential step in understanding your customers and delivering effective customer service. A buyer persona is a detailed profile of an ideal customer that helps you understand their needs, preferences, behaviors, and motivations. By developing buyer personas, you can gain insights into your customers' perspectives and create a more targeted and personalized customer experience.

In this section, we will discuss the importance of developing buyer personas and provide a step-by-step guide on how to create them.

Why are Buyer Personas Important?

Buyer personas provide a deep understanding of your customers' wants and needs, allowing you to tailor your customer service to their specific preferences. By creating accurate and detailed buyer personas, you can:

Personalize your marketing efforts: Knowing your customers' preferences and behaviors allows you to create marketing campaigns that resonate with them, increasing the likelihood of a successful outcome.

Customize your customer service: Understanding your customers' needs and pain points can help you provide more effective customer service, leading to higher satisfaction rates.

Identify new opportunities: Developing buyer personas can reveal new customer segments that you may have previously overlooked, helping you identify new growth opportunities.

How to Create Buyer Personas

Creating buyer personas involves a thorough process of research and analysis. Here is a step-by-step guide on how to create effective buyer personas:

Step 1: Conduct Market Research

To develop accurate buyer personas, you must first conduct market research to understand your customer base better. You can do this by:

Collecting data on your existing customers: Use customer relationship management (CRM) software to collect data on your existing customers, including demographics, purchase history, and communication preferences.

Analyzing website analytics: Analyze your website analytics to determine the most popular pages, search terms, and referral sources.

Conducting surveys and interviews: Conduct surveys and interviews with your customers to gather qualitative data on their preferences, motivations, and behaviors.

Studying social media: Analyze your social media activity to see what types of content generate the most engagement and what people are saying about your brand.

Step 2: Identify Common Characteristics

After conducting market research, you can begin to identify common characteristics among your customers. This may include demographic data such as age, gender, income, and location, as well as psychographic data such as values, interests, and lifestyle.

Step 3: Create the Persona

With the data collected in the previous steps, you can begin to create your buyer personas. Each persona should include the following information:

Name and title: Give your persona a name and a job title that reflects their role and position.

Background: Include relevant background information, such as their age, gender, income, and education level.

Goals: Outline the persona's goals and motivations, including their pain points and challenges.

Behaviors: Describe the persona's behaviors, including their decision-making process and communication preferences.

Influencers: Identify the people or sources that influence the persona's decision-making, such as family members, friends, or industry experts.

Step 4: Validate Your Personas

Once you have created your buyer personas, it is essential to validate them with your target audience. You can do this by:

Conducting surveys: Send your personas to a sample of your target audience and ask for their feedback.

Analyzing website analytics: Analyze your website analytics to determine if your personas align with your actual customer base.

Conducting interviews: Conduct interviews with your customers to validate the accuracy of your personas.

Conclusion

Developing accurate and detailed buyer personas is crucial for understanding your customers and providing effective customer service. By conducting thorough market research and creating detailed personas, you can gain insights into your customers' preferences, behaviors, and motivations. This can lead to more personalized marketing efforts, customized customer service, and ultimately, increased customer satisfaction and loyalty.

However, it is important to note that buyer personas should not be seen as a one-time task. As markets and customer preferences evolve, so should your personas. Regularly reviewing and updating your personas can ensure that they remain relevant and effective in guiding your customer service efforts.

In addition, it is important to remember that personas are not meant to be definitive representations of all customers. Rather, they serve as a tool to help you understand common patterns and behaviors among your target audience. It is important to also consider individual differences and to be open to feedback and input from customers themselves.

Overall, developing buyer personas is a valuable process for any business seeking to provide effective customer service. By gaining insights into your customers' needs, preferences, and behaviors, you can tailor your marketing and service efforts to better meet their expectations and build strong relationships.

Exercise: Identifying customer needs and preferences for a specific product or service

One of the most important aspects of providing effective customer service is understanding your customers' needs and preferences. This exercise will walk you through the process of identifying customer needs and preferences for a specific product or service, using a step-by-step approach.

Step 1: Define the product or service
To begin, you need to define the product or service you will be focusing on. This could be a physical product, such as a piece of technology or a piece of clothing, or it could be a service, such as a haircut or a gym membership.

Step 2: Identify your target customer
Next, you need to identify your target customer. Who is your product or service intended for? What are their demographics (age, gender, income level, etc.)? What are their psychographics (personality traits, values, interests, etc.)? You can use the buyer personas you developed in the previous section to help you with this step.

Step 3: Conduct market research

Once you have identified your target customer, you need to conduct market research to gather data about their needs and preferences. This can include:

Surveys: You can create a survey to gather information from your target customers about their needs and preferences. Surveys can be distributed through email, social media, or other channels.

Focus groups: Focus groups are small groups of people who are brought together to discuss a specific product or service. This can be a great way to gather in-depth feedback and insights from your target customers.

Interviews: You can conduct one-on-one interviews with your target customers to gather more detailed information about their needs and preferences.

Observation: You can observe your target customers as they use your product or service, to gain insights into how they interact with it and what they find important.

Step 4: Analyze the data

Once you have gathered data through market research, you need to analyze it to identify common themes and patterns. Look for trends in the data that can help you understand your customers' needs and preferences.

Step 5: Develop a customer needs and preferences profile

Based on your analysis of the data, develop a customer needs and preferences profile. This should include information about your target customer's needs and preferences, as well as any pain points or challenges they may be facing. Use this profile to inform your customer service strategy and ensure that you are providing the best possible experience for your customers.

Example Exercise:

Let's say that you are the manager of a high-end shoe store. Your target customer is a middle-aged woman with a high income level and a strong interest in fashion. Your goal is to identify your target customer's needs and preferences when it comes to shoes.

Step 1: Define the product or service

Your product is high-end shoes for women.

Step 2: Identify your target customer

Your target customer is a middle-aged woman with a high income level and a strong interest in fashion.

Step 3: Conduct market research
You decide to conduct a survey of your target customers to gather information about their needs and preferences. The survey includes questions about their shoe size, favorite shoe styles, favorite shoe brands, and any pain points or challenges they may be facing when it comes to buying shoes.

After conducting the survey, you also decide to hold a focus group to gather more in-depth feedback. The focus group includes five middle-aged women who fit your target customer profile. During the focus group, you ask them questions about their shoe buying habits, what they look for in a pair of shoes, and what challenges they have faced in the past when buying shoes.

Step 4: Analyze the data
After gathering data through the survey and focus group, you analyze the data to identify common themes and patterns.

You find that your target customers are looking for high-quality shoes that are comfortable, stylish, and durable. They prefer classic styles such as pumps, flats, and boots, but are also interested in trendy styles. They are willing to pay a premium for shoes that meet their needs and preferences.

Your survey also reveals that your target customers value personalized service and recommendations from store staff. They appreciate being greeted warmly when they enter the store and having staff help them find shoes that fit well and match their style preferences.

The focus group feedback confirms that your target customers have had challenges finding shoes that fit well and are comfortable. They often have to try on multiple pairs before finding the right fit, which can be time-consuming and frustrating.

Step 5: Use the insights to improve your product and service
Based on the insights you have gathered, you can make several improvements to your product and service:

Stock more classic shoe styles such as pumps, flats, and boots, but also include trendy styles to appeal to a wider range of customers.

Emphasize high-quality materials and construction to ensure that your shoes are durable and comfortable.

Train your staff to provide personalized service, including greeting customers warmly and helping them find shoes that fit well and match their style preferences.

Consider offering a shoe fitting service to help customers find the right fit more quickly and easily.

By using these insights to improve your product and service, you can better meet the needs and preferences of your target customers and increase customer satisfaction and loyalty.

CHAPTER 4: ACTIVE LISTENING SKILLS

Active listening is a crucial skill in the field of customer service. It involves not only hearing what the customer is saying but also understanding their needs, concerns, and emotions. Active listening helps to build trust, establish rapport, and ultimately leads to better customer satisfaction.

In this chapter, we will discuss the importance of active listening in customer service and provide practical tips and techniques to improve your listening skills. We will explore the various barriers to effective listening and provide strategies to overcome them. We will also discuss the role of body language, empathy, and questioning in active listening.

Why Active Listening is Important in Customer Service

Active listening is a critical component of customer service. It helps to build strong relationships with customers by demonstrating empathy, understanding, and a willingness to help. When customers feel that they are being heard and understood, they are more likely to feel satisfied with the service they receive and are more likely to return in the future.

Active listening also allows customer service representatives to gather critical information about the customer's needs, preferences, and concerns. By actively listening, service representatives can identify the root cause of the customer's problem and provide a more effective solution. This not only leads to better customer satisfaction but also helps to improve the overall efficiency of the customer service process.

Barriers to Effective Listening

There are several barriers to effective listening that can prevent customer service representatives from truly hearing and understanding the customer's needs. These barriers include:

Distractions: External distractions such as noise, interruptions, or background activity can make it difficult to focus on the customer's message.

Prejudices and biases: Preconceived notions or biases about the customer or the issue at hand can lead to a lack of empathy and a failure to truly hear what the customer is saying.

Emotional barriers: Strong emotions such as anger or frustration can make it difficult for the customer service representative to remain objective and listen actively.

Information overload: Too much information or a lack of organization can make it difficult to process the customer's message effectively.

Language barriers: Differences in language or dialect can make it difficult to understand the customer's message clearly.

Strategies to Overcome Barriers to Effective Listening

To overcome these barriers and improve active listening skills, customer service representatives can use several strategies, including:

Minimizing distractions: Eliminating external distractions such as noise or interruptions can help to improve focus and concentration.

Being aware of prejudices and biases: Recognizing and acknowledging personal biases and prejudices can help to minimize their impact on the listening process.

Managing emotions: Practicing emotional intelligence and empathy can help to manage strong emotions and remain objective when listening to the customer.

Practicing effective note-taking: Taking notes during the conversation can help to organize and remember the customer's message.

Clarifying language: Paraphrasing or repeating the customer's message can help to ensure that it is understood correctly.

The Role of Body Language, Empathy, and Questioning in Active Listening

Effective active listening involves not only listening to what the customer is saying but also paying attention to nonverbal cues and demonstrating empathy and understanding. Body language, empathy, and questioning can all play a crucial role in active listening.

Body language: Paying attention to the customer's body language can help to identify emotions and attitudes that may not be expressed verbally. By matching their body language and posture, the customer service representative can demonstrate empathy and build rapport.

Empathy: Showing empathy involves understanding and sharing the customer's emotions and feelings. By acknowledging their feelings and demonstrating a desire to help, the customer service representative can establish trust and build a stronger relationship with the customer.

Questioning: Asking open-ended questions can help to gather more information about the customer's needs and preferences. This not only helps to build rapport and understanding, but also allows the representative to provide more personalized assistance. Open-ended questions encourage the customer to provide more detailed and descriptive answers, which can help the representative to better understand their needs and provide more effective solutions.

Paraphrasing: Paraphrasing involves summarizing what the customer has said in a way that shows the representative has actively listened and understood their needs. This can help to confirm the representative's understanding and show the customer that their needs and concerns have been heard and acknowledged.

Reflecting: Reflecting involves taking the customer's statements and emotions and reflecting them back in a way that shows the representative is actively listening and understanding their perspective. This can help to build trust and empathy, and can also help to diffuse potentially tense situations by demonstrating a willingness to understand and resolve any issues.

Clarifying: Clarifying involves asking questions to ensure that the representative has understood the customer's needs and concerns accurately. This can help to avoid misunderstandings and ensure that the representative is providing the correct information and solutions.

Summarizing: Summarizing involves recapping the key points of the conversation to ensure that both parties are on the same page and that the representative has understood the customer's needs and concerns accurately. This can help to ensure that the customer receives the correct information and solutions, and can also help to avoid misunderstandings and miscommunication.

Overall, active listening skills are an essential component of effective customer service. By paying attention to the customer's verbal and nonverbal cues, demonstrating empathy, asking open-ended questions, paraphrasing, reflecting, clarifying, and summarizing, the representative can build trust, establish rapport, and provide more personalized assistance. These skills are especially important in situations where the customer may be upset or frustrated, as they can help to diffuse potentially tense situations and provide a more positive customer experience.

The importance of active listening in customer service

Customer service is a critical aspect of any business, as it can make or break a customer's experience with a company. Providing excellent customer service involves more than just resolving issues and answering questions; it also requires active listening skills. Active listening is the process of fully concentrating on what the customer is saying, both verbally and nonverbally, and responding appropriately.

In this section, we will explore the importance of active listening in customer service, including the benefits it provides to both the customer and the business. We will also discuss the various techniques and strategies that customer service representatives can use to improve their active listening skills.

Body:

Understanding Active Listening
Active listening is the process of fully concentrating on what the customer is saying and responding appropriately. It involves not just hearing the customer's words but also paying attention to their tone, body language, and other nonverbal cues.

Benefits of Active Listening in Customer Service
Effective active listening can benefit both the customer and the business. The benefits for the customer include feeling heard, valued, and understood, which can lead to increased customer satisfaction, loyalty, and repeat business. For the business, active listening can result in better customer retention, increased sales, and a positive reputation.

Techniques for Improving Active Listening Skills
There are several techniques that customer service representatives can use to improve their active listening skills, including:

a. Paying attention to the customer's body language: Paying attention to the customer's body language can help to identify emotions and attitudes that may not be expressed verbally. By matching their body language and posture, the customer service representative can demonstrate empathy and build rapport.

b. Empathy: Showing empathy involves understanding and sharing the customer's emotions and feelings. By acknowledging their feelings and demonstrating a desire to help, the customer service representative can establish trust and build a stronger relationship with the customer.

c. Questioning: Asking open-ended questions can help to gather more information about the customer's needs and preferences. This not only helps to build rapport but also allows the customer service representative to provide more personalized service.

d. Reflective listening: Reflective listening involves paraphrasing or summarizing the customer's words to show that the customer service representative has understood what was said. This can help to clarify any misunderstandings and ensure that the customer feels heard and valued.

e. Avoiding distractions: Active listening requires full concentration on the customer's words and nonverbal cues. Customer service representatives should avoid distractions such as checking their phone or computer while interacting with the customer.

Challenges of Active Listening
Active listening can be challenging for customer service representatives due to various factors such as time constraints, language barriers, and dealing with difficult customers. However, by developing their active listening skills, customer service representatives can overcome these challenges and provide excellent service to all customers.

Conclusion:

Active listening is a critical component of effective customer service. By fully concentrating on what the customer is saying, responding appropriately, and using various techniques and strategies, customer service representatives can provide personalized, empathetic service that leads to increased customer satisfaction, loyalty, and repeat business. Active listening requires practice and effort, but the benefits it provides to both the customer and the business make it well worth the investment.

Techniques for active listening, such as paraphrasing and clarifying

Active listening is a crucial skill for anyone in customer service, as it allows representatives to fully understand a customer's needs and concerns, and provide effective solutions. One of the key components of active listening is the use of specific techniques, such as paraphrasing and clarifying. In this section, we will explore these techniques in detail and provide examples of how they can be used effectively.

Paraphrasing

Paraphrasing is the process of restating the customer's message in your own words. It allows the representative to confirm their understanding of what the customer is saying and also demonstrates that the representative is actively engaged in the conversation.

To effectively paraphrase, the representative should listen carefully to what the customer is saying and then restate the message using different words. It is important to avoid simply repeating the customer's words verbatim, as this can come across as robotic and insincere.

For example, if a customer says, "I'm having trouble with my internet connection," a representative could paraphrase by saying, "So it sounds like you're experiencing issues with your internet service, is that correct?" This shows the customer that the representative is actively listening and trying to understand their problem.

Paraphrasing can also be used to summarize longer messages or to break down complex information into smaller, more manageable pieces. For example, a representative might say, "Let me make sure I understand everything. You're saying that you've been having issues with your internet connection for the past week, and you've already tried resetting your modem, is that correct?"

By using paraphrasing in this way, representatives can ensure that they fully understand the customer's message and are able to provide appropriate solutions.

Clarifying

Clarifying is another technique that can be used in active listening. It involves asking questions to ensure that the representative fully understands the customer's message.

When using clarifying, representatives should ask open-ended questions that encourage the customer to provide more information. This can help to identify any underlying issues or concerns that may not have been initially expressed.

For example, if a customer says, "I'm not happy with the service I received," a representative could use clarifying by saying, "Can you tell me more about what specifically you were unhappy with?" This allows the customer to provide more detail and can help the representative to identify the root cause of the problem.

Clarifying can also be used to confirm understanding. For example, a representative might say, "So, just to make sure I understand, you're saying that you need a replacement for your damaged product, is that correct?"

By using clarifying in this way, representatives can ensure that they fully understand the customer's message and can provide the appropriate solutions.

Combining Paraphrasing and Clarifying

Paraphrasing and clarifying are often used together in active listening to ensure that the representative fully understands the customer's message. For example, a representative might say, "So, if I understand correctly, you're saying that you've been experiencing issues with your internet connection for the past week, and you've already tried resetting your modem. Is there anything else you'd like to add or clarify?"

By using both techniques in this way, representatives can demonstrate that they are fully engaged in the conversation and are committed to understanding and addressing the customer's concerns.

Exercises and Questions:

Why is active listening important in customer service?

Explain the technique of paraphrasing and provide an example of how it can be used effectively in customer service.

How can clarifying be used to identify underlying issues or concerns?

How can paraphrasing and clarifying be used together in active listening?

Can you think of a time when you used paraphrasing or clarifying in a customer service situation?

How to use open-ended questions to gather information

In customer service, the ability to gather information effectively is essential. Open-ended questions are a valuable tool for customer service representatives as they allow them to collect detailed and specific information from customers. These questions encourage customers to share their thoughts and feelings, providing insights that would not be obtained through closed-ended questions. This section will discuss the benefits of using open-ended questions in customer service, how to ask open-ended questions effectively, and provide examples of open-ended questions in different customer service scenarios.

Benefits of Open-Ended Questions:

Open-ended questions allow customer service representatives to gather more detailed and specific information from customers. They provide customers with the opportunity to express themselves freely and share their thoughts and feelings in greater detail. Additionally, open-ended questions can help to uncover underlying concerns or issues that may not have been initially apparent. By using open-ended questions, customer service representatives can gain a deeper understanding of the customer's needs and provide more personalized and effective solutions.

Effective Techniques for Asking Open-Ended Questions:

Asking open-ended questions can be challenging for customer service representatives, particularly when the customer is upset or agitated. However, there are several techniques that can be used to ask open-ended questions effectively:

Start with an open-ended question: Begin the conversation with a broad, open-ended question that encourages the customer to share their thoughts and feelings. For example, "Can you tell me more about the issue you are experiencing?" or "What prompted you to contact us today?"

Use probing questions: Follow up with probing questions that delve deeper into the customer's responses. For example, "What specifically is causing you frustration?" or "Can you provide more details about the product you are having trouble with?"

Avoid closed-ended questions: Closed-ended questions can limit the amount of information obtained from the customer. Avoid questions that can be answered with a simple "yes" or "no." Instead, opt for questions that require the customer to provide more detail and explanation.

Listen actively: Active listening involves fully concentrating on what the customer is saying and providing verbal and nonverbal cues to indicate understanding. Pay attention to the customer's tone of voice, body language, and the words they use to express themselves. This can provide valuable insights into their thoughts and feelings.

Examples of Open-Ended Questions in Different Scenarios:

Sales: "Can you tell me about the features you are looking for in a product?" or "How will this product fit into your current business operations?"

Technical Support: "What specifically is happening when you encounter the error message?" or "Can you provide more details about the steps you have taken so far to resolve the issue?"

Customer Complaints: "What specifically was the issue you encountered?" or "Can you walk me through what happened leading up to the issue?"

Customer Feedback: "Can you tell me more about what you enjoyed about your experience with us?" or "What suggestions do you have for us to improve our services?"

Conclusion:

Open-ended questions are a valuable tool for customer service representatives as they allow them to gather detailed and specific information from customers. Effective techniques for asking open-ended questions include starting with a broad question, using probing questions, avoiding closed-ended questions, and listening actively. By using open-ended questions, customer service representatives can gain a deeper understanding of the customer's needs and provide more personalized and effective solutions.

Exercise: Practicing active listening with a partner or group

Active listening is a skill that can be honed with practice. It is not enough to simply understand the theory behind active listening; you must also practice it in real-life scenarios to develop and master the skill. The following exercise is designed to help you practice active listening with a partner or a group.

Instructions:

Find a partner or form a group of three to five people.
Decide who will be the speaker and who will be the listener(s) for the first round.
The speaker will choose a topic they want to discuss, and the listener(s) will actively listen and respond using active listening techniques.
The speaker will talk for two to three minutes, while the listener(s) will actively listen and take notes on what they hear.
Once the speaker has finished, the listener(s) will paraphrase what they heard, clarifying any misunderstandings and reflecting back the main points of the speaker's message.

The speaker will then confirm whether the listener(s) understood their message or if they need to provide additional information or clarification.

Swap roles and repeat the exercise until each person has had a chance to be the speaker and the listener(s).

Tips for Success:

Be fully present and focused on the speaker. Avoid distractions such as checking your phone or looking around the room.

Use nonverbal cues such as nodding, maintaining eye contact, and leaning forward to show that you are engaged in the conversation.

Practice active listening techniques such as paraphrasing, summarizing, and clarifying to demonstrate that you are actively listening and understanding the speaker's message.

Avoid interrupting the speaker, and wait for them to finish before responding.

Be patient and understanding if the speaker needs to take a moment to collect their thoughts or clarify their message.

Examples:

Example 1:

Speaker: "I'm really struggling with my workload. I have so much to do, and I feel like I can't keep up."

Listener: "It sounds like you're feeling overwhelmed with your workload. Can you tell me more about the tasks that are causing you the most stress?"

Example 2:

Speaker: "I'm excited to start my new job, but I'm also nervous about meeting my new coworkers and learning the ropes."

Listener: "It sounds like you have mixed feelings about starting your new job. What are you most excited about, and what are your concerns?"

Exercises:

Practice active listening with a partner or group using the instructions and tips provided above.

Reflect on your experience practicing active listening. What did you find challenging, and what came easily to you? How do you think this exercise will help you in your future interactions with customers and colleagues?

Take turns choosing different topics to discuss, such as personal interests, current events, or customer service scenarios, to practice active listening in a variety of contexts.

CHAPTER 5: EFFECTIVE COMMUNICATION TECHNIQUES

Effective communication is a fundamental aspect of any successful organization or business. It is essential for building strong relationships with customers, employees, stakeholders, and partners. Poor communication can lead to misunderstandings, mistakes, conflicts, and lost opportunities. Effective communication techniques are the foundation for establishing trust, promoting collaboration, achieving goals, and providing excellent customer service. In this chapter, we will explore various communication techniques that can enhance your ability to communicate effectively and build strong relationships.

Section 1: The Importance of Effective Communication

Communication is the process of conveying information, ideas, feelings, or messages from one person to another. Effective communication involves sending and receiving messages accurately, clearly, and concisely. It requires the use of appropriate verbal and nonverbal language, active listening, empathy, and feedback. Effective communication is critical in business because it helps to:

Build Relationships: Effective communication helps to build trust, mutual understanding, and respect between parties. When people feel heard and understood, they are more likely to collaborate, share ideas, and work together towards a common goal.

Improve Productivity: Effective communication can improve productivity by reducing misunderstandings, clarifying expectations, and providing timely feedback. It can help to streamline processes, avoid errors, and achieve goals efficiently.

Enhance Customer Satisfaction: Effective communication is essential for providing excellent customer service. It helps to understand customers' needs, provide relevant information, and resolve issues promptly. Customers who feel heard and valued are more likely to become loyal, repeat customers.

Manage Conflicts: Effective communication is critical for managing conflicts and resolving disputes. It can help to identify the root cause of the conflict, clarify expectations, and find mutually acceptable solutions.

Build a Positive Work Environment: Effective communication is essential for creating a positive work environment. It can help to foster teamwork, increase job satisfaction, and reduce turnover rates.

Section 2: Verbal Communication Techniques

Verbal communication is the use of words to convey information, ideas, or feelings. Effective verbal communication involves using clear and concise language, speaking at an appropriate pace and tone, and being mindful of the context and audience. Some verbal communication techniques include:

Active Listening: Active listening involves paying attention to the speaker, asking clarifying questions, and reflecting on what was said. It helps to show interest, understand the speaker's perspective, and avoid misunderstandings.

Paraphrasing: Paraphrasing involves restating the speaker's message in your own words. It helps to confirm understanding, clarify meaning, and demonstrate empathy.

Clarifying: Clarifying involves asking questions to gain a better understanding of the speaker's message. It helps to avoid misunderstandings, provide feedback, and promote dialogue.

Summarizing: Summarizing involves restating the key points of the speaker's message. It helps to reinforce understanding, provide closure, and facilitate next steps.

Empathizing: Empathizing involves acknowledging the speaker's feelings and showing understanding. It helps to build rapport, establish trust, and demonstrate care.

Section 3: Nonverbal Communication Techniques

Nonverbal communication is the use of body language, facial expressions, gestures, and tone of voice to convey meaning. Effective nonverbal communication involves being aware of your body language, tone of voice, and facial expressions, and using them appropriately. Some nonverbal communication techniques include:

Eye Contact: Eye contact helps to establish rapport, show interest, and build trust. It can also convey confidence, sincerity, and attentiveness.

Facial Expressions: Facial expressions can convey emotions, such as happiness, sadness, anger, or surprise. It can also convey interest, attention, or disinterest.

Gestures: Gestures can enhance and clarify verbal communication by emphasizing key points, conveying emotion, or signaling understanding. However, it's important to use gestures appropriately and not to overdo it, as it can become distracting or even offensive.

Posture: Posture can communicate confidence, assertiveness, or insecurity. Standing or sitting up straight can convey a sense of confidence, while slouching or hunching over can convey insecurity or disinterest.

Proximity: Proximity refers to the distance between people and can communicate intimacy, aggression, or formality. Standing too close to someone can be perceived as invasive, while standing too far away can be perceived as cold or disinterested.

Tone of Voice: Tone of voice can communicate emotions, attitudes, and intentions. A friendly, upbeat tone can convey warmth and enthusiasm, while a monotonous tone can convey boredom or disinterest.

It's important to note that nonverbal communication can vary across cultures, and what may be appropriate in one culture may not be in another. For example, in some cultures, direct eye contact is seen as a sign of respect and attentiveness, while in others it may be seen as aggressive or disrespectful.

Overall, effective nonverbal communication involves being aware of your own nonverbal cues and how they may be perceived, as well as being able to interpret and respond appropriately to the nonverbal cues of others. By doing so, you can enhance your communication skills and build stronger relationships with others.

Some exercises and questions to consider:

Practice making eye contact with someone during a conversation. How does it change the dynamic of the conversation?

Experiment with using different facial expressions during a conversation. How do people react to different expressions?

Pay attention to your own posture during a conversation. How does it affect your level of confidence and engagement in the conversation?

Pay attention to the proximity between you and others during a conversation. How does it affect the level of intimacy or formality in the conversation?

Listen to the tone of voice of others during a conversation. How does it convey their emotions or attitudes towards the conversation topic?

The role of clear and concise communication in customer service

Clear and concise communication is critical in customer service. Effective communication helps to build trust, reduce misunderstandings, and create a positive customer experience. In this section, we will explore the importance of clear and concise communication in customer service, the challenges that can arise when communication is unclear, and strategies for improving communication skills.

Importance of Clear and Concise Communication:

Clear and concise communication is essential in customer service for several reasons. Firstly, it helps to establish trust and build a relationship with the customer. When customers feel that their questions and concerns are being heard and understood, they are more likely to feel satisfied with the service they receive.

Secondly, clear communication helps to reduce misunderstandings. Misunderstandings can lead to frustration, anger, and a negative customer experience. When communication is clear, the customer is more likely to understand what is being said and what is expected of them.

Thirdly, clear communication helps to create a positive customer experience. When customers feel that they are being listened to and understood, they are more likely to have a positive view of the company and the service they receive. This positive experience can lead to repeat business and word-of-mouth referrals.

Challenges of Unclear Communication:

Unclear communication can lead to a host of challenges in customer service. For example, if a customer is not sure what is expected of them or does not understand the information being presented, they may become frustrated or angry. This can lead to a negative customer experience and damage to the company's reputation.

Unclear communication can also lead to misunderstandings. When customers misunderstand the information being presented to them, they may make incorrect assumptions or take inappropriate actions. This can lead to confusion, wasted time, and unnecessary expenses.

Strategies for Improving Communication Skills:

Improving communication skills is essential for providing excellent customer service. Here are some strategies that can be used to improve communication skills:

Active Listening: Active listening involves fully engaging with the customer and listening to what they are saying. This means paying attention to both verbal and nonverbal cues, asking clarifying questions, and demonstrating that you understand what the customer is saying.

Clear Language: Using clear, simple language can help to ensure that the customer understands the information being presented to them. Avoid using technical jargon or complex terminology unless it is necessary.

Empathy: Demonstrating empathy involves acknowledging the customer's feelings and concerns. This can help to build rapport with the customer and make them feel heard and understood.

Body Language: Using appropriate body language can help to reinforce the message being conveyed. This includes maintaining eye contact, using open body posture, and using appropriate facial expressions.

Tone of Voice: The tone of voice used when communicating with customers can impact how the message is received. Using a friendly and positive tone can help to create a positive customer experience.

Examples:

Example 1: A customer calls a bank to inquire about a loan. The customer service representative uses technical jargon and complex terminology, causing the customer to become confused and frustrated.

Solution: The customer service representative should use clear, simple language that the customer can understand. They should avoid using technical jargon unless it is necessary and explain any complex terminology that is used.

Example 2: A customer visits a store to return a defective product. The store clerk is dismissive and does not demonstrate empathy for the customer's situation.

Solution: The store clerk should demonstrate empathy by acknowledging the customer's frustration and concern. They should apologize for the inconvenience and work to find a solution that meets the customer's needs.

Exercise:

Choose a scenario in which communication was unclear, and discuss the challenges that arose as a result.

Identify strategies that could have been used to improve communication in the scenario you chose.

Practice active listening by engaging in a role-playing activity with a partner or group. One person will play the role of a customer with a complaint, and the other person will play the role of a customer service representative. The customer should express their concerns and the representative should actively listen, paraphrase, and clarify any misunderstandings. Then, switch roles and repeat the activity.

Additional Exercises:

Write down a recent customer service experience that you had, and analyze the communication that took place. Was the communication clear and concise? Were there any misunderstandings? What could have been done differently to improve the communication?

Watch a video or read a case study about a customer service experience. Analyze the communication that took place and identify areas where communication could have been improved. What strategies could have been used to improve the communication in this scenario?

Role-play a customer service scenario with a partner or group, where one person is a customer with a complex problem and the other person is a customer service representative. The representative should actively listen, ask clarifying questions, and work with the customer to find a solution to their problem.

Practice using clear and concise language by writing out a script for a customer service interaction. Edit the script to remove any unnecessary language or jargon, and ensure that the language used is clear and easy to understand.

Attend a customer service training workshop or seminar, where you can learn and practice effective communication techniques with other professionals in the field.

The importance of empathy and positivity in communication

In any customer service interaction, empathy and positivity are key factors that can make a big difference in the outcome. Empathy allows a customer service representative to understand and relate to the customer's situation, while positivity helps to maintain a constructive and optimistic environment. This section will explore the importance of empathy and positivity in communication, how they affect customer service interactions, and practical ways to apply them in customer service situations.

Part 1: The Importance of Empathy in Communication
Empathy is the ability to understand and share the feelings of others. In customer service, empathy is critical to building rapport with customers and developing a positive relationship. When customers feel that they are understood and that their needs are being taken into account, they are more likely to trust the representative and be satisfied with the outcome. Empathy can help to de-escalate a situation by showing the customer that their concerns are valid and that the representative is working to find a solution.

For example, imagine a customer who is upset because they have received a faulty product. The customer service representative can show empathy by acknowledging the customer's frustration, apologizing for the inconvenience caused, and showing a willingness to help the customer find a solution. By expressing empathy, the representative can help to calm the customer down and make them feel heard.

Part 2: The Importance of Positivity in Communication
Positivity is the practice of focusing on the good in a situation and finding constructive solutions to problems. In customer service, positivity is critical to maintaining a professional and optimistic environment, even in challenging situations. Positivity can help to build trust and credibility with customers, and it can also help to inspire confidence in a representative's ability to solve problems.

For example, imagine a customer who is experiencing a technical issue with a product. The customer service representative can show positivity by maintaining a friendly and helpful demeanor, remaining patient and understanding throughout the interaction, and focusing on finding a solution rather than dwelling on the problem. By maintaining a positive attitude, the representative can help the customer to feel more comfortable and confident in the representative's ability to resolve the issue.

Part 3: Applying Empathy and Positivity in Customer Service Situations

Now that we have established the importance of empathy and positivity in communication, let us explore some practical ways to apply them in customer service situations.

Active Listening

Active listening is a communication technique that involves fully concentrating on and understanding the speaker's message before responding. By actively listening to a customer, a representative can demonstrate empathy by showing that they are genuinely interested in the customer's concerns and are willing to take the time to understand their situation. Active listening can also help to identify underlying issues or concerns that may not be immediately apparent.

Acknowledge and Apologize

Acknowledging the customer's concerns and apologizing for any inconvenience caused can go a long way in showing empathy and diffusing a potentially tense situation. Even if the representative is not directly responsible for the issue, acknowledging the customer's frustration and showing a willingness to help can help to de-escalate the situation.

Provide Solutions

When a customer brings up an issue, it is important to focus on finding a solution rather than dwelling on the problem. By providing clear and actionable solutions, a representative can show positivity and inspire confidence in the customer's ability to resolve the issue.

Follow Up

Following up with the customer after the initial interaction can show empathy and a willingness to ensure that the issue has been fully resolved. A quick phone call or email can help to solidify the relationship and demonstrate a commitment to the customer's satisfaction.

Conclusion:

In conclusion, empathy and positivity are critical components of effective communication in customer service. By demonstrating empathy, representatives can show that they understand and care about the customer's concerns. By maintaining a positive attitude, representatives can inspire confidence and create a pleasant experience for the customer, even in challenging situations. These qualities can help to build rapport, trust, and loyalty with customers, which can ultimately lead to increased sales and revenue.

It's important to remember that empathy and positivity are not just words, but actions. They require effort and intentionality to be effectively conveyed.

Representatives must be willing to actively listen to customers, acknowledge their feelings and concerns, and respond in a way that shows empathy and positivity.

To develop these skills, representatives can undergo training programs that teach active listening, empathy, and positivity. These programs can provide representatives with the tools and strategies necessary to effectively communicate with customers in a positive and empathetic way.

In addition, organizations can create a positive work culture that encourages and supports empathy and positivity in communication. By recognizing and rewarding representatives who demonstrate these qualities, organizations can create an environment that values and prioritizes effective communication.

In today's competitive market, effective communication is essential for success in customer service. By prioritizing empathy and positivity in communication, organizations can create a customer-centric culture that sets them apart from their competitors. Customers will appreciate the effort that representatives put into understanding and addressing their needs, and they will be more likely to return in the future.

Overall, the importance of empathy and positivity in communication cannot be overstated. Representatives who demonstrate these qualities can build lasting relationships with customers and contribute to the success of their organizations. It's up to organizations to prioritize these qualities and provide the necessary training and support to ensure that representatives are equipped to communicate effectively with customers.

Strategies for communicating effectively in different situations (e.g. phone, email, in-person)

In customer service, it's important to know how to effectively communicate with customers in different situations. Communication methods such as phone, email, and in-person interactions require different approaches to ensure successful communication. In this section, we will discuss various strategies for communicating effectively in different situations.

Communication Strategies for Phone Conversations:

When communicating with customers over the phone, there are several strategies you can use to ensure effective communication. First, it's important to have a clear and friendly tone of voice. This can be achieved by speaking clearly and with a smile on your face, even though the customer cannot see you.

Active listening is another key strategy for effective phone communication. This involves focusing on the customer's words and responding appropriately. It's important to avoid interrupting the customer and to repeat back their concerns to ensure understanding.

In addition, using positive language can help diffuse difficult situations and leave customers feeling satisfied with their experience. Instead of saying "I don't know," say "Let me find out for you." Instead of saying "I can't do that," say "Here's what I can do for you."

Communication Strategies for Email Correspondence:

Email communication requires a different set of strategies to ensure effective communication. The first step is to write a clear and concise subject line that summarizes the purpose of the email. This helps the customer understand the purpose of the email and prioritize it accordingly.

When writing the body of the email, it's important to keep it brief and to the point. Use short paragraphs and bullet points to break up the text and make it easier to read. Use proper grammar and spelling, and avoid using slang or abbreviations that the customer may not understand.

Active listening is also important in email correspondence. Ensure that you read and fully understand the customer's email before responding. Respond promptly, and use a friendly and professional tone. Use the customer's name if possible, and end the email with a polite closing.

Communication Strategies for In-Person Interactions:

In-person interactions provide an opportunity to connect with the customer on a personal level. It's important to approach the customer with a friendly and welcoming demeanor, and to maintain eye contact and good body posture throughout the interaction.

Active listening is also important in in-person interactions. It's important to focus on the customer's words, maintain eye contact, and provide verbal and nonverbal cues to show that you are actively listening.

Nonverbal communication is also important in in-person interactions. Smiling, nodding, and using appropriate facial expressions can help build rapport with the customer and make them feel more comfortable.

Finally, it's important to use positive language and avoid negative language. Instead of saying "I can't do that," say "Here's what I can do for you." Instead of saying "That's not my job," say "Let me see if I can find someone who can help you with that."

Conclusion:

Effective communication is key to successful customer service. By using the appropriate communication strategies for different situations, you can ensure that your customers feel heard and valued. Remember to use active listening, positive language, and appropriate nonverbal communication to create a positive experience for your customers.

Exercise: Role-playing common customer service scenarios and practicing effective communication techniques

Effective communication is crucial in any customer service setting. It is essential to have strong communication skills to provide a positive customer experience and resolve conflicts quickly and efficiently. Role-playing common customer service scenarios and practicing effective communication techniques can help customer service representatives develop the skills they need to communicate effectively in a variety of situations.

Role-playing Common Customer Service Scenarios:

Role-playing is an effective way to practice communication skills and prepare for real-life scenarios. By role-playing common customer service scenarios, representatives can develop their communication skills and gain confidence in their ability to handle different situations.

Some common customer service scenarios that can be role-played include:

Dealing with an Angry Customer: In this scenario, the representative needs to remain calm, acknowledge the customer's frustration, and offer a solution to their problem.

Responding to a Complaint: In this scenario, the representative needs to actively listen to the customer's complaint, ask questions to understand the problem, and offer a solution that addresses the issue.

Handling a Request for a Refund: In this scenario, the representative needs to explain the refund policy clearly, listen to the customer's reason for the refund, and offer a satisfactory solution.

Upselling a Product or Service: In this scenario, the representative needs to understand the customer's needs, explain the benefits of the product or service, and address any concerns the customer may have.

Practicing Effective Communication Techniques:

Effective communication techniques can help customer service representatives handle different situations with confidence and professionalism. Some effective communication techniques include:

Active Listening: Active listening is a technique that involves paying close attention to what the customer is saying, asking questions to clarify their concerns, and summarizing the conversation to ensure understanding. By actively listening, representatives can understand the customer's needs and provide a solution that meets their expectations.

Using Positive Language: Using positive language can help create a positive customer experience. Positive language includes phrases like "I can help you with that," "I understand your concern," and "Let me see what I can do." By using positive language, representatives can demonstrate that they care about the customer's needs and are willing to help.

Empathy: Empathy involves understanding and acknowledging the customer's emotions and concerns. By showing empathy, representatives can build trust and create a positive customer experience. Empathetic phrases include "I understand how frustrating that can be" and "I'm sorry you're having a hard time with this."

Clear and Concise Communication: Clear and concise communication is essential in any customer service situation. Representatives should use simple language and avoid technical jargon or complicated explanations. By communicating clearly and concisely, representatives can ensure that the customer understands the solution and feels satisfied with the outcome.

Conclusion:

In conclusion, role-playing common customer service scenarios and practicing effective communication techniques can help customer service representatives develop the skills they need to communicate effectively in a variety of situations. By using techniques like active listening, using positive language, showing empathy, and communicating clearly and concisely, representatives can provide a positive customer experience and build trust with their customers. It is essential for representatives to continue practicing these techniques to maintain their communication skills and provide excellent customer service.

CHAPTER 6: PROBLEM-SOLVING STRATEGIES IN CUSTOMER SERVICE

As customer service representatives, we are often faced with complex issues and problems that require effective problem-solving skills. From dealing with unhappy customers to resolving technical issues, the ability to solve problems in a timely and efficient manner is critical for maintaining customer satisfaction and loyalty.

In this chapter, we will discuss the key strategies and techniques that can be used to solve problems in customer service. We will explore various problem-solving models and frameworks, as well as practical tips for identifying, analyzing, and resolving customer issues. We will also discuss the importance of effective communication and collaboration in problem-solving, and how to build a problem-solving culture within a customer service team.

By the end of this chapter, readers will have a solid understanding of the problem-solving process and the skills needed to tackle even the most challenging customer service problems. Whether you are a seasoned customer service professional or just starting out in the field, this chapter will provide you with valuable insights and tools to enhance your problem-solving abilities and deliver exceptional customer service.

Identifying and defining customer problems

Customer service is a critical component of any successful business. Customers expect high-quality service that meets their needs and addresses their concerns. However, not every interaction with a customer will be smooth sailing. Customers may experience problems or issues that require the intervention of customer service representatives.

In such cases, it is important for customer service representatives to have a set of problem-solving strategies in place to identify and address customer problems effectively. This chapter will cover some of the essential problem-solving strategies that can be employed in customer service.

Identifying and Defining Customer Problems:

The first step in effective problem-solving in customer service is identifying and defining the problem. A clear understanding of the customer's problem is necessary to provide a solution that meets their needs. In this section, we will explore some of the ways that customer service representatives can identify and define customer problems.

Active Listening:
Active listening is a crucial skill for customer service representatives to have. It involves paying close attention to the customer's words and their tone of voice to understand their problem fully. It also involves asking clarifying questions to ensure that the customer's issue is clearly understood. Active listening helps customer service representatives to identify the root cause of the problem and find an appropriate solution.

Asking Open-Ended Questions:
Asking open-ended questions is another effective way to identify and define customer problems. Open-ended questions allow customers to provide detailed responses, which can help customer service representatives understand the problem better. For example, instead of asking "Did the product arrive damaged?" a customer service representative might ask "What was the issue with the product when it arrived?" This approach allows customers to provide more detail and can help identify the underlying problem.

Analyzing Trends and Patterns:
Analyzing trends and patterns can also be an effective way to identify and define customer problems. By examining customer complaints, customer service representatives can identify common issues that customers are experiencing. This approach can help businesses proactively address issues before they become widespread.

Using Data and Analytics:
Data and analytics can also be useful in identifying and defining customer problems. By examining customer feedback and complaints, businesses can identify patterns and trends that can be used to improve products or services. Customer service representatives can use this data to provide targeted solutions to customers and to identify broader issues that require attention.

Conclusion:

Identifying and defining customer problems is an essential first step in effective problem-solving in customer service. Active listening, asking open-ended questions, analyzing trends and patterns, and using data and analytics are all useful strategies for identifying and defining customer problems. By understanding the problem fully, customer service representatives can provide targeted solutions that meet the customer's needs and address their concerns.

The importance of taking ownership of customer problems

In the field of customer service, the ability to identify and solve customer problems effectively is paramount to a successful business. In order to deliver outstanding service, it is essential for customer service representatives to take ownership of customer problems and handle them with care and urgency. This means acknowledging the issue, taking responsibility for resolving it, and following through until the customer is satisfied with the outcome. In this section, we will explore the importance of taking ownership of customer problems, the benefits of doing so, and strategies for effectively handling customer issues.

Why Taking Ownership of Customer Problems is Important:

Taking ownership of customer problems is crucial for several reasons. First and foremost, it helps to build trust and strengthen relationships with customers. When a customer has an issue, they want to feel that their concerns are being taken seriously and that they are being treated with respect. By taking ownership of the problem, the customer service representative is showing the customer that their issue matters and that they are committed to finding a solution.

Secondly, taking ownership of customer problems can help to prevent the problem from escalating. When a customer feels that their problem is not being addressed, they may become frustrated and angry. This can lead to negative reviews, complaints to management, and even legal action in some cases. By taking ownership of the problem and working to resolve it, the customer service representative can prevent these negative outcomes from occurring.

Finally, taking ownership of customer problems can lead to increased customer loyalty and retention. When customers feel that their issues are being addressed and resolved promptly and effectively, they are more likely to remain loyal to the business and continue to make future purchases. This can lead to increased revenue and a stronger customer base for the business.

Strategies for Taking Ownership of Customer Problems:

In order to take ownership of customer problems effectively, there are several strategies that customer service representatives can use. First, it is important to actively listen to the customer and understand the issue from their perspective. This involves asking open-ended questions, paraphrasing the customer's concerns, and clarifying any misunderstandings.

Once the issue has been identified, the customer service representative should take responsibility for resolving it. This means acknowledging the issue and taking immediate action to find a solution. It may involve consulting with other team members or managers to find the best course of action.

During the problem-solving process, it is important to keep the customer informed and updated on the progress being made. This can be done through regular communication, such as email or phone calls. It is also important to set realistic expectations and timelines for resolving the issue.

Once the problem has been resolved, it is important to follow up with the customer to ensure that they are satisfied with the outcome. This can involve asking for feedback or offering incentives for future purchases. By following up with the customer, the business can demonstrate its commitment to customer satisfaction and build trust and loyalty.

Conclusion:

Taking ownership of customer problems is an essential part of providing outstanding customer service. By actively listening to the customer, taking responsibility for resolving the issue, and following through until the customer is satisfied, customer service representatives can build trust, prevent problems from escalating, and increase customer loyalty and retention. By implementing these strategies, businesses can create a culture of customer service excellence and establish themselves as leaders in their respective industries.

Techniques for resolving customer problems (e.g. offering solutions, apologizing, following up)

Resolving customer problems is an essential part of providing excellent customer service. Customers who have experienced a problem want a resolution to their issue, and it is the responsibility of customer service representatives to ensure that they receive one. In this section, we will discuss various techniques that can be used to resolve customer problems, including offering solutions, apologizing, and following up.

Offering Solutions:

One of the most effective techniques for resolving customer problems is to offer solutions. When a customer presents a problem, the customer service representative should immediately begin to brainstorm possible solutions. Ideally, the representative will be able to offer a solution that meets the customer's needs and resolves the problem. However, if the representative is unable to provide a solution that satisfies the customer, they should explain the options that are available and work with the customer to identify the best course of action.

It is essential to provide clear and concise explanations of potential solutions, including any limitations or drawbacks. The representative should also explain the expected outcomes of each solution, including how it will resolve the customer's problem. If the customer has questions about the proposed solution, the representative should be prepared to answer them. Overall, offering solutions is an effective way to resolve customer problems and ensure customer satisfaction.

Apologizing:

In some cases, apologizing is an appropriate technique for resolving customer problems. Apologizing shows the customer that their problem is being taken seriously and can help to defuse a potentially tense situation. Apologizing should be done sincerely, and the representative should take responsibility for any mistakes or issues that may have caused the problem.

It is important to note that apologizing does not necessarily mean accepting blame or fault. Rather, apologizing acknowledges that the customer is unhappy and shows a willingness to work towards a resolution. It is also important to follow up the apology with concrete actions to address the problem.

Following Up:

Following up is another essential technique for resolving customer problems. After a solution has been offered, it is important to follow up with the customer to ensure that the problem has been resolved to their satisfaction. This not only shows the customer that their issue is important but also provides an opportunity to address any lingering concerns or issues that the customer may have.

Following up can be done via phone, email, or other communication channels. The representative should inquire if the customer is satisfied with the resolution and ask if there is anything else that can be done to improve their experience. If the customer has any additional concerns or issues, the representative should work to address them promptly.

Conclusion:

In conclusion, resolving customer problems is a critical part of providing excellent customer service. Techniques such as offering solutions, apologizing, and following up are effective ways to resolve customer issues and ensure customer satisfaction. Customer service representatives who can effectively resolve customer problems are more likely to have satisfied customers and build positive relationships with them. By implementing these techniques, representatives can ensure that customers are not only satisfied with the resolution of their problem but also feel valued and respected.

Exercise: Analyzing a real customer service problem and developing a plan for resolving it

One of the best ways to learn problem-solving techniques in customer service is to analyze a real-world customer service problem and develop a plan for resolving it. In this exercise, we will go through the steps involved in analyzing a customer service problem and developing a plan for resolving it.

Step 1: Identify the Problem
The first step in resolving a customer service problem is to identify the problem. The problem may be obvious, such as a customer complaint, or it may be more subtle, such as a decrease in sales. Once you have identified the problem, you need to gather more information about it. This may involve speaking to the customer or observing their behavior, analyzing sales data, or talking to employees who interact with customers.

Example: Let's say that a restaurant has received several complaints from customers about the quality of the food.

Step 2: Define the Problem
Once you have gathered information about the problem, you need to define it. This involves clarifying the problem, understanding its scope, and identifying the underlying causes.

Example: After speaking to customers and analyzing the food preparation process, the problem is defined as a lack of consistency in the quality of the food. The underlying causes are identified as variability in the skill level of the kitchen staff and inadequate training.

Step 3: Brainstorm Solutions

Once you have defined the problem, you need to brainstorm solutions. This involves generating as many possible solutions as you can, without evaluating them. It's important to encourage creativity and avoid judgment at this stage.

Example: Possible solutions to the problem of inconsistent food quality include:

Providing additional training to the kitchen staff
Hiring more experienced staff
Simplifying the menu to reduce complexity
Changing the food suppliers
Implementing a quality control system

Step 4: Evaluate Solutions
After generating possible solutions, it's time to evaluate them. This involves considering the advantages and disadvantages of each solution and assessing their feasibility.

Example: After evaluating the possible solutions, the restaurant decides to implement a quality control system that involves regular tasting sessions and feedback from customers. This solution addresses the underlying causes of the problem and is feasible for the restaurant to implement.

Step 5: Implement the Solution
Once you have selected a solution, it's time to implement it. This involves developing an action plan, assigning responsibilities, and setting a timeline for implementation.

Example: The restaurant develops an action plan for implementing the quality control system, assigns responsibilities to the kitchen staff and management, and sets a timeline for implementation over the next month.

Step 6: Evaluate the Outcome
After implementing the solution, it's important to evaluate the outcome to determine whether the problem has been resolved. This involves monitoring the situation, gathering feedback from customers, and analyzing data to assess the effectiveness of the solution.

Example: After implementing the quality control system, the restaurant monitors food quality through regular tastings and feedback from customers. The data shows that the quality of the food has improved, and there are no further complaints from customers about inconsistency.

Conclusion:

Resolving customer service problems requires a systematic approach that involves identifying and defining the problem, brainstorming solutions, evaluating the solutions, implementing the solution, and evaluating the outcome. By following these steps, you can develop a plan for resolving any customer service problem and improve the overall customer experience.

CHAPTER 7: HANDLING DIFFICULT CUSTOMERS

In customer service, dealing with difficult customers is an inevitable challenge. These customers can be frustrating, angry, or dissatisfied, and they can make it difficult to provide satisfactory service. In this chapter, we will explore techniques for handling difficult customers and providing effective solutions to their problems. We will discuss the common types of difficult customers and the underlying reasons for their behavior. We will also provide strategies for calming angry customers, resolving complaints, and restoring customer trust.

Understanding Difficult Customers

Difficult customers come in many forms, and it is important to understand their behavior in order to handle them effectively. The following are some common types of difficult customers:

The Complainer - This customer is always unhappy and complains about everything. They may be dissatisfied with the service or product, or they may simply be looking for someone to vent their frustrations on.

The Demander - This customer is demanding and expects immediate solutions to their problems. They may become angry if their demands are not met promptly.

The Nitpicker - This customer is overly critical and finds fault with everything. They may be looking for flaws in the service or product and are difficult to please.

The Abusive - This customer is rude, aggressive, and may use profanity or threats. They may be angry about the service or product, or they may have personal issues that are causing them to behave this way.

The Silent - This customer is quiet and unresponsive. They may be dissatisfied with the service or product, but they are reluctant to speak up.

Understanding the underlying reasons for difficult customer behavior can help service providers address the root cause of the problem. Common reasons for difficult customer behavior include:

Dissatisfaction with the service or product

Misunderstanding of the service or product
Personal issues or emotions
Unrealistic expectations
Past negative experiences

Calming Angry Customers

Angry customers can be challenging to deal with, but it is important to remain calm and professional. The following are some strategies for calming angry customers:

Listen - Allow the customer to vent their frustrations and actively listen to their concerns. This can help the customer feel heard and understood.

Apologize - Apologize for the customer's negative experience, even if the issue was not directly caused by the service provider.

Empathize - Show empathy for the customer's situation and acknowledge their feelings.

Offer Solutions - Offer solutions to the customer's problem and work with them to find a satisfactory resolution.

Stay Calm - Remain calm and professional, even if the customer becomes angry or aggressive.

Escalate if Necessary - If the customer is unreasonable or abusive, it may be necessary to escalate the issue to a higher authority.

Resolving Complaints

Effective complaint resolution is essential for customer satisfaction and retention. The following are some strategies for resolving customer complaints:

Acknowledge the Problem - Acknowledge the customer's complaint and take responsibility for resolving the issue.

Investigate - Investigate the problem and gather relevant information. This can help service providers understand the root cause of the issue and develop an appropriate solution.

Communicate - Communicate with the customer throughout the process to keep them informed of the progress and any potential solutions.

Offer Solutions - Offer solutions to the customer's problem and work with them to find a satisfactory resolution.

Follow Up - Follow up with the customer after the issue has been resolved to ensure their satisfaction and build trust.

Restoring Customer Trust

Difficult customer interactions can damage customer trust, but there are strategies for restoring it. The following are some techniques for restoring customer trust:

Apologize - Apologizing is often the first step in restoring customer trust. A sincere and timely apology can go a long way in diffusing a difficult situation and showing the customer that their concerns are taken seriously. However, it's important to note that simply saying "I'm sorry" is not enough. The apology needs to be specific and demonstrate an understanding of the customer's concerns.

Offer a solution - Once you have apologized, it's important to offer a solution to the customer's problem. This can help to rebuild trust by demonstrating that you are committed to resolving the issue and ensuring that the customer is satisfied. The solution offered should be tailored to the specific problem and should be communicated clearly and concisely.

Follow up - Following up with the customer after the interaction can also help to restore trust. This shows the customer that you value their business and are committed to ensuring that they are satisfied with the outcome. It's important to follow up in a timely manner and to communicate any updates or progress made towards resolving the issue.

Listen - Listening to the customer's concerns is also an important aspect of restoring trust. It's important to actively listen to the customer's perspective and to show empathy for their situation. This can help to de-escalate the situation and show the customer that you are genuinely interested in resolving the issue.

Train employees - Providing employees with training on how to handle difficult customers can also be an effective way to restore trust. This can include techniques for de-escalating situations, active listening, and problem-solving. By providing employees with the tools they need to handle difficult interactions, they can be better equipped to handle customer complaints and rebuild trust.

Handling difficult customers is a challenging but important aspect of customer service. While it can be tempting to avoid difficult interactions, it's important to remember that how these interactions are handled can have a significant impact on customer loyalty and satisfaction. By following the strategies outlined in this chapter, customer service professionals can effectively handle difficult customers and maintain positive customer relationships. It's also important to remember that handling difficult customers is not a one-size-fits-all approach, and it's important to tailor strategies to the specific situation and customer involved.

The different types of difficult customers and how to identify them

In customer service, dealing with difficult customers can be challenging, but it is an essential skill for customer service representatives to develop. Understanding the different types of difficult customers can help customer service representatives identify the best strategies to use when interacting with them. In this section, we will explore some of the most common types of difficult customers and how to identify them.

The Angry Customer
Angry customers are the most common type of difficult customer. They are upset and may express their frustration with raised voices or aggressive body language. They are often triggered by a perceived wrongdoing on the part of the company, such as a late delivery or a faulty product. In some cases, the customer's anger may be justified, but in other cases, it may be misplaced.
To identify an angry customer, look for signs of agitation, such as clenched fists or a raised voice. They may also use aggressive language or make threats. The key to dealing with an angry customer is to remain calm and empathetic while addressing their concerns.

The Indecisive Customer
Indecisive customers are those who have a hard time making decisions. They may ask a lot of questions or seek reassurance before making a purchase. They may also change their minds frequently or ask for additional information that they may not need.
To identify an indecisive customer, look for signs of uncertainty, such as hesitation, confusion, or an inability to make a decision. The key to dealing with an indecisive customer is to be patient and to provide clear and concise information to help them make a decision.

The Demanding Customer

Demanding customers are those who have high expectations and may be difficult to please. They may have specific requests or may demand immediate attention or special treatment. They may also be overly critical or demanding of the service they receive.

To identify a demanding customer, look for signs of entitlement, such as making unreasonable requests or expecting immediate attention. The key to dealing with a demanding customer is to remain professional and to set clear boundaries while trying to meet their needs.

The Perfectionist Customer

Perfectionist customers are those who have high standards and expect nothing less than perfection. They may be overly critical of minor issues or may demand that everything be done exactly as they want it.

To identify a perfectionist customer, look for signs of nitpicking or an obsessive focus on details. The key to dealing with a perfectionist customer is to be patient and to explain any limitations or constraints that may prevent you from meeting their expectations.

The Complaining Customer

Complaining customers are those who have a habit of finding fault with everything. They may be overly critical of minor issues or may complain about things that are outside of your control.

To identify a complaining customer, look for signs of negativity or a focus on the negative aspects of a situation. The key to dealing with a complaining customer is to remain positive and to focus on finding solutions to their concerns.

In conclusion, identifying different types of difficult customers is an important skill for customer service representatives to develop. By understanding the different types of difficult customers and their behavior patterns, customer service representatives can tailor their responses and use the most effective strategies to address their concerns.

Strategies for de-escalating difficult situations

Handling difficult customers is an essential part of providing customer service. One of the most important skills for a customer service representative to possess is the ability to de-escalate a tense situation. This involves recognizing the signs of escalating behavior and taking action to calm the customer down. In this section, we will discuss several strategies for de-escalating difficult situations.

Active Listening

Active listening is an important tool for de-escalating difficult situations. When a customer is upset, it is important to give them your full attention and demonstrate that you are listening to them. This can involve making eye contact, nodding your head, and paraphrasing their concerns to show that you understand their perspective. Active listening can help to defuse tension and make the customer feel heard and valued.

Empathy

Empathy is another key strategy for de-escalating difficult situations. When a customer is upset, it is important to put yourself in their shoes and try to understand their perspective. This can involve acknowledging their feelings and expressing sympathy for their situation. By demonstrating empathy, you can help to defuse the customer's emotions and build rapport with them.

Stay Calm

In a tense situation, it is important to remain calm and composed. If you become agitated or defensive, it can escalate the situation and make the customer feel more frustrated. Instead, take a deep breath and remain composed. This can help to defuse the tension and make the customer feel more at ease.

Use Positive Language

Positive language is an important tool for de-escalating difficult situations. Instead of using negative language, such as "I can't do that," use positive language, such as "Let me see what I can do to help." This can help to convey a sense of willingness to help and can make the customer feel more at ease.

Offer Solutions

When a customer is upset, it is important to offer solutions to their problem. This can involve suggesting alternatives or offering to escalate the issue to a supervisor. By offering solutions, you can demonstrate a willingness to help and show that you are taking the customer's concerns seriously.

Know When to Escalate

In some cases, it may be necessary to escalate a difficult situation to a supervisor or manager. This can involve transferring the customer to a higher level of support or involving another department to help resolve the issue. Knowing when to escalate is an important skill for de-escalating difficult situations, as it can help to ensure that the customer's concerns are addressed in a timely and effective manner.

In conclusion, de-escalating difficult situations is an essential skill for providing effective customer service. By using active listening, empathy, positive language, and offering solutions, customer service representatives can help to defuse tension and build rapport with customers. Additionally, knowing when to escalate is an important skill that can help to ensure that the customer's concerns are addressed in a timely and effective manner.

The importance of staying calm and professional

As a customer service representative, it is important to remain calm and professional even in the most challenging situations. Staying calm and professional helps to de-escalate difficult situations, fosters better communication, and helps to build trust with customers.

When a customer is upset, it is easy to become defensive and react emotionally. However, reacting emotionally will only escalate the situation and make it harder to resolve. It is essential to remain calm, listen to the customer's concerns, and respond in a professional manner. This approach can help to turn a difficult situation around and leave the customer feeling satisfied with the service they received.

Staying calm and professional can also help to maintain control of the conversation. When a customer is angry, they may try to dominate the conversation and take control. However, by remaining calm and professional, the customer service representative can maintain control of the conversation and steer it towards a resolution.

Furthermore, staying calm and professional is a reflection of the company's culture and values. A customer who receives calm and professional service is more likely to have a positive perception of the company and be more likely to continue doing business with them.

In order to remain calm and professional, it is important to practice good self-care. This includes getting enough sleep, eating well, and taking breaks as needed. Customer service representatives who are tired, hungry, or stressed are more likely to react emotionally in difficult situations. Taking care of oneself can help to reduce stress and promote a calm and professional demeanor.

Overall, staying calm and professional is essential for effective customer service. It helps to de-escalate difficult situations, maintain control of the conversation, and promote a positive perception of the company. By practicing good self-care and remaining calm and professional, customer service representatives can provide the best service possible to their customers.

Examples:

Example 1:

A customer is upset because their order was delayed, and they need it for a time-sensitive project. The customer service representative apologizes for the delay, explains the reason for the delay, and offers to expedite the shipping at no additional cost. The customer begins to calm down, and the representative continues to provide excellent service by ensuring that the customer receives their order in time for their project.

Example 2:

A customer is upset because they received a damaged product. The customer service representative apologizes for the inconvenience, asks the customer to send a photo of the damage, and offers to send a replacement product or a refund. The customer is initially angry, but the representative remains calm and professional throughout the conversation. The customer ultimately feels heard and appreciated for their feedback.

Exercise:

Imagine that you are a customer service representative and a customer calls in, upset because they received the wrong product. How would you respond to the customer in a calm and professional manner?

Questions:

Why is it important to stay calm and professional in customer service?

What are some ways that staying calm and professional can benefit both the customer and the company?

What are some strategies for practicing good self-care in customer service?

How can staying calm and professional help to maintain control of the conversation?

What are some examples of situations where staying calm and professional can be challenging, and how can a customer service representative respond effectively in these situations?

Exercise: Role-playing difficult customer scenarios and practicing de-escalation techniques

One of the most effective ways to prepare for difficult customer interactions and to develop de-escalation skills is through role-playing exercises. Role-playing allows customer service representatives to practice responding to challenging situations in a safe and controlled environment, where they can receive feedback and guidance on how to improve their communication skills.

To conduct a role-playing exercise, managers or trainers can create a series of scenarios that reflect the most common types of difficult customers that employees are likely to encounter. These scenarios should be based on real-life situations that employees have encountered, and should involve a range of customer personalities and communication styles.

For example, a scenario might involve a customer who is angry and aggressive, or one who is frustrated and overwhelmed. The customer might be demanding, rude, or unreasonable, and the scenario should reflect the level of difficulty that the employee might face in a real-life situation.

Once the scenarios have been developed, employees can be paired up to play the roles of the customer and the customer service representative. Managers or trainers can provide guidance and feedback throughout the exercise, and can help employees to develop their de-escalation skills and communication techniques.

During the role-playing exercise, employees should be encouraged to:

Listen actively - Customer service representatives should listen carefully to the customer's concerns and complaints, and should acknowledge their feelings and emotions.

Empathize - Employees should try to understand the customer's perspective and show empathy for their situation, even if they do not agree with their behavior or demands.

Stay calm and professional - Customer service representatives should remain calm and professional, even in the face of aggressive or abusive behavior. They should avoid reacting defensively or taking the customer's behavior personally.

Use positive language - Employees should use positive language and avoid negative or confrontational statements. They should focus on finding a solution to the customer's problem, rather than on blaming or criticizing the customer.

Offer solutions - Employees should offer practical solutions to the customer's problem, and should be prepared to negotiate and compromise if necessary.

Follow up - After the interaction, employees should follow up with the customer to ensure that their problem has been resolved and to check if they are satisfied with the outcome.

Role-playing exercises can be conducted in a group setting or one-on-one, and can be tailored to the specific needs and challenges of each employee. They can also be repeated over time to reinforce learning and to help employees to develop their skills and confidence.

In addition to role-playing exercises, managers and trainers can also provide employees with training and resources on de-escalation techniques, communication skills, and conflict resolution. This can include workshops, online training modules, and coaching sessions.

Ultimately, the goal of role-playing and training exercises is to help customer service representatives to build strong relationships with customers, to resolve problems and conflicts effectively, and to create a positive and supportive customer experience. By practicing de-escalation techniques and developing effective communication skills, employees can improve their performance and increase customer satisfaction, loyalty, and retention.

Exercise:

What are some benefits of role-playing exercises for customer service representatives?

Why is active listening important in de-escalating difficult customer interactions?

How can customer service representatives show empathy for a customer's situation?

What are some examples of positive language that employees can use in difficult customer interactions?

How can follow-up help to reinforce positive customer experiences?

CHAPTER 8: DEALING WITH COMPLAINTS AND CONFLICT

In the world of customer service, dealing with complaints and conflict is an inevitable part of the job. Whether you are a business owner, a store manager, a shift supervisor, or a customer service representative, it is essential to know how to handle difficult situations in a professional and effective manner. The ability to manage conflict and complaints is not only important for maintaining customer satisfaction, but also for building trust and loyalty with your customers.

This chapter will provide you with a comprehensive overview of how to deal with complaints and conflict in a customer service environment. We will cover a range of topics, from understanding the psychology of complaining customers to learning de-escalation techniques and strategies for resolving conflicts.

Section 1: Understanding Complaints and Conflict

The first step in dealing with complaints and conflict is to understand the psychology behind these behaviors. Complaints and conflicts arise when customers feel that their expectations have not been met or that they have been treated unfairly. When customers feel dissatisfied, they may become confrontational or aggressive in their behavior.

It is important to recognize that complaints and conflicts are not personal attacks on you or your business, but rather a natural response to perceived grievances. By understanding the underlying causes of complaints and conflicts, you can develop empathy for your customers and respond to their concerns in a constructive manner.

Section 2: De-escalation Techniques

De-escalation techniques are essential for managing difficult situations with customers. These techniques involve recognizing and responding to the emotional state of the customer, and taking steps to calm them down and diffuse the situation. Some common de-escalation techniques include active listening, acknowledging the customer's concerns, and offering apologies or solutions.

It is important to remain calm and professional in these situations, even if the customer becomes angry or aggressive. Your goal should be to de-escalate the situation and find a resolution that satisfies the customer.

Section 3: Strategies for Resolving Conflict

In some cases, de-escalation techniques may not be enough to resolve a conflict. When this happens, it is important to have strategies in place for resolving the conflict. These strategies may involve finding common ground with the customer, offering alternative solutions, or involving a third party mediator.

The key to resolving conflicts is to remain calm and focused on finding a mutually satisfactory solution. It is important to listen to the customer's concerns and work together to find a resolution that meets their needs while also protecting the interests of your business.

Section 4: Best Practices for Handling Complaints and Conflict

In addition to understanding the psychology of complaints and conflict, and having de-escalation techniques and strategies in place, there are several best practices that can help you effectively handle difficult situations with customers. These best practices include:

Responding promptly and professionally to complaints and conflicts
Empathizing with the customer and acknowledging their concerns
Offering apologies and solutions to resolve the issue
Following up with the customer to ensure their satisfaction
Documenting complaints and conflicts for future reference
By following these best practices, you can effectively manage complaints and conflict in your customer service interactions and build stronger relationships with your customers.

In conclusion, dealing with complaints and conflict is an essential part of customer service. By understanding the psychology behind these behaviors, using de-escalation techniques, and having strategies and best practices in place, you can effectively manage difficult situations with customers and build stronger relationships with them. In the next sections, we will delve deeper into these topics and provide you with the tools and skills you need to handle complaints and conflict in a professional and effective manner.

The importance of addressing customer complaints and conflict

Every business, regardless of size or industry, will encounter complaints and conflict at some point. Dealing with these situations can be challenging, especially when emotions are running high. However, addressing customer complaints and conflict is crucial for maintaining a positive reputation and retaining customers.

In this chapter, we will discuss the importance of addressing customer complaints and conflict and provide strategies for handling difficult situations. We will also explore the benefits of effectively addressing complaints and conflict and how to prevent future issues.

The Importance of Addressing Customer Complaints and Conflict

Ignoring customer complaints and conflict can lead to negative consequences for a business. Customers who feel ignored or undervalued are likely to take their business elsewhere, resulting in lost revenue and a damaged reputation.

On the other hand, addressing complaints and conflict in a timely and effective manner can have numerous benefits. For instance, it can help to build customer loyalty, increase customer satisfaction, and improve the overall reputation of a business. Addressing complaints and conflict can also provide opportunities for businesses to learn from their mistakes and improve their products or services.

It is important to note that addressing complaints and conflict is not just about resolving the specific issue at hand. It is also about demonstrating to customers that their concerns are being taken seriously and that their business is valued. When customers feel heard and understood, they are more likely to continue doing business with a company and recommend it to others.

Strategies for Handling Difficult Situations

Dealing with difficult customers can be challenging, but there are several strategies that customer service representatives can use to effectively handle these situations.

Listen actively
Active listening involves paying close attention to what the customer is saying and asking clarifying questions to ensure that their concerns are fully understood. When customers feel heard and understood, they are more likely to remain calm and work with the representative to find a resolution.

Stay calm and professional
Remaining calm and professional can help to de-escalate tense situations and prevent them from escalating further. It is important for customer service representatives to maintain a professional demeanor, even when dealing with difficult customers.

Acknowledge the customer's concerns
Acknowledging the customer's concerns shows that their issue is being taken seriously and that the representative understands the importance of finding a resolution. This can help to build trust and establish a positive rapport with the customer.

Apologize when appropriate
Apologizing for any inconvenience or frustration caused by the issue can go a long way in diffusing tense situations. However, it is important to only apologize when appropriate and avoid taking responsibility for issues that are beyond the representative's control.

Offer solutions
Offering solutions that address the customer's concerns can help to find a resolution and prevent the issue from escalating further. It is important to provide options that are feasible and realistic, and to follow through on any promises made.

Preventing Future Issues

While addressing customer complaints and conflict is important, preventing these issues from occurring in the first place is even more beneficial. Here are some strategies that businesses can use to prevent future issues:

Provide clear communication
Clear communication can help to prevent misunderstandings and ensure that customers know what to expect. This includes providing clear instructions, setting realistic expectations, and keeping customers informed throughout the process.

Train employees in customer service skills
Proper training in customer service skills can help employees to effectively handle difficult situations and provide exceptional customer service. This can include training in active listening, conflict resolution, and empathy.

Encourage customer feedback

Encouraging customer feedback can help businesses to identify potential issues before they escalate and address them in a timely manner. This can include surveys, feedback forms, and social media monitoring.

Address issues promptly

Addressing issues promptly can prevent them from escalating and becoming bigger problems. This means acknowledging the customer's concerns and taking action to resolve the issue as soon as possible. Businesses can establish clear protocols for how to handle customer complaints and conflicts, including who is responsible for addressing them and how they should be documented and resolved.

Implement quality control measures

Implementing quality control measures can help businesses identify potential issues before they occur. This can include conducting regular checks on products and services, reviewing customer feedback and complaints, and making necessary changes to prevent similar issues from occurring in the future.

Offer incentives for positive behavior

Offering incentives for positive behavior can encourage customers to continue to do business with a company and provide feedback that can help the business improve. This can include discounts, rewards programs, and special promotions for customers who provide feedback or refer others to the business.

In conclusion, addressing customer complaints and conflict is an important part of providing exceptional customer service. Not only does it help to resolve immediate issues, but it also shows customers that the business values their concerns and is committed to providing a positive experience. However, preventing these issues from occurring in the first place is even more beneficial, and businesses can use a variety of strategies to do so, including clear communication, employee training, customer feedback, prompt issue resolution, quality control measures, and incentives for positive behavior. By implementing these strategies, businesses can improve their overall customer service and create a positive reputation in the marketplace.

Techniques for handling complaints effectively (e.g. active listening, offering solutions, following up)

Techniques for handling complaints effectively are essential for maintaining positive customer relationships and preventing further issues. The following techniques can help customer service representatives to effectively address customer complaints:

Active Listening

Active listening is the process of fully concentrating on what the customer is saying and understanding their perspective. It involves giving the customer your full attention and responding to their concerns in a thoughtful and empathetic manner. Active listening can help to de-escalate tense situations and make customers feel heard and understood.

Examples of active listening techniques include:

Paraphrasing: Restating the customer's complaint in your own words to show that you understand their perspective.

Asking open-ended questions: Asking questions that encourage the customer to share more information about their complaint and how they feel.

Using nonverbal cues: Nodding, maintaining eye contact, and using affirmative sounds (such as "uh-huh") to show that you are listening.

Offering Solutions

Offering solutions is an important part of handling complaints effectively. Customers want their problems to be solved, and providing solutions can help to turn a negative experience into a positive one. When offering solutions, it's important to consider the customer's needs and preferences, and to provide options when possible.

Examples of effective solutions include:

Refunds or exchanges: If the customer has received a defective or unsatisfactory product, offering a refund or exchange can help to resolve the issue.

Discounts or vouchers: Offering discounts or vouchers for future purchases can help to compensate customers for their inconvenience and encourage them to continue doing business with your company.

Apologies: Sometimes a sincere apology can go a long way in resolving a customer's complaint. Apologizing for the inconvenience or frustration caused by the issue can help to show that your company values the customer's experience.

Following Up

Following up after a complaint has been resolved can help to reinforce the customer's positive experience and show that your company values their feedback. Following up can also provide an opportunity to address any lingering concerns and ensure that the customer is satisfied with the resolution.

Examples of effective follow-up techniques include:

Email or phone call: Following up with a personalized email or phone call can help to show that your company values the customer's experience and wants to ensure their satisfaction.

Surveys: Sending a survey to the customer after their complaint has been resolved can provide valuable feedback on the customer's experience and help to identify areas for improvement.

Offering incentives: Offering incentives (such as discounts or vouchers) for completing a survey or providing feedback can encourage customers to share their experiences and provide valuable insights for your company.

It's important to note that not all complaints can be resolved with a simple solution, and some issues may require more time and effort to address. However, by using active listening, offering solutions, and following up, customer service representatives can effectively handle complaints and prevent further issues.

Examples:

A customer contacts a company to complain about a defective product they received. The customer service representative listens actively to the customer's complaint, empathizes with their frustration, and offers a replacement product or refund. The representative also follows up with an email to ensure that the customer received their replacement and is satisfied with the resolution.

A customer contacts a company to complain about a delayed delivery. The customer service representative listens actively to the customer's complaint, apologizes for the inconvenience, and offers a discount on their next purchase as compensation. The representative also follows up with a phone call to ensure that the customer received their delivery and to address any further concerns.

The role of empathy in conflict resolution

The role of empathy in conflict resolution is crucial, particularly in the field of customer service. Empathy refers to the ability to understand and share the feelings of others. It involves not only understanding the perspective of the customer but also showing that you care about their situation.

Empathy can be particularly effective in conflict resolution because it helps to defuse anger and frustration. When a customer feels that their concerns are being heard and acknowledged, they are more likely to be receptive to finding a solution. On the other hand, if a customer feels that their concerns are being ignored or dismissed, they are more likely to become even more upset and escalate the situation.

To demonstrate empathy, customer service representatives must first listen actively to the customer's concerns. This means giving the customer their full attention, maintaining eye contact, and using body language to signal that you are engaged and attentive. It also means asking questions to clarify the customer's concerns and demonstrating that you understand their perspective.

In addition to active listening, customer service representatives can also use empathy statements to show that they care about the customer's situation. For example, instead of saying "I understand," which can come across as dismissive, they might say "I can imagine how frustrating that must be for you." This statement not only acknowledges the customer's frustration but also demonstrates that the representative is empathizing with the customer's experience.

Another important aspect of empathy in conflict resolution is validating the customer's emotions. This involves acknowledging the customer's feelings and letting them know that it is understandable for them to feel that way. For example, if a customer is upset because they received a defective product, the representative might say something like "I can understand why you would be upset about this. It's frustrating to receive a product that doesn't work properly."

Once the customer feels heard and validated, the customer service representative can begin working with them to find a solution to their problem. This may involve offering a refund, exchange, or other resolution that addresses the customer's concerns. By demonstrating empathy throughout the process, the representative can help to defuse the conflict and create a positive outcome for the customer.

Empathy is not only important for resolving conflicts but also for preventing them in the first place. By showing empathy in their interactions with customers, businesses can build trust and loyalty, and customers are less likely to become upset or frustrated in the first place.

However, it is important to note that empathy is not a panacea for all customer service issues. In some cases, the customer's concerns may be beyond the control of the representative, or the customer may be unreasonable or difficult to please. In these situations, it is still important to demonstrate empathy and respect, while also setting appropriate boundaries and managing the customer's expectations.

In conclusion, empathy plays a critical role in conflict resolution in the customer service industry. By demonstrating empathy, customer service representatives can defuse anger and frustration, build trust and loyalty, and create positive outcomes for customers. However, it is important to remember that empathy is only one tool in the customer service representative's toolkit and that it must be used in conjunction with other skills and strategies to effectively manage customer complaints and conflicts.

Exercise: Analyzing a real customer complaint and developing a plan for addressing it

One of the best ways to learn how to effectively handle customer complaints is to practice. In this exercise, we will analyze a real customer complaint and develop a plan for addressing it.

Step 1: Analyzing the Complaint

The first step in addressing a customer complaint is to understand the issue. Let's consider the following customer complaint:

"I am extremely unhappy with the service I received at your store. The employee who assisted me was rude and unhelpful, and I was left feeling frustrated and ignored. I would like a refund for my purchase and an apology for the poor customer service."

To effectively address this complaint, we need to break it down and understand the specific issues that the customer is raising. In this case, the customer is unhappy with the service they received, specifically citing the employee's behavior as the problem. They are requesting a refund for their purchase and an apology for the poor customer service.

Step 2: Developing a Plan for Addressing the Complaint

Now that we understand the customer's specific issues, we can develop a plan for addressing the complaint. Here are some steps we might take:

Apologize to the customer: The first step in addressing the customer's complaint is to apologize for the poor service they received. This can be done verbally or in writing, depending on the situation.

Investigate the issue: Once we have apologized, we need to investigate the issue and determine what went wrong. We can do this by speaking with the employee involved, reviewing security footage, or speaking with other employees who were present.

Provide a resolution: Once we have identified the issue, we need to provide a resolution to the customer. This might include offering a refund, a replacement product, or a discount on future purchases.

Follow up with the customer: Finally, we need to follow up with the customer to ensure that they are satisfied with the resolution. This can be done through a phone call, email, or in-person conversation.

Step 3: Applying the Plan

Now that we have developed a plan for addressing the customer's complaint, it's time to put it into action. Here's how we might apply the plan in this situation:

Apologize to the customer: We would start by apologizing to the customer for the poor service they received. This might involve speaking with them in person, calling them on the phone, or sending an email.

Investigate the issue: Next, we would investigate the issue to determine what went wrong. We might speak with the employee involved, review security footage, or speak with other employees who were present.

Provide a resolution: Based on our investigation, we would determine an appropriate resolution to offer the customer. In this case, we might offer a full refund for the purchase and a discount on future purchases.

Follow up with the customer: Finally, we would follow up with the customer to ensure that they are satisfied with the resolution. We might call them on the phone a few days after the initial conversation or send an email to check in.

Handling customer complaints can be challenging, but it is an essential part of providing excellent customer service. By analyzing a real customer complaint and developing a plan for addressing it, you can gain valuable experience and develop skills that will help you handle similar situations in the future. Remember to always listen to the customer, empathize with their situation, and work towards finding a resolution that satisfies both the customer and the business.

CHAPTER 9: THE POWER OF EMPATHY IN CUSTOMER SERVICE

Empathy is the ability to understand and share the feelings of others. It is an important skill in customer service because it allows customer service representatives to connect with customers on a personal level, build trust and rapport, and ultimately resolve issues more effectively. Empathy is not just about sympathizing with customers or feeling sorry for them. It's about putting yourself in their shoes, understanding their perspective, and using that understanding to guide your actions.

In this chapter, we will explore the importance of empathy in customer service and provide practical tips and strategies for developing and demonstrating empathy in customer interactions. We will discuss the benefits of empathy, how to cultivate empathy, and how to apply empathy in customer interactions to improve the customer experience.

Section 1: The Benefits of Empathy in Customer Service

Empathy has numerous benefits in customer service. First, empathy helps to build trust and rapport with customers. When customers feel that the representative understands their perspective, they are more likely to trust that the representative has their best interests in mind. This can lead to increased customer loyalty and repeat business.

Second, empathy helps to de-escalate tense situations. When a customer is upset or frustrated, showing empathy can help to calm them down and make them feel heard. This can diffuse the situation and make it easier to resolve the issue.

Third, empathy can help to uncover underlying issues or needs. When a customer shares their experience or concern, demonstrating empathy can help to draw out additional information that may be relevant to resolving the issue. This can help to identify root causes and prevent similar issues from occurring in the future.

Section 2: Cultivating Empathy in Customer Service

Empathy is a skill that can be developed and honed over time. Here are some tips for cultivating empathy in customer service:

Practice active listening: Active listening involves paying close attention to the customer's words, tone, and body language. It requires focusing on the customer's message and avoiding distractions or interruptions. Active listening shows the customer that you are interested in their perspective and value their input.

Put yourself in the customer's shoes: To demonstrate empathy, it's important to understand the customer's perspective. Imagine yourself in their position and think about how you would feel in their situation. This can help you to relate to the customer's emotions and experiences.

Avoid making assumptions: It's important to avoid making assumptions about the customer's feelings or intentions. Instead, ask clarifying questions to ensure that you understand the customer's perspective.

Use open-ended questions: Open-ended questions encourage the customer to share more information and provide greater insight into their concerns. These types of questions also demonstrate that you are interested in the customer's perspective and value their input.

Section 3: Applying Empathy in Customer Interactions

Demonstrating empathy in customer interactions requires more than just understanding the customer's perspective. It requires taking action based on that understanding. Here are some strategies for applying empathy in customer interactions:

Acknowledge the customer's feelings: When a customer expresses frustration or dissatisfaction, it's important to acknowledge their feelings. This can be as simple as saying, "I understand that this is frustrating for you." Acknowledging the customer's feelings shows that you are listening and that you care.

Offer solutions that address the customer's concerns: Empathy is not just about sympathizing with the customer, it's about taking action to address their concerns. When offering solutions, it's important to focus on the customer's needs and preferences.

Follow up with the customer: Following up with the customer after the issue has been resolved shows that you care about their experience and are committed to ensuring their satisfaction. It also provides an opportunity to reinforce the relationship and build trust.

Provide personalized attention: Customers want to feel valued and appreciated. By providing personalized attention, you can make them feel important and valued. This can be done by addressing them by name, asking them how their day is going, or remembering their preferences.

Be patient and understanding: Dealing with angry or frustrated customers can be challenging, but it's important to remain patient and understanding. Remember that the customer is upset because they have an issue that needs to be resolved. By remaining calm and patient, you can help to defuse the situation and find a solution.

Use active listening: Active listening is a technique that involves fully concentrating on what the customer is saying and then responding in a way that demonstrates that you have understood their concerns. This can be done by paraphrasing their statements, asking clarifying questions, and providing feedback.

Take ownership of the issue: When a customer has an issue, it's important to take ownership of it and work to resolve it as quickly and effectively as possible. This involves being accountable for the issue and taking steps to address it, rather than blaming others or making excuses.

Stay positive: Maintaining a positive attitude can help to diffuse tense situations and create a more positive experience for the customer. This can be done by using positive language, such as "I'm confident we can find a solution," and expressing gratitude for the customer's patience and understanding.

By applying these strategies, you can demonstrate empathy in customer interactions and create a more positive experience for your customers. However, it's important to remember that empathy is not a one-time event, but rather an ongoing commitment to understanding and addressing the needs of your customers. By consistently demonstrating empathy, you can build strong relationships with your customers and improve the overall success of your business.

Defining empathy and its role in customer service

Empathy is an essential component of effective customer service. It refers to the ability to understand and share the feelings of another person. When it comes to customer service, empathy is the ability to understand and share the feelings of a customer who is experiencing a problem or a difficult situation.

Empathy is often confused with sympathy, but the two concepts are distinct. Sympathy refers to feeling sorry for someone, while empathy involves understanding and sharing the feelings of someone else. Empathy requires active listening, observation, and an ability to put oneself in the other person's shoes.

The role of empathy in customer service is multifaceted. It helps build trust and rapport with customers, enhances the customer experience, and promotes customer loyalty. Empathy is particularly important in situations where customers are unhappy, frustrated, or angry. In such situations, empathizing with the customer can help defuse the situation and find a satisfactory resolution.

Empathy is also important in understanding the customer's perspective. Customers want to feel that their concerns and opinions are valued and that the company cares about their needs. Empathy can help customer service representatives to gain a deeper understanding of the customer's situation and develop solutions that address the customer's needs and concerns.

For example, a customer may call a customer service representative to report a problem with a product. Instead of simply apologizing and offering a refund or replacement, the customer service representative can use empathy to understand the customer's frustration and offer a personalized solution that meets the customer's needs. This may involve offering a discount on a future purchase or providing additional support to ensure the product works as expected.

In addition, empathy can help customer service representatives to anticipate and proactively address customer needs. By understanding the customer's perspective, customer service representatives can identify potential issues before they become major problems and offer solutions that prevent further frustration or inconvenience for the customer.

Overall, empathy is a critical component of effective customer service. It helps build trust and rapport with customers, enhances the customer experience, and promotes customer loyalty. In the following sections, we will explore strategies for demonstrating empathy in customer interactions and the benefits of doing so.

The benefits of showing empathy to customers

Empathy is a crucial aspect of customer service that can have significant benefits for both the customer and the business. When customers feel understood and valued, they are more likely to remain loyal to the business and recommend it to others. In this section, we will explore the benefits of showing empathy to customers in more detail.

Improved Customer Satisfaction

Empathy is the ability to understand and share the feelings of another person. When customers are upset or frustrated, showing empathy can help them feel heard and valued. By acknowledging their feelings and demonstrating a willingness to help, you can turn a negative experience into a positive one. This can lead to increased customer satisfaction and loyalty.

For example, imagine a customer contacts a clothing store to inquire about a damaged item they received in the mail. The customer is upset because they were looking forward to wearing the item to a special event. Instead of dismissing the customer's concerns or making excuses, the customer service representative acknowledges the customer's frustration and offers a solution that meets their needs. The customer is happy with the outcome and feels valued by the business.

Increased Customer Loyalty

When customers feel valued and understood, they are more likely to remain loyal to the business. This means they are more likely to continue purchasing products or services from the business and recommend it to others.

According to a study by PwC, 73% of customers cite customer experience as an important factor in their purchasing decisions. By showing empathy and providing excellent customer service, businesses can differentiate themselves from competitors and build long-term relationships with their customers.

For example, imagine a customer contacts a bank to report a fraudulent charge on their credit card. The customer service representative not only helps the customer dispute the charge but also takes the time to explain how to monitor their account for future fraudulent activity. The customer appreciates the extra effort and feels more loyal to the bank.

Improved Employee Engagement

Empathy is not just important for customers; it also plays a role in employee engagement. When employees feel supported and valued, they are more likely to be engaged and committed to their work.

According to a study by Gallup, engaged employees are more productive, provide better customer service, and are less likely to leave their jobs. By promoting empathy and providing employees with the tools they need to deliver excellent customer service, businesses can improve employee engagement and create a positive work environment.

For example, imagine a retail store that values empathy and encourages employees to put themselves in the customer's shoes. The store provides employees with training on how to handle difficult customer situations and recognizes and rewards employees who demonstrate empathy in their interactions with customers. The employees feel valued and motivated to provide excellent customer service.

Reduced Customer Churn

Customer churn refers to the number of customers who stop doing business with a company over a period of time. By showing empathy and providing excellent customer service, businesses can reduce customer churn and retain more customers.

According to a study by NewVoiceMedia, poor customer service is the leading cause of customer churn, with 44% of customers switching to a competitor after a poor customer service experience. By investing in customer service and promoting empathy, businesses can reduce the likelihood of losing customers and increase their lifetime value.

For example, imagine a customer contacts a cable company to report a service outage. The customer service representative not only apologizes for the inconvenience but also provides regular updates on the status of the outage and offers a discount on the customer's next bill. The customer is satisfied with the resolution and is less likely to switch to a competitor.

In conclusion, showing empathy to customers can have significant benefits for both the customer and the business. By improving customer satisfaction, increasing customer loyalty, improving employee engagement, and reducing customer churn, businesses can create a positive customer experience that leads to long-term success.

Techniques for showing empathy (e.g. active listening, using positive language, validating customer concerns)

Techniques for showing empathy are essential for customer service representatives and other professionals who interact with customers on a regular basis. Empathy allows these individuals to understand and relate to their customers' needs and concerns, leading to a more positive and productive customer experience. In this section, we will explore several techniques for showing empathy, including active listening, using positive language, and validating customer concerns.

Active Listening

Active listening is a critical component of showing empathy. It involves fully concentrating on what the customer is saying, without interrupting or imposing one's own ideas or opinions. Active listening requires focus, attention, and a willingness to understand the customer's perspective. When done correctly, active listening can help build trust and rapport with the customer, leading to a more positive and productive interaction.

One way to practice active listening is to repeat back what the customer has said in your own words. This helps ensure that you have understood the customer's perspective and can respond appropriately. Another technique is to ask clarifying questions to gain a deeper understanding of the customer's concerns and needs.

Using Positive Language

Using positive language is another effective technique for showing empathy. Positive language focuses on what can be done, rather than what cannot. It avoids negative or critical statements and instead focuses on constructive solutions.

For example, instead of saying "I can't do that," a customer service representative might say "Here are some other options we can explore." Using positive language not only shows empathy by focusing on solutions, but it can also help de-escalate tense or difficult situations.

Validating Customer Concerns

Validating customer concerns is an important technique for showing empathy. It involves acknowledging the customer's perspective and demonstrating that their concerns are valid and understood. This can help build trust and rapport with the customer and create a more positive and productive interaction.

One way to validate customer concerns is to summarize what the customer has said and repeat it back to them. This demonstrates that you have listened and understood their perspective. Another technique is to empathize with the customer by expressing your understanding of how they feel. For example, "I can understand why you might feel frustrated in this situation."

Exercises and Questions:

Why is active listening an essential technique for showing empathy?
How can positive language help de-escalate difficult situations in customer service?

What are some techniques for validating customer concerns?

Think about a recent interaction you had with a customer. Did you use any of the techniques discussed in this section? How did they impact the interaction?

Provide an example of a situation where using positive language could be helpful in a customer service interaction.

In conclusion, techniques for showing empathy are essential for anyone who interacts with customers on a regular basis. Active listening, using positive language, and validating customer concerns are just a few examples of effective techniques for showing empathy. By practicing these techniques, customer service representatives and other professionals can build trust and rapport with customers and create more positive and productive interactions.

Exercise: Practicing empathy in customer service scenarios

Practicing empathy in customer service scenarios is essential to building strong relationships with customers and providing excellent service. Empathy is the ability to understand and share the feelings of another person, and it is a critical component of effective communication in customer service. The following exercises will help you develop your empathy skills and apply them in real-world situations.

Exercise 1: Active Listening

Active listening is a technique that involves paying close attention to what the customer is saying and responding in a way that shows you understand their perspective. In this exercise, you will practice active listening by engaging in a role-play scenario with a partner.

Find a partner and choose a customer service scenario to role-play. For example, one of you can pretend to be a customer with a complaint, and the other can be a customer service representative.

Start the role-play and focus on actively listening to your partner. Listen to what they say, and try to understand their perspective. Ask open-ended questions to clarify their concerns and show that you are engaged.

Respond to your partner in a way that demonstrates empathy. Use positive language, validate their concerns, and offer solutions that address their needs.

Switch roles and repeat the exercise.

Exercise 2: Using Positive Language

Using positive language is an essential technique for showing empathy in customer service. Positive language involves using words and phrases that convey a helpful and supportive attitude. In this exercise, you will practice using positive language by completing a worksheet.

Download and print the Positive Language Worksheet (link provided).

Read the customer service scenarios on the worksheet and circle the negative language.

Rewrite the sentences using positive language. For example, instead of saying "I can't do that," say "Let me see what I can do to help you."

Discuss your answers with a partner and share your strategies for using positive language in customer service scenarios.

Exercise 3: Validating Customer Concerns

Validating customer concerns is a technique that involves acknowledging the customer's feelings and demonstrating that you understand their perspective. In this exercise, you will practice validating customer concerns by completing a role-play scenario with a partner.

Find a partner and choose a customer service scenario to role-play. For example, one of you can pretend to be a customer with a complaint, and the other can be a customer service representative.

Start the role-play and listen to your partner's concerns. Acknowledge their feelings and demonstrate that you understand their perspective.

Validate your partner's concerns by restating their problem in your own words. For example, "It sounds like you're frustrated because you haven't received your order yet."

Respond to your partner's concerns by offering solutions that address their needs.

Switch roles and repeat the exercise.

Exercise 4: Building Empathy Skills

Building empathy skills is an ongoing process that involves self-reflection and practice. In this exercise, you will reflect on your experiences and identify areas for improvement.

Think of a recent customer service interaction you had, either as a customer or a customer service representative.

Reflect on the interaction and identify what worked well and what could be improved.

Write down your reflections in a journal or notebook.

Identify one area for improvement and set a goal to practice that skill in your next customer service interaction.

Conclusion

Practicing empathy in customer service scenarios is essential to building strong relationships with customers and providing excellent service. Active listening, using positive language, and validating customer concerns are all techniques that can help you show empathy in your interactions with customers. By practicing these techniques and reflecting on your experiences, you can continue to build your empathy skills and provide exceptional customer service.

CHAPTER 10: BUILDING STRONG RELATIONSHIPS WITH CUSTOMERS

In the world of business, customer relationships are key to success. Building strong relationships with customers not only fosters brand loyalty but also creates a positive image of the company in the customer's mind. It is not only about providing excellent customer service but also about understanding the customer's needs, wants, and expectations. To build strong relationships with customers, companies need to focus on understanding the customer's perspective and meeting their needs. In this chapter, we will explore the importance of building strong relationships with customers, how to develop a customer-focused mindset, and the various strategies companies can use to build strong relationships with customers.

Why Building Strong Relationships with Customers is Important

The importance of building strong relationships with customers cannot be overstated. The following are some of the reasons why companies should focus on building strong relationships with their customers:

Increased customer loyalty: Customers are more likely to stay loyal to a brand that they feel connected to. By building strong relationships with customers, companies can foster brand loyalty and keep their customers coming back.

Positive brand image: Building strong relationships with customers can create a positive image of the company in the customer's mind. Customers are more likely to recommend a company that they have a positive relationship with to their friends and family, which can lead to new customers and increased revenue.

Increased customer lifetime value: Customers who have a strong relationship with a company are more likely to spend more money on that company's products or services over time. This can increase the customer's lifetime value to the company and ultimately lead to increased revenue.

Developing a Customer-Focused Mindset

To build strong relationships with customers, companies need to develop a customer-focused mindset. This means that companies should focus on understanding the customer's perspective and meeting their needs. The following are some of the ways companies can develop a customer-focused mindset:

Listen to the customer: Listening to the customer is essential in developing a customer-focused mindset. Companies should listen to their customers' feedback and use it to improve their products and services.

Empathize with the customer: Empathy is the ability to understand and share the feelings of others. By empathizing with the customer, companies can develop a deeper understanding of their needs and expectations.

Put the customer first: Companies should prioritize the customer's needs and expectations over their own. This means that companies should be willing to go above and beyond to ensure that the customer is satisfied.

Strategies for Building Strong Relationships with Customers

There are several strategies that companies can use to build strong relationships with their customers. The following are some of the most effective strategies:

Provide excellent customer service: Providing excellent customer service is essential in building strong relationships with customers. Companies should be responsive to customer inquiries, provide timely and accurate information, and resolve customer issues quickly.

Use positive language: Using positive language can help to create a positive image of the company in the customer's mind. Companies should avoid negative language and instead focus on using positive language to communicate with customers.

Personalize the customer experience: Personalizing the customer experience can help to create a stronger connection between the customer and the company. Companies should use customer data to personalize their interactions with customers and tailor their products and services to meet their individual needs.

Validate customer concerns: Validating customer concerns can help to build trust with customers. Companies should listen to customer complaints and take steps to address their concerns.

Use active listening: Active listening is the ability to fully concentrate on what is being said and understand the message being conveyed. By using active listening techniques, companies can better understand their customers' needs and expectations.

Exercise: Practicing Building Strong Relationships with Customers

To practice building strong relationships with customers, students can role-play customer service scenarios to further develop skills in building strong relationships with customers, it is helpful to practice through role-playing customer service scenarios. In this exercise, students can take on the roles of both the customer and the customer service representative.

In each scenario, the customer should present a specific issue or concern, and the customer service representative should use their skills in empathy and active listening to address the concern and work towards a resolution. The scenarios can range from simple inquiries to more complex issues, such as complaints or product defects.

It is important to encourage students to approach these scenarios with an open mind and to practice active listening, asking open-ended questions, and responding with empathy and positive language. This exercise can help students build confidence in their ability to handle challenging customer service situations and build stronger relationships with customers.

In addition to role-playing scenarios, students can also benefit from real-world experience in customer service. Encourage students to seek out opportunities to gain practical experience, such as volunteering at a non-profit organization or working part-time in a customer service role.

By practicing building strong relationships with customers, students can develop the skills necessary to excel in the field of customer service and provide exceptional service to customers.

The importance of building relationships with customers

In today's highly competitive business landscape, building strong relationships with customers is essential for long-term success. Companies that prioritize customer relationships and consistently provide exceptional customer service are more likely to retain customers, increase sales, and build a positive reputation. In this section, we will discuss the importance of building relationships with customers and explore the benefits of doing so.

Increased Customer Loyalty

One of the main benefits of building strong relationships with customers is increased customer loyalty. When customers feel valued and appreciated, they are more likely to continue doing business with a company. They may also be more inclined to refer friends and family to the company, which can lead to new customers and increased sales. In fact, according to a study by Temkin Group, customers who have a positive emotional experience with a company are 6 times more likely to recommend the company to others.

Improved Customer Retention

Another benefit of building strong relationships with customers is improved customer retention. Customers who feel connected to a company and its values are more likely to remain loyal over time. By building a relationship with customers, companies can also gain valuable feedback that can help them improve their products or services, leading to even greater customer satisfaction.

Increased Sales

Building strong relationships with customers can also lead to increased sales. When customers trust a company and feel connected to its brand, they are more likely to purchase additional products or services. Additionally, loyal customers may be willing to pay a premium price for a company's products or services, which can lead to increased revenue.

Positive Reputation

Companies that prioritize building relationships with customers also benefit from a positive reputation. Customers are more likely to share positive experiences with others, which can lead to new customers and increased sales. In contrast, negative experiences can quickly spread through social media and other online channels, damaging a company's reputation.

Competitive Advantage

Finally, companies that build strong relationships with customers gain a competitive advantage in their industry. By providing exceptional customer service and building a positive reputation, these companies are more likely to stand out in a crowded market. This can lead to increased market share, increased revenue, and greater long-term success.

In summary, building relationships with customers is essential for long-term success in today's business landscape. Companies that prioritize customer relationships are more likely to retain customers, increase sales, and build a positive reputation. By providing exceptional customer service and building a strong brand, companies can gain a competitive advantage and ensure long-term success.

Examples:

Example 1: A restaurant that focuses on building strong relationships with customers

A restaurant owner who understands the importance of building relationships with customers might train staff members to remember the names and preferences of regular customers. They may offer personalized recommendations or invite customers to special events. By providing exceptional customer service and building a strong rapport with customers, the restaurant can create a loyal customer base that returns time and time again.

Example 2: A small business owner who prioritizes customer relationships

A small business owner who prioritizes building relationships with customers might send personalized thank-you notes after a purchase or offer exclusive discounts to repeat customers. By showing customers that they are valued and appreciated, the business owner can increase customer loyalty and build a positive reputation in the community.

Exercises:

Why is building relationships with customers important for long-term success in business?

How can building strong relationships with customers lead to increased sales?

What are some strategies that companies can use to build strong relationships with customers?

How can companies use customer feedback to improve their products or services?

Can you think of a time when a positive customer experience led you to recommend a company to others? What made that experience so memorable?

Techniques for building rapport and trust (e.g. remembering customer details, personalizing communication)

Building rapport and trust with customers is an essential aspect of creating a positive customer experience. When customers feel that they are heard, understood, and valued, they are more likely to become loyal, repeat customers. One way to build rapport and trust is by personalizing communication and remembering customer details. In this section, we will discuss techniques for building rapport and trust, including the importance of personalization and remembering customer details.

Personalization

Personalization refers to the process of customizing interactions with customers to meet their unique needs and preferences. Personalization helps build rapport and trust because customers feel that they are being heard and that their needs are being met. Personalization can take many forms, such as using a customer's name, tailoring recommendations based on previous purchases, or acknowledging a customer's preferences.

One example of personalization is when a customer walks into a store, and an employee greets them by name. This simple gesture can make the customer feel welcome and valued. Similarly, when an online retailer recommends products based on a customer's previous purchases, it shows that the retailer is paying attention to the customer's needs and preferences.

Remembering Customer Details

Remembering customer details is another way to build rapport and trust. When a customer feels that an employee remembers them, they feel valued and respected. Remembering customer details can take many forms, such as remembering their name, their preferences, or their previous interactions with the company.

For example, a bank teller who remembers a customer's name and inquires about their family can make the customer feel valued and appreciated. Similarly, a sales associate who remembers a customer's shoe size and suggests new styles based on their previous purchases can make the customer feel understood and heard.

Techniques for Remembering Customer Details

Remembering customer details can be challenging, particularly for employees who interact with many customers each day. However, there are several techniques that employees can use to help remember customer details.

One technique is to take notes after each interaction. For example, a customer service representative could make a note of a customer's name and the reason for their call. These notes can be reviewed before the next interaction, making it easier to remember important details.

Another technique is to use mnemonics or other memory aids. For example, a sales associate could associate a customer's name with a particular color or object to help remember it.

Finally, employees can use technology to help remember customer details. For example, a CRM system can store customer information, such as their name, contact information, and purchase history. When an employee interacts with the customer, they can review this information to refresh their memory.

Building rapport and trust with customers is essential for creating a positive customer experience. Personalization and remembering customer details are two techniques that can help build rapport and trust. By customizing interactions and remembering important details, employees can make customers feel valued and appreciated. These techniques require effort and practice but are well worth the effort as they lead to loyal, repeat customers.

The role of follow-up and ongoing communication in relationship-building

The relationship between a business and its customers is not a one-time interaction. It is an ongoing process that requires consistent communication and follow-up. By providing follow-up and ongoing communication, businesses can build strong relationships with their customers, foster trust, and increase customer loyalty.

One effective way to maintain ongoing communication with customers is to utilize customer relationship management (CRM) software. CRM software is designed to manage a company's interactions with current and potential customers. It allows businesses to keep track of customer information, including their contact details, preferences, and previous interactions with the company. By using this information, businesses can tailor their communication with customers to make it more personal and relevant.

Another technique for building relationships with customers through ongoing communication is to send regular newsletters or updates. These can be used to share information about new products or services, special promotions, or company news. Newsletters can also be used to provide value to customers by sharing industry news or helpful tips related to the products or services the company provides.

Personalized follow-up communication is also critical for building strong relationships with customers. For example, a customer who has recently made a purchase may receive a follow-up call or email thanking them for their business and checking in to see if they are satisfied with their purchase. This type of personalized communication shows the customer that the company values their business and is interested in their satisfaction.

In addition to personalized follow-up communication, businesses can also utilize automated follow-up communication. For example, a customer who has not made a purchase in a while may receive an automated email or text message reminding them of the company's products or services. Automated communication can be an effective way to stay top-of-mind with customers without requiring a significant investment of time or resources.

It is important to note that follow-up and ongoing communication should not be intrusive or pushy. Customers may quickly become annoyed if they feel that they are being bombarded with communication from a company. Instead, businesses should focus on providing value to their customers through their communication efforts.

In summary, the role of follow-up and ongoing communication in relationship-building cannot be overstated. By utilizing CRM software, sending regular newsletters, providing personalized follow-up communication, and utilizing automated follow-up communication, businesses can build strong relationships with their customers, foster trust, and increase customer loyalty. However, it is important to ensure that communication efforts are tailored to the customer's needs and preferences, and that they provide value to the customer.

Exercise: Developing a plan for building relationships with a specific set of customers

One of the key aspects of building strong relationships with customers is identifying specific groups of customers and developing targeted strategies for building relationships with them. In this exercise, students will develop a plan for building relationships with a specific set of customers, using the techniques and principles discussed in the previous sections.

Step 1: Identify the Target Customer Group

The first step in developing a plan for building relationships with a specific set of customers is to identify the target customer group. This could be a group of customers who have specific needs or characteristics that set them apart from other customers. For example, the target group might be high-income customers who are interested in luxury goods, or it might be young families with children who are looking for affordable and convenient products.

Once the target group has been identified, it is important to gather information about their needs, preferences, and behaviors. This can be done through customer surveys, focus groups, or by analyzing customer data.

Step 2: Define the Objectives of the Plan

Once the target customer group has been identified, the next step is to define the objectives of the plan. These objectives should be specific, measurable, and achievable. They should also be aligned with the overall goals of the organization.

For example, the objectives of a plan to build relationships with high-income customers might be to increase sales to this group by 10% over the next year, to improve customer satisfaction ratings among this group, or to increase the number of repeat purchases from this group.

Step 3: Develop a Strategy for Building Relationships

With the target group and objectives in mind, the next step is to develop a strategy for building relationships with this group of customers. This strategy should be tailored to the specific needs and preferences of the target group.

One effective strategy for building relationships with customers is to personalize communication and interactions with them. This might involve addressing customers by name, remembering their preferences, and sending them personalized offers or recommendations based on their past purchases or behavior.

Another strategy is to provide excellent customer service at every touchpoint. This means being responsive to customer inquiries and complaints, providing timely and accurate information, and going above and beyond to meet their needs and expectations.

Step 4: Implement the Plan

Once the strategy has been developed, the next step is to implement the plan. This might involve training customer service staff to interact with the target group in a specific way, developing marketing campaigns tailored to this group, or adjusting product offerings to better meet their needs.

It is important to monitor the effectiveness of the plan over time and make adjustments as necessary. This might involve gathering feedback from customers, analyzing sales and customer data, or conducting additional research to better understand the target group.

Step 5: Evaluate the Results

Finally, it is important to evaluate the results of the plan to determine whether it has been successful in achieving its objectives. This might involve analyzing sales and customer data, gathering feedback from customers, or conducting surveys or focus groups to assess customer satisfaction.

Based on the results of the evaluation, adjustments can be made to the plan as necessary to improve its effectiveness over time.

Developing a plan for building relationships with a specific set of customers is an important aspect of effective customer service. By identifying a target group, defining specific objectives, developing a tailored strategy, implementing the plan, and evaluating the results, organizations can build strong relationships with their customers and improve customer satisfaction and loyalty.

PART 2 ADVANCED CUSTOMER SERVICE TECHNIQUES:

As businesses grow and competition intensifies, it becomes increasingly important to go beyond the basics of customer service and implement more advanced techniques to build strong relationships with customers. This is where advanced customer service techniques come into play.

Part 2 of this textbook will cover advanced customer service techniques that can help businesses stand out from their competitors and create loyal customers. These techniques will require more effort, resources, and expertise, but the rewards are worth it in terms of increased customer satisfaction, loyalty, and revenue.

The section will cover various topics such as building trust and rapport with customers, personalizing communication, managing customer expectations, handling difficult customers, and measuring customer satisfaction. The goal is to equip students with the skills and knowledge they need to excel in their customer service roles and make a positive impact on their organizations.

Throughout this section, we will use examples from a range of industries, including retail, hospitality, banking, and healthcare, to illustrate how these techniques can be applied in different settings. We will also provide exercises, case studies, and discussion questions to help students develop a deeper understanding of the concepts and apply them in practical situations.

By the end of this section, students will have a solid foundation in advanced customer service techniques and be able to apply them in a wide range of customer-facing roles. They will also understand the importance of continuous improvement and ongoing training in the field of customer service, as well as the impact that excellent customer service can have on a business's success.

CHAPTER 11: PROVIDING EXCEPTIONAL FACE-TO-FACE CUSTOMER SERVICE

Providing exceptional face-to-face customer service is an important skill for customer service representatives to develop. When customers visit a physical store or location, they expect to be treated with courtesy and respect. In addition, customers want their needs to be met quickly and efficiently. This requires that customer service representatives possess excellent communication skills, knowledge of the products and services they provide, and the ability to anticipate customer needs.

This chapter will provide an overview of the skills required for providing exceptional face-to-face customer service. The chapter will begin by discussing the importance of creating a positive first impression and how to do so. Then, it will cover how to listen actively to customers and ask the right questions to identify their needs. It will also address the importance of body language and non-verbal communication in customer interactions. Finally, the chapter will discuss strategies for resolving customer complaints and ensuring that customers leave the store feeling satisfied.

Creating a Positive First Impression

The first impression a customer has of a business is critical in shaping their overall perception of the company. Therefore, it is essential that customer service representatives create a positive first impression. This can be achieved by being well-groomed and dressed professionally, greeting customers with a warm and friendly smile, and using appropriate language when addressing customers.

In addition, customer service representatives should be aware of their body language and the signals they are sending to customers. For example, crossing arms or standing with hands on hips can convey a negative or defensive attitude, while nodding and maintaining eye contact can signal active listening and engagement.

Listening Actively to Customers

Active listening is an essential skill for customer service representatives. It involves focusing on what the customer is saying, understanding their needs, and responding appropriately. To listen actively, customer service representatives should give the customer their undivided attention, avoid interrupting, and provide feedback to show that they understand what the customer is saying.

Asking the Right Questions

Asking the right questions is also important in identifying customer needs. Open-ended questions, such as "How can I help you today?" or "What brings you to our store?" encourage customers to share more information and provide insights into their needs. Closed-ended questions, such as "Would you like me to show you some options?" can help narrow down the customer's needs and preferences.

Body Language and Non-Verbal Communication

In addition to verbal communication, body language and non-verbal communication can also impact customer interactions. Positive body language, such as smiling, nodding, and maintaining eye contact, can help build rapport and establish trust with customers. On the other hand, negative body language, such as avoiding eye contact or crossing arms, can create a negative impression and hinder effective communication.

Resolving Customer Complaints

Even with exceptional customer service, complaints can still arise. The key is to handle complaints in a way that satisfies the customer and resolves the issue. This can be achieved by actively listening to the customer's concerns, acknowledging their frustration, and proposing solutions that meet their needs. It is important to remember that a successful resolution to a customer complaint can often turn a negative experience into a positive one and increase customer loyalty.

In conclusion, providing exceptional face-to-face customer service requires a combination of communication skills, product knowledge, and the ability to anticipate customer needs. By creating a positive first impression, listening actively, asking the right questions, using positive body language and non-verbal communication, and resolving complaints effectively, customer service representatives can provide exceptional service that meets customer needs and builds long-term relationships.

Techniques for greeting and engaging customers in person

In today's fast-paced world, where technology has taken over most of our communication, face-to-face interaction has become more important than ever before.

Especially in the customer service industry, where the first impression of a business is formed by the interaction between the customer and the employee. Therefore, it is essential to have the right techniques for greeting and engaging customers in person.

This chapter will explore the techniques that are used to create a welcoming and positive environment when engaging with customers face-to-face. We will discuss the importance of making a great first impression, non-verbal communication, active listening, and other strategies to engage with customers effectively.

The Importance of Making a Great First Impression

First impressions are critical when it comes to customer service. It can be challenging to recover from a bad first impression, and it can negatively impact the customer's experience with the business. Therefore, it is essential to make a great first impression by greeting the customer with a smile, introducing yourself, and being attentive to their needs.

Greeting the Customer

The greeting is the first opportunity to make a positive impression on the customer. A simple greeting can set the tone for the entire interaction, and it can make the customer feel welcomed and valued. It is crucial to greet the customer with a smile and an enthusiastic tone of voice.

For example, instead of saying, "Can I help you?" try saying "Good morning, how can I assist you today?" This approach shows that you are friendly and willing to help the customer, which can make them feel more comfortable.

Introducing Yourself

Introducing yourself is another important technique to make a great first impression. When you introduce yourself, it creates a more personal connection between you and the customer. It also helps to establish trust and credibility.

For example, "Hello, my name is John. How may I assist you?" This approach shows that you are willing to take ownership of the customer's needs and that you are responsible for helping them.

Being Attentive to the Customer's Needs

Being attentive to the customer's needs is another essential technique for making a great first impression. Listening to their needs and showing a genuine interest in helping them can create a positive impression and build trust.

For example, "I understand you are looking for a specific product. Let me show you where it is located and answer any questions you may have." This approach shows that you are willing to go the extra mile to assist the customer and that you are invested in their needs.

Non-Verbal Communication

Non-verbal communication plays a vital role in face-to-face interactions. It includes body language, facial expressions, and tone of voice. Non-verbal communication can either enhance or detract from the customer's experience, so it is essential to be aware of it.

Body Language

Body language includes gestures, posture, and eye contact. It can communicate a lot about a person's mood, attitude, and confidence. For example, standing up straight with your shoulders back and maintaining eye contact can convey confidence, while slouching and avoiding eye contact can convey insecurity.

Facial Expressions

Facial expressions can also communicate a lot about a person's emotions and attitude. Smiling, nodding, and maintaining an open and friendly facial expression can create a welcoming environment for the customer.

Tone of Voice

The tone of voice is another crucial aspect of non-verbal communication. It includes the volume, pitch, and inflection of a person's voice. It can communicate a lot about a person's mood and attitude. A warm and friendly tone of voice can create a welcoming environment for the customer, while a cold and indifferent tone of voice can make the customer feel unwelcome.

Active Listening

Active listening is an essential technique for engaging with customers in person. It involves focusing on the customer's words, interpreting them accurately, and responding appropriately. Active listening means giving your full attention to the customer and making sure you understand what they are saying before responding. This technique is crucial for building rapport with the customer and making them feel heard and valued.

Active listening involves several steps. First, it is important to give the customer your full attention. This means making eye contact, nodding your head, and giving verbal cues to indicate that you are listening. Second, it is essential to focus on the customer's words and avoid distractions. This means putting away any devices or other distractions and focusing solely on the customer.

Third, it is crucial to interpret the customer's words accurately. This means paraphrasing what the customer has said to ensure that you have understood them correctly. For example, if a customer says, "I'm looking for a dress for a wedding," you might respond by saying, "So you need a dress for a formal occasion, is that right?" This demonstrates to the customer that you are actively listening and trying to understand their needs.

Finally, it is essential to respond appropriately to the customer's words. This means providing relevant information, offering assistance, and answering any questions the customer may have. By responding appropriately, you can build trust with the customer and create a positive customer service experience.

Empathy

Empathy is another critical component of engaging with customers in person. Empathy means understanding and sharing the customer's feelings and emotions. When a customer feels understood and valued, they are more likely to have a positive experience with your business.

To demonstrate empathy, it is essential to put yourself in the customer's shoes and try to understand their perspective. This means being patient, kind, and compassionate. It also means using active listening techniques to understand the customer's needs and concerns.

For example, if a customer is upset about a product that did not meet their expectations, you might say, "I understand that you're frustrated with the product. Let's see if we can find a solution that works for you." This shows the customer that you understand their frustration and are willing to work with them to find a solution.

Non-Verbal Cues

In addition to verbal communication, non-verbal cues can also play a significant role in engaging with customers in person. Non-verbal cues include body language, facial expressions, and gestures. These cues can communicate a lot about a person's mood and attitude, even if they are not saying anything.

To communicate effectively with customers, it is essential to pay attention to your own non-verbal cues and be aware of the customer's non-verbal cues. This means maintaining good eye contact, smiling, and using open body language. It also means being aware of the customer's body language and facial expressions, which can indicate their mood and level of engagement.

For example, if a customer is frowning and crossing their arms, it may indicate that they are unhappy or defensive. In this case, it is important to use active listening techniques and demonstrate empathy to address the customer's concerns and improve their experience.

Engaging with customers in person requires a range of techniques, including active listening, empathy, and effective use of non-verbal cues. By using these techniques, you can create a positive customer service experience that builds trust and loyalty with your customers. Remember, every interaction with a customer is an opportunity to create a lasting impression and build a relationship that can benefit your business in the long term.

Strategies for creating a positive and welcoming environment

Creating a positive and welcoming environment is crucial for engaging with customers in person. It can help build rapport and trust with the customer, which can lead to increased loyalty and repeat business. Here are some strategies for creating a positive and welcoming environment:

Smile: A warm and genuine smile can go a long way in making a customer feel welcome. It shows that you are happy to see them and are eager to assist them. Make sure to maintain eye contact while smiling to make the interaction feel more personal.

Use positive body language: Body language is an important aspect of non-verbal communication. It can convey a lot about a person's mood and attitude. Positive body language includes open posture, relaxed shoulders, and a friendly facial expression. Avoid crossing your arms or looking away from the customer as it can create a negative impression.

Use the customer's name: Using a customer's name can create a personal connection and make them feel valued. It shows that you are interested in them as an individual and not just as a customer. However, make sure to use their name appropriately and avoid being too familiar.

Provide a comfortable environment: Providing a comfortable environment can make the customer feel at ease and help them relax. This can be achieved by providing comfortable seating, good lighting, and a pleasant ambiance.

Anticipate customer needs: Anticipating customer needs and proactively offering assistance can make the customer feel valued and appreciated. It shows that you are attentive to their needs and are willing to go the extra mile to provide excellent service.

Use positive language: Using positive language can create a positive and welcoming environment. Avoid using negative language, such as "I can't" or "I don't know," as it can create a negative impression. Instead, use positive language, such as "Let me find out for you" or "I'll be happy to assist you."

Personalize the interaction: Personalizing the interaction can make the customer feel valued and appreciated. This can be achieved by using the customer's name, referencing previous interactions, and asking about their preferences.

Provide a warm farewell: Providing a warm farewell can leave a positive lasting impression on the customer. It shows that you appreciate their business and are looking forward to their next visit. Make sure to thank them for their business and wish them a pleasant day.

Example Exercise:

Identify three ways in which you can create a positive and welcoming environment for customers in person.

Describe how you would personalize the interaction with a customer who is a regular at your establishment.

Explain why using positive language is important when interacting with customers.

Evaluate the effectiveness of using a customer's name in creating a positive and welcoming environment.

Develop a plan for anticipating customer needs in a retail environment.

Tips for handling customer inquiries and complaints face-to-face

Customer inquiries and complaints are inevitable in any customer service role. As a customer service representative, it is essential to handle them efficiently and effectively. A face-to-face interaction can be challenging to handle, as it requires interpersonal skills, patience, and a professional attitude. Here are some tips for handling customer inquiries and complaints face-to-face:

Listen actively
One of the critical skills in handling customer inquiries and complaints is active listening. Active listening involves paying full attention to what the customer is saying without interrupting or judging. This allows the customer to express themselves fully and feel heard. It also gives the representative the chance to understand the problem correctly and respond appropriately. Active listening is essential in establishing trust and building rapport with the customer.

Stay calm and composed
It is essential to stay calm and composed when dealing with customers, especially when handling complaints. A calm and professional demeanor helps to de-escalate any tense situations and reassure the customer that their concerns are being taken seriously. It also helps to prevent any miscommunication or misunderstandings that may arise from a heated exchange.

Empathize with the customer
Empathy is a crucial aspect of providing excellent customer service. It involves putting yourself in the customer's shoes and understanding their perspective. When dealing with complaints, it is essential to empathize with the customer and acknowledge their feelings. This helps to show the customer that you understand their situation and are working to resolve their issue.

Apologize if necessary
Apologizing is an essential part of handling customer complaints. It shows that you acknowledge the customer's problem and are taking responsibility for the situation. A sincere apology can go a long way in diffusing a tense situation and restoring trust with the customer. However, it is important to ensure that the apology is appropriate and does not admit fault if it is not warranted.

Offer a solution

After understanding the customer's issue, it is essential to offer a solution that addresses their concerns. The solution should be relevant to the problem and should be communicated clearly and concisely. It is also important to offer alternatives if the initial solution is not feasible or acceptable to the customer.

Follow up

Following up with the customer after their inquiry or complaint has been resolved shows that you care about their experience and value their feedback. It also provides an opportunity to ensure that the solution provided was effective and to address any further concerns or questions the customer may have.

Example:

As a shift supervisor at a retail store, you received a complaint from a customer about a product they purchased. The customer was unhappy with the quality of the product and was seeking a refund. Here is an example of how to handle the situation using the tips provided above:

Listen actively: Listen to the customer's complaint without interruption, allowing them to express their concerns fully.

Stay calm and composed: Remain calm and professional throughout the interaction, even if the customer is upset or frustrated.

Empathize with the customer: Show empathy by acknowledging the customer's frustration and validating their concerns.

Apologize if necessary: If the quality of the product was below standard, apologize for the inconvenience and assure the customer that you will do your best to resolve the issue.

Offer a solution: Offer a solution that addresses the customer's concerns, such as a refund or exchange of the product.

Follow up: Follow up with the customer after the issue has been resolved to ensure their satisfaction and address any further concerns they may have.

Exercises:

Describe a situation where a customer came to you with a complaint about a product or service. How did you handle the situation?

Explain the importance of active listening when handling customer inquiries and complaints face-to-face.

Active listening is a crucial skill for customer service representatives when dealing with customer inquiries and complaints face-to-face. It involves fully concentrating on what the customer is saying, not interrupting, and seeking clarification if necessary. Active listening ensures that the customer feels heard, understood, and valued, which can help to deescalate the situation and resolve the issue.

When a customer is unhappy with a product or service, they often feel frustrated, angry, or disappointed. As a customer service representative, it is essential to remain calm and professional, even when the customer is upset. Active listening helps to create a positive and respectful environment where the customer can express their concerns and feel that they are being heard. By actively listening to the customer's complaint, you can gain a better understanding of the issue and work with the customer to find a resolution.

In addition to actively listening to the customer, it is also important to use nonverbal cues to communicate your attention and interest. Maintain eye contact with the customer, nod occasionally to show that you are listening, and use appropriate facial expressions to convey empathy and understanding.

When handling customer inquiries and complaints face-to-face, it is also essential to acknowledge the customer's emotions. Customers often feel frustrated, angry, or disappointed, and acknowledging these feelings can help to deescalate the situation. Use empathetic statements such as "I can understand how frustrating that must be for you" or "I'm sorry that you've had a negative experience" to demonstrate that you are taking the customer's concerns seriously.

In summary, active listening is an essential technique for handling customer inquiries and complaints face-to-face. It involves fully concentrating on what the customer is saying, using nonverbal cues to communicate your attention and interest, and acknowledging the customer's emotions. By actively listening to the customer, you can gain a better understanding of the issue and work with the customer to find a resolution that meets their needs.

Exercise: Role-playing common face-to-face customer service scenarios

Role-playing is a great way to practice and improve your customer service skills. By simulating real-life scenarios, you can learn how to handle difficult situations and build your confidence when interacting with customers.

Here are some common face-to-face customer service scenarios that you can use for role-playing exercises:

The Unhappy Customer: A customer comes to you with a complaint about a product or service. They are upset and want a resolution.

The Confused Customer: A customer comes to you with a question about a product or service. They are confused and need help understanding the information.

The Demanding Customer: A customer comes to you with a request that is beyond the scope of your job responsibilities. They are persistent and want you to fulfill their request.

The Indecisive Customer: A customer comes to you with a lot of questions and is having trouble making a decision. They are unsure about which product or service to choose.

The Angry Customer: A customer comes to you with a complaint about a product or service. They are very angry and are demanding an immediate solution.

To begin the exercise, divide the participants into pairs. One person will play the role of the customer, while the other person will play the role of the customer service representative. Provide each pair with a scenario and give them some time to prepare. Once they are ready, they can begin the role-playing exercise.

During the exercise, it is important to pay attention to the following:

Active listening: Encourage the customer service representative to actively listen to the customer's concerns and respond appropriately.

Empathy: Encourage the customer service representative to show empathy towards the customer's situation.

Problem-solving: Encourage the customer service representative to come up with a solution that addresses the customer's needs and concerns.

Professionalism: Encourage the customer service representative to maintain a professional demeanor at all times, even in difficult situations.

Time management: Encourage the customer service representative to manage their time effectively and prioritize tasks accordingly.

After the exercise, have each pair switch roles and repeat the exercise with a different scenario. This will give each participant the opportunity to practice both roles.

By role-playing common face-to-face customer service scenarios, you can develop your skills and build your confidence when interacting with customers. These exercises can also help you identify areas for improvement and give you the opportunity to practice new strategies and techniques.

Exercises:

Choose one of the scenarios listed above and role-play the scenario with a partner.

Reflect on your role-playing experience. What did you learn from the exercise? What did you do well, and what could you improve on?

Choose a different scenario and repeat the role-playing exercise with a different partner. What strategies did you use in this scenario that were effective? What strategies could you improve on?

Discuss with your partner the importance of active listening, empathy, problem-solving, professionalism, and time management when handling customer inquiries and complaints face-to-face. How can these skills help you improve your interactions with customers?

CHAPTER 12: BEST PRACTICES FOR SERVING CUSTOMERS FROM BEHIND THE COUNTER

Serving customers from behind the counter can be a challenging task for any business. Customers have high expectations when they visit a store or business and they want to receive top-notch service. In this chapter, we will discuss the best practices for serving customers from behind the counter. We will explore different strategies that businesses can use to provide excellent customer service and build a loyal customer base.

The Importance of Excellent Customer Service

Excellent customer service is critical for the success of any business. When customers receive good service, they are more likely to return to the business, spend more money, and recommend the business to others. On the other hand, when customers receive poor service, they are less likely to return and more likely to share their negative experiences with others. In today's competitive business environment, it's essential to provide excellent customer service to stay ahead of the competition.

Best Practices for Serving Customers from Behind the Counter

Greet customers warmly: The first impression is crucial, and greeting customers warmly sets the tone for the rest of their visit. When customers feel welcomed and valued, they are more likely to have a positive experience.

Listen actively: Listening actively means paying attention to what the customer is saying and responding appropriately. It's important to let the customer speak and not interrupt them. By listening actively, the customer feels heard and valued, and their concerns are addressed effectively.

Be knowledgeable: Customers expect employees to be knowledgeable about the products and services they offer. Employees should be able to answer questions and provide recommendations to help customers make informed decisions.

Offer solutions: When customers have a problem, they want a solution. Employees should be empowered to offer solutions that meet the customer's needs.

Be friendly and professional: Employees should maintain a friendly and professional demeanor at all times. Even if the customer is upset or difficult, it's important to remain calm and professional.

Maintain a clean and organized workspace: Customers notice the cleanliness and organization of a business. A clean and organized workspace creates a positive impression and contributes to the overall customer experience.

Follow up: Following up with customers after their visit shows that the business values their feedback and wants to ensure their satisfaction.

Conclusion

In conclusion, serving customers from behind the counter requires a set of best practices to ensure excellent customer service. By greeting customers warmly, listening actively, being knowledgeable, offering solutions, being friendly and professional, maintaining a clean and organized workspace, and following up, businesses can provide an exceptional customer experience. These practices can help businesses build a loyal customer base and stay ahead of the competition.

The role of speed and efficiency in serving customers from behind the counter

Providing excellent customer service is a critical aspect of any business that wants to retain customers and attract new ones. Customers expect to be served in a timely and efficient manner, particularly when they are in a hurry or have a busy schedule. Serving customers quickly and efficiently from behind the counter is crucial in ensuring customer satisfaction and loyalty. In this section, we will explore the role of speed and efficiency in serving customers from behind the counter, including the benefits of fast service, potential drawbacks, and best practices for balancing speed with quality.

Benefits of Fast Service:

One of the most significant benefits of providing fast and efficient service to customers is customer satisfaction. Customers appreciate businesses that value their time and can quickly provide the products or services they need. Fast service can also lead to repeat business and positive reviews, which can ultimately lead to increased revenue for the business.

Additionally, fast service can reduce wait times, which can help prevent customers from becoming frustrated or irritable. This is particularly true for customers who are in a hurry or have a busy schedule. When customers are served quickly, they are more likely to have a positive experience and leave with a favorable impression of the business.

Potential Drawbacks:

While fast service can provide significant benefits to businesses, there are also potential drawbacks that need to be considered. For example, serving customers too quickly can lead to mistakes or oversights that can result in negative experiences for customers. This can ultimately lead to a loss of business and negative reviews.

Another potential drawback is that prioritizing speed can lead to a lack of focus on quality. Businesses that focus solely on speed may cut corners, neglecting important details or quality control measures that could result in negative consequences.

Best Practices for Balancing Speed with Quality:

The key to providing excellent customer service from behind the counter is to balance speed with quality. There are several best practices that businesses can follow to achieve this balance, including:

Prioritize Training and Development: Providing employees with the proper training and development is crucial in ensuring that they can serve customers efficiently while still maintaining high levels of quality. Employees should be trained on best practices for serving customers quickly, while still prioritizing quality.

Streamline Processes: Businesses can streamline their processes by removing unnecessary steps and automating certain tasks. This can help save time and increase efficiency, ultimately allowing employees to serve customers more quickly.

Use Technology: Utilizing technology, such as point-of-sale systems, can help businesses serve customers quickly and efficiently. For example, having a streamlined and user-friendly POS system can help employees quickly process transactions, reducing wait times for customers.

Monitor and Measure Performance: To ensure that employees are balancing speed with quality, businesses should monitor and measure their performance regularly. This can help identify areas where employees may need additional training or where processes may need to be adjusted.

In conclusion, providing fast and efficient service to customers from behind the counter is critical in ensuring customer satisfaction and loyalty. However, it is essential to balance speed with quality to avoid potential drawbacks such as mistakes or oversights that can result in negative experiences for customers. By prioritizing training and development, streamlining processes, utilizing technology, and monitoring and measuring performance, businesses can achieve the right balance of speed and quality, resulting in positive experiences for customers and increased revenue for the business.

Techniques for handling orders and payments quickly and accurately

Speed and accuracy are two essential components of excellent customer service from behind the counter. Customers expect fast and efficient service when placing an order and making a payment. Failing to provide speedy and accurate service can lead to frustration and disappointment, which can ultimately drive customers away. Therefore, it is important to develop techniques to handle orders and payments quickly and accurately to meet customer expectations and improve customer satisfaction.

Preparing in Advance
One technique for handling orders and payments quickly and accurately is to prepare in advance. This involves ensuring that all necessary items and equipment are readily available before customers arrive. This could include pre-filling order forms, arranging cash or card machines, and preparing change in the register.

For example, imagine a coffee shop that serves many customers in a short amount of time. The baristas could prepare their workstations before the rush hour by setting up cups, straws, and lids in advance. This would allow them to serve customers quickly without wasting time searching for items during peak hours.

Implementing Clear Communication
Effective communication is a key component of providing efficient customer service. Clear communication can help prevent misunderstandings and delays, thereby improving the speed and accuracy of order-taking and payment processing.

One way to ensure clear communication is to use simple and concise language when taking orders. It is important to repeat the order back to the customer to confirm that it is correct. Additionally, when processing payments, it is important to clearly explain the transaction process and provide a receipt.

Streamlining the Payment Process
Another technique for handling orders and payments quickly and accurately is to streamline the payment process. This can involve various strategies, such as offering multiple payment options, utilizing contactless payments, and having a designated person to handle payments.

For example, some retail stores allow customers to pay using their mobile devices to reduce waiting times. This not only speeds up the payment process but also offers convenience to customers who may not want to carry cash or credit cards.

Training Employees on Order Taking and Payment Processing
Training employees on order-taking and payment processing can also contribute to speed and accuracy. This training can include teaching employees how to use the necessary equipment, how to handle cash, and how to process payments using different payment methods. Providing ongoing training can ensure that employees stay up-to-date with the latest payment technologies and techniques.

Using Technology to Assist in Order Taking and Payment Processing
Technology can be used to assist in order-taking and payment processing. For example, a point-of-sale (POS) system can be used to automate the payment process, allowing for quick and accurate processing of payments. Additionally, self-service kiosks can be used to allow customers to place their orders and make payments without interacting with an employee.

Handling orders and payments quickly and accurately is essential for providing excellent customer service from behind the counter. By preparing in advance, implementing clear communication, streamlining the payment process, training employees, and using technology, businesses can improve their efficiency and meet customer expectations. Remember, speed and accuracy are key components of successful customer service, so it is important to prioritize these aspects in your business strategy.

The importance of maintaining a clean and organized workspace

In customer service, maintaining a clean and organized workspace is essential. It not only presents a professional appearance to customers, but it also improves efficiency and productivity. A cluttered workspace can lead to confusion and delays in serving customers, while a clean and organized workspace can help employees work more efficiently and quickly.

In this section, we will discuss the importance of maintaining a clean and organized workspace in customer service and explore some techniques for achieving it.

Why is a Clean and Organized Workspace Important?

A clean and organized workspace is important for several reasons:

Professional Appearance: A clean and organized workspace presents a professional appearance to customers. When customers enter a business, they expect to see a clean and organized workspace. A cluttered workspace can create a negative impression and make customers feel uncomfortable.

Efficiency: A clean and organized workspace can improve efficiency by reducing the time it takes to find necessary items. When everything is in its place, employees can easily locate what they need and serve customers quickly.

Safety: A cluttered workspace can create safety hazards. Items left on the floor can cause tripping, while stacked items can fall and injure employees or customers.

Productivity: A clean and organized workspace can increase productivity. When employees know where everything is located, they can work more efficiently and get more done in less time.

Techniques for Maintaining a Clean and Organized Workspace

Regular Cleaning: Regular cleaning is essential to maintaining a clean and organized workspace. Daily cleaning tasks should include wiping down surfaces, sweeping or vacuuming floors, and removing trash.

Organization: Items should be organized in a logical and efficient manner. This means keeping frequently used items within reach and storing less frequently used items in a designated storage area.

Decluttering: Decluttering involves removing unnecessary items from the workspace. Items that are not needed should be removed to prevent clutter and make space for essential items.

Labeling: Labeling can help employees locate items quickly and easily. This can be especially useful in storage areas where items may be stacked or stored in containers.

Storage: Storage solutions should be tailored to the specific needs of the business. This may involve shelving, cabinets, or other storage solutions.

Encourage Employee Participation: Employees should be encouraged to maintain a clean and organized workspace. This can be achieved by setting cleaning schedules and holding employees accountable for their workspaces.

Clean as you Go: One of the easiest ways to maintain a clean and organized workspace is to clean as you go. This means putting items away immediately after use and wiping down surfaces as needed.

In customer service, maintaining a clean and organized workspace is essential. It not only presents a professional appearance to customers, but it also improves efficiency and productivity. By following the techniques outlined in this section, businesses can create a workspace that is clean, organized, and conducive to excellent customer service.

Exercise: Analyzing a real behind-the-counter customer service problem and developing a plan for addressing it

Customer service is a critical aspect of any business, and it is especially important for those who work behind the counter. From fast food restaurants to retail stores, the people who work behind the counter are often the face of the company and the first point of contact for customers. As such, it is essential for them to be able to handle a wide variety of customer service problems in a professional and effective manner. In this exercise, we will analyze a real behind-the-counter customer service problem and develop a plan for addressing it.

Step 1: Identify the Problem
The first step in addressing any customer service problem is to identify it. Take some time to observe and gather data about the customer service problem you want to address. This could involve talking to customers and employees, analyzing customer feedback, or reviewing sales data. Once you have a clear understanding of the problem, define it as precisely as possible. For example, a common behind-the-counter customer service problem is long wait times for orders.

Step 2: Analyze the Problem

The next step is to analyze the problem in more detail. Identify the root cause(s) of the problem and any contributing factors. Consider the impact of the problem on customers, employees, and the business as a whole. For example, long wait times can result in frustrated customers, reduced sales, and stressed employees. Use tools such as fishbone diagrams or process maps to visualize the problem and its causes.

Step 3: Develop a Plan for Addressing the Problem
Once you have a clear understanding of the problem, it is time to develop a plan for addressing it. This could involve making changes to processes, policies, or training programs. Consider the resources that will be needed to implement the plan and any potential obstacles that may arise. Develop a timeline for implementing the plan and identify metrics for measuring its success. For example, a plan for addressing long wait times might involve streamlining the ordering process, adding additional staff during peak hours, and providing training to employees on how to handle high-volume periods.

Step 4: Implement and Monitor the Plan
Once the plan has been developed, it is time to implement it. Assign responsibilities and communicate the plan to all employees who will be involved in its implementation. Monitor progress regularly and adjust the plan as needed. Keep in mind that it may take some time to see results, so be patient and continue to gather data on the problem.

Step 5: Evaluate the Plan's Effectiveness
After the plan has been in place for a sufficient amount of time, evaluate its effectiveness. Use the metrics identified in step 3 to measure success. Determine if the plan has addressed the root cause(s) of the problem and if it has improved the customer service experience. If the plan has been successful, continue to monitor the situation to ensure that the problem does not reoccur. If the plan has not been successful, go back to step 3 and revise the plan accordingly.

Analyzing a real behind-the-counter customer service problem and developing a plan for addressing it is an essential exercise for anyone working in customer service. By identifying and addressing customer service problems, businesses can improve the customer experience, increase sales, and boost employee morale. Remember to be thorough in your analysis, develop a plan that is realistic and achievable, and evaluate the plan's effectiveness. Customer service is a critical part of any business, and by taking a proactive approach to addressing problems, businesses can improve the bottom line while ensuring customer satisfaction.

CHAPTER 13: STOCKING SHELVES AND MERCHANDISING FOR OPTIMAL CUSTOMER EXPERIENCE

Merchandising plays a crucial role in ensuring that customers have a positive experience when they visit a store. Stocking shelves and organizing merchandise in a way that is visually appealing and easy to navigate can make a big difference in how customers perceive the store and their willingness to return in the future. In this chapter, we will explore the best practices for stocking shelves and merchandising to optimize the customer experience.

Section 1: Understanding the Importance of Merchandising

Merchandising is the process of planning and executing the presentation of products to customers in a way that maximizes sales. The ultimate goal of merchandising is to create a visually appealing shopping environment that encourages customers to spend more time in the store and purchase more products. Effective merchandising requires an understanding of customer behavior, as well as an eye for design and a willingness to experiment with different strategies.

One of the most important aspects of merchandising is the layout of the store. A well-planned layout should make it easy for customers to navigate the store, find what they are looking for, and discover new products. It should also create a sense of flow that encourages customers to move through the store and explore different areas.

In addition to the layout of the store, other elements of merchandising that can impact the customer experience include the lighting, color scheme, and overall ambiance of the store. A bright, welcoming atmosphere can make customers feel more comfortable and encourage them to stay longer, while a dark or cluttered environment can be a turnoff.

Section 2: Best Practices for Stocking Shelves

Stocking shelves is a critical part of effective merchandising. When done correctly, it ensures that products are available when customers want to purchase them, and that the store always looks full and inviting. Here are some best practices for stocking shelves:

Keep products front and center: Products that are prominently displayed are more likely to catch the attention of customers. Use eye-catching signage and make sure that products are arranged in a way that is visually appealing.

Group products strategically: Grouping products by category or theme can help customers find what they are looking for more easily. For example, grouping all of the cleaning products together in one area of the store can make it easier for customers to find what they need.

Ensure that shelves are always stocked: Running out of products can be frustrating for customers, so it is important to ensure that shelves are always fully stocked. Regularly check inventory levels and order more products as needed.

Rotate products regularly: Rotating products can help keep the store looking fresh and encourage customers to try new things. Consider moving products to different areas of the store or featuring them in special displays to keep things interesting.

Keep shelves clean and organized: A cluttered, disorganized shelf can be overwhelming for customers and make it difficult for them to find what they are looking for. Keep shelves clean and organized to make it easy for customers to find what they need.

Section 3: Merchandising Strategies for Optimal Customer Experience

There are a number of different merchandising strategies that can be used to optimize the customer experience. Some of the most effective include:

Using endcaps: Endcaps are displays located at the end of aisles that can be used to showcase featured products. They are highly visible and can be a great way to draw attention to new or popular products.

Creating themed displays: Themed displays can be used to create a sense of excitement and anticipation in the store. For example, a back-to-school display might feature school supplies, backpacks, and lunchboxes.

Using signage: Signage can be used to highlight sales, promotions, and new products. It can also be used to provide information about the products, such as pricing and ingredients. Clear and informative signage can help customers find what they are looking for more easily and can also increase sales.

Grouping products by use or occasion: Grouping products together based on their intended use or occasion can make it easier for customers to find what they need. For example, grouping all the ingredients for a certain recipe in one area can make it easier for customers to find everything they need to make the dish.

Creating visually appealing displays: Visually appealing displays can be used to catch the customer's eye and encourage them to purchase a product. This can include using colors that pop, arranging products in an aesthetically pleasing way, and using lighting to highlight certain products.

Using cross-merchandising: Cross-merchandising involves placing complementary products near each other to encourage customers to purchase both. For example, placing crackers and cheese near each other can encourage customers to purchase both items together.

In addition to these strategies, there are a few other tips to keep in mind when merchandising for optimal customer experience. First, it is important to keep the store clean and organized. Customers are more likely to enjoy their shopping experience and make purchases when the store is tidy and easy to navigate. It is also important to regularly rotate merchandise to keep the store looking fresh and new. Finally, it can be helpful to get feedback from customers about their shopping experience and use that feedback to make improvements.

Exercises:

Visit a local store and evaluate its merchandising strategies. Which strategies do they use, and how effective do you think they are?

Create a themed display for a holiday or season of your choice. What products would you include, and how would you arrange them to create an attractive display?

Develop a plan for improving the merchandising in a store that you are familiar with. What changes would you make, and how do you think these changes would improve the customer experience?

The impact of product placement and organization on customer experience

In today's highly competitive retail environment, the success of a business often depends on its ability to provide customers with a positive shopping experience. This includes everything from the friendliness of the staff to the quality of the products on offer. However, one often overlooked aspect of the customer experience is the impact of product placement and organization.

Product placement refers to the way that products are arranged and displayed within a store, while organization refers to the overall layout and flow of the store. These factors can have a significant impact on how customers perceive a store, how long they spend there, and how likely they are to make a purchase.

In this section, we will explore the importance of product placement and organization in creating a positive customer experience. We will examine the ways in which these factors can influence customer behavior and provide practical tips for optimizing product placement and organization in your store.

The Psychology of Product Placement

To understand the importance of product placement, it is first necessary to understand the psychology behind how customers make purchasing decisions. Research has shown that customers are heavily influenced by a range of factors, including visual cues, social norms, and emotional associations.

Visual cues, such as product placement and signage, can play a particularly powerful role in influencing customer behavior. One study found that customers were more likely to purchase products that were located at eye level or within easy reach, as these were perceived as being more convenient and desirable. Similarly, products that were displayed in an attractive or eye-catching way were more likely to be noticed and purchased.

Social norms also play a role in customer behavior. Customers are often influenced by the behavior of others around them, particularly when it comes to purchasing decisions. For example, if a customer sees that a particular product is selling quickly or is popular with other customers, they are more likely to perceive it as desirable and may be more inclined to purchase it themselves.

Finally, emotional associations can also influence customer behavior. Products that are associated with positive emotions, such as happiness or excitement, are more likely to be purchased than those associated with negative emotions, such as sadness or anger.

The Impact of Product Placement and Organization on Customer Experience

Given the importance of visual cues and emotional associations in customer behavior, it is clear that product placement and organization can have a significant impact on the customer experience. For example, a store that is cluttered and disorganized may be perceived as uninviting and difficult to navigate, which can lead to a negative customer experience and a lower likelihood of making a purchase.

On the other hand, a store that is well-organized and visually appealing is more likely to create a positive customer experience and increase the likelihood of making a purchase. This includes factors such as the placement of products, the use of signage and displays, and the overall layout of the store.

One key factor to consider when optimizing product placement and organization is the concept of "planograms". A planogram is a visual representation of how products should be arranged and displayed within a store. By using a planogram, retailers can ensure that products are placed in the most effective locations and that the overall layout of the store is optimized for customer flow and convenience.

Another important factor to consider is the use of color and lighting. Research has shown that certain colors and lighting can have a significant impact on customer behavior. For example, warm colors such as red and orange are often associated with excitement and impulse purchases, while cool colors such as blue and green are associated with calmness and relaxation.

Practical Tips for Optimizing Product Placement and Organization

Now that we have a better understanding of the psychology behind product placement and organization, let's explore some practical tips for optimizing these factors in your store:

Use a planogram: As mentioned earlier, a planogram can be an incredibly useful tool for optimizing product placement and organization. By mapping out the layout of your store and carefully planning where each product will be displayed, you can create a visually appealing and intuitive shopping experience for your customers. There are a variety of different planogram software options available, and many of them are designed specifically for retailers.

Consider the customer journey: When designing your store layout and product placement strategy, it's important to think about the customer journey. This includes considering factors such as the flow of traffic, the most commonly visited areas of the store, and the overall path that customers are likely to take. By understanding the customer journey, you can strategically place products and displays in a way that maximizes their impact and encourages customers to make additional purchases.

Organize products by category: One of the simplest ways to optimize product organization is to group items by category. For example, all of the canned goods should be located in one area, while all of the bakery items should be in another. This makes it easier for customers to find what they are looking for and ensures that items are logically organized.

Focus on high-traffic areas: Another effective strategy is to focus on high-traffic areas of your store when selecting which products to feature. For example, items that are frequently purchased or that are particularly popular might be displayed prominently near the entrance or checkout area. This can help to draw customers' attention and increase the likelihood of additional purchases.

Consider the height of displays: When placing products on shelves, it's important to consider the height of the display. Items that are displayed at eye level are more likely to be noticed by customers, while items that are located on lower or higher shelves may be overlooked. Keep this in mind when selecting which products to feature and where to place them in your store.

Pay attention to lighting: Lighting can also play a role in product placement and organization. Bright, well-lit areas are more likely to draw customers' attention, while dimly lit areas may be overlooked. Consider investing in high-quality lighting fixtures and strategically placing them throughout your store to create a welcoming and visually appealing atmosphere.

Regularly review and update your strategy: Finally, it's important to regularly review and update your product placement and organization strategy. As customer preferences and shopping habits change, so too should your approach to product placement. Consider conducting regular audits of your store layout and seeking feedback from customers to identify areas for improvement and opportunities for growth.

By following these practical tips and leveraging the psychological principles of product placement and organization, you can create a shopping experience that is both visually appealing and optimized for customer engagement and sales.

Techniques for keeping shelves and displays organized and attractive

Keeping your store organized and attractive is key to providing a positive customer experience. In this section, we will explore some techniques for keeping shelves and displays organized and visually appealing.

Regularly restock shelves: Ensure that your shelves are always well-stocked with products. Customers are more likely to purchase items that are easily accessible and in stock. Keeping your shelves regularly restocked also creates a sense of abundance and variety, making your store feel more inviting and exciting.

Use signage and labels: Signage and labels are essential tools for guiding customers to the products they are looking for. Use clear, bold signage to make it easy for customers to navigate your store and find what they need. Use labels to indicate product details such as price, brand, and ingredients. Labels also help to keep shelves organized and reduce confusion for both customers and employees.

Keep shelves clean and tidy: Clean and well-maintained shelves not only enhance the overall appearance of your store, but they also make it easier for customers to find products. Make sure that all products are facing forward and are in their correct location. Remove any damaged or expired products from the shelves and dispose of them properly.

Use creative displays: Displays are an effective way to draw attention to featured products and increase sales. Use creative displays to highlight seasonal or holiday items, new products, or items that are on sale. Consider creating themed displays that tell a story or showcase complementary products. Use eye-catching colors, textures, and props to make your displays visually appealing and engaging.

Monitor inventory levels: Regularly monitoring your inventory levels will help you keep track of what products need to be restocked and which products are not selling well. This information can help you make informed decisions about product placement and display.

Use lighting: Lighting is an often-overlooked aspect of shelf and display organization. Proper lighting can enhance the appearance of products and make them more appealing to customers. Use bright, natural lighting to showcase products and create a welcoming atmosphere in your store.

Train employees: Your employees play a crucial role in keeping your store organized and visually appealing. Train your employees to regularly check and restock shelves, keep displays clean and tidy, and create eye-catching displays. Encourage them to be creative and use their own ideas for improving the overall appearance of the store.

By implementing these techniques, you can keep your store organized and visually appealing, enhancing the overall customer experience.

By implementing these techniques, you can keep your store organized and visually appealing, enhancing the overall customer experience. However, there are additional techniques that you can use to maintain and enhance the aesthetic appeal of your shelves and displays. These techniques include:

Use color: Color can be a powerful tool in attracting and retaining customers. Using vibrant and complementary colors can draw attention to products and make them more visually appealing. It is important to use color strategically and in a way that is consistent with your brand image.

Group products by color or theme: Grouping products by color or theme can make it easier for customers to find what they are looking for and create a visually appealing display. For example, grouping all red products together can create a bold statement on the shelf, while grouping products by a specific theme, such as a beach or tropical theme, can create a cohesive and attractive display.

Rotate products: Regularly rotating products on your shelves and displays can keep your store looking fresh and new, and can also encourage customers to try new products. Consider rotating products based on the season or upcoming holidays.

Use lighting: Lighting can play an important role in creating an attractive display. Proper lighting can enhance the appearance of products and draw attention to specific areas of the store. It is important to use lighting that is consistent with your brand image and that is appropriate for the products being displayed.

Keep shelves and displays clean and well-maintained: Maintaining clean and well-organized shelves and displays is essential for creating a positive customer experience. Regularly dusting and cleaning shelves, ensuring that products are properly aligned and faced forward, and removing expired or damaged products can all help to create an attractive and inviting display.

Overall, keeping your store organized and visually appealing is essential for enhancing the customer experience. By using these techniques and others like them, you can create an environment that is not only visually appealing, but also easy to navigate and conducive to purchasing.

The importance of monitoring inventory levels and restocking efficiently

Maintaining an efficient and effective inventory management system is crucial to the success of any retail business. A poorly managed inventory system can lead to stockouts, overstocking, lost sales, and dissatisfied customers. Thus, it is essential to monitor inventory levels and restock efficiently to ensure that products are available when customers need them.

The importance of monitoring inventory levels
Inventory monitoring involves tracking the quantity, location, and status of products in a store. The process of monitoring inventory levels allows retailers to identify trends, predict future demand, and make informed purchasing decisions. By monitoring inventory levels, retailers can avoid stockouts and overstocking, which can have a significant impact on the customer experience.

For instance, consider a customer who walks into a store and is unable to find the product they need because it is out of stock. This can be frustrating for the customer, and they may decide to take their business elsewhere. On the other hand, if a store overstocks a product, it may lead to a surplus of unsold inventory, which can lead to waste and a loss of profit.

The benefits of restocking efficiently
Restocking efficiently involves replenishing inventory levels based on demand and trends. Retailers can use sales data to identify which products are selling well and need to be restocked. Efficient restocking ensures that products are available when customers need them and helps to avoid stockouts.

Efficient restocking also helps retailers to manage their inventory levels effectively. When retailers are able to replenish inventory levels based on demand, they can avoid overstocking and reduce the risk of unsold inventory. By reducing the risk of unsold inventory, retailers can increase profitability and reduce waste.

Techniques for monitoring inventory levels and restocking efficiently
Retailers can use several techniques to monitor inventory levels and restock efficiently. Here are some examples:

a) Inventory management software: Retailers can use inventory management software to track inventory levels, monitor trends, and make informed purchasing decisions. Inventory management software can help retailers to automate many of the tasks involved in inventory management, saving time and reducing errors.

b) ABC analysis: This technique involves classifying products based on their value and the level of demand. Products that are high in value and high in demand should be given priority when restocking inventory.

c) Just-in-time (JIT) inventory management: JIT inventory management involves restocking inventory levels based on actual demand, rather than forecasting demand. This technique can help to reduce the risk of overstocking and unsold inventory.

d) Cycle counting: Cycle counting involves counting a small sample of inventory on a regular basis to ensure that inventory levels are accurate. This technique can help to identify discrepancies between inventory levels and sales data, enabling retailers to make informed restocking decisions.

Challenges of monitoring inventory levels and restocking efficiently
Despite the benefits of monitoring inventory levels and restocking efficiently, there are several challenges that retailers may face. These include:

a) Lack of data: Retailers may not have access to accurate data on sales and inventory levels, making it difficult to make informed purchasing decisions.

b) Seasonal demand: Retailers may experience fluctuations in demand based on seasonal trends. This can make it difficult to predict demand and restock efficiently.

c) Supply chain disruptions: Supply chain disruptions can impact the availability of products and lead to stockouts.

d) Shrinkage: Shrinkage refers to the loss of inventory due to theft, damage, or other factors. Shrinkage can impact inventory levels and make it difficult to restock efficiently.

Monitoring inventory levels and restocking efficiently are essential components of effective inventory management. By implementing the techniques outlined in this section, retailers can ensure that products are available when customers want them, reducing the risk of stockouts and lost sales. Additionally, effective inventory management can help retailers control costs and minimize waste, ensuring that their business is profitable and sustainable over the long term.

However, it's important to remember that inventory management is an ongoing process that requires regular attention and adjustment. Retailers must stay vigilant to changes in customer demand, trends in the marketplace, and fluctuations in the supply chain, adapting their inventory levels and restocking strategies accordingly.

In addition, retailers must also keep in mind the importance of customer experience in their inventory management efforts. For example, maintaining attractive displays and keeping shelves organized can help create a positive shopping environment that encourages customers to make purchases. On the other hand, stockouts, cluttered displays, and messy shelves can all detract from the customer experience and harm a retailer's reputation.

Ultimately, effective inventory management is about finding the right balance between maintaining sufficient stock levels to meet customer demand, while also minimizing costs and waste. By using data-driven analysis, leveraging technology, and adopting best practices in inventory management, retailers can create a more efficient and profitable business that meets the needs of their customers and delivers a superior shopping experience.

Exercise: Analyzing a real merchandising problem and developing a plan for improving it

Now that we've explored various techniques for optimizing product placement, organization, and inventory management, it's time to apply this knowledge to a real-world merchandising problem.

For this exercise, imagine that you are a store manager at a clothing retailer. Your store has been experiencing a decrease in sales over the past few months, and you suspect that merchandising may be a contributing factor. Your task is to analyze the current merchandising setup and develop a plan for improving it to enhance the overall customer experience and increase sales.

Step 1: Analyze the Current Merchandising Setup
To begin, take a thorough look at the current merchandising setup in your store. Consider the following questions:

How are products arranged on the shelves and displays? Are they organized in a logical and visually appealing way?
Are the products easy to find? Are there any dead spots where products are not selling?
Are products restocked in a timely manner? Are there any inventory issues?
Are there any particular products that seem to be selling well or poorly? Why might this be?
Take note of any issues or opportunities for improvement that you identify.

Step 2: Develop a Plan for Improving the Merchandising Setup
Based on your analysis, develop a plan for improving the merchandising setup in your store. Consider the following strategies:

Reorganize the Product Displays:
Consider reorganizing the product displays to create a more visually appealing and easy-to-navigate layout. This might include grouping related products together, highlighting new or popular items, and ensuring that each display has a clear focal point.

Optimize Product Placement:
Review the product placement strategy to ensure that the most desirable and high-margin products are placed in prime locations. Consider using cross-merchandising techniques to encourage customers to purchase complementary products.

Monitor Inventory Levels:
Set up a system for monitoring inventory levels in real-time, so you can quickly restock popular items and avoid running out of stock. Consider using software tools to help automate this process.

Train Staff:
Provide training to store staff on effective merchandising techniques and the importance of maintaining a clean and organized store. Encourage staff to provide feedback on the current setup and any issues they encounter.

Collect Customer Feedback:
Gather feedback from customers on their shopping experience and use this to inform future merchandising decisions. Consider using surveys, focus groups, or online reviews to gather this feedback.

Step 3: Implement and Monitor the Plan
Once you have developed your plan, it's time to put it into action. Implement the changes gradually and monitor their effectiveness over time. Make adjustments as needed based on sales data, customer feedback, and other metrics.

Effective merchandising is essential for maintaining a successful retail operation. By taking a strategic approach to product placement, organization, and inventory management, retailers can create a visually appealing and easy-to-navigate store that enhances the overall customer experience and drives sales. This exercise provides a framework for analyzing real merchandising problems and developing effective solutions to address them.

CHAPTER 14: PROVIDING EXCELLENT CUSTOMER SERVICE ON THE PHONE

In today's world, customer service is more important than ever before. Customers expect prompt and efficient service, and they demand it from every company they interact with. The phone is one of the most popular and convenient channels for customers to reach out to businesses for support and service. Therefore, it is crucial for companies to provide excellent customer service on the phone.

Providing excellent customer service on the phone requires a specific set of skills and techniques. Unlike in-person interactions, phone conversations lack the visual cues and body language that we use to communicate. Therefore, it is essential to focus on tone of voice, language, and listening skills to ensure customer satisfaction. In this chapter, we will discuss the best practices for providing excellent customer service on the phone.

We will start by exploring the importance of phone etiquette, including proper greetings, listening skills, and speaking techniques. Next, we will discuss how to handle difficult customer situations and provide solutions that meet their needs. We will also cover strategies for handling high call volumes and managing customer expectations. Finally, we will discuss the importance of follow-up and feedback in maintaining excellent customer service.

Throughout the chapter, we will use examples from a variety of industries and perspectives, including business owners, managers, and customer service representatives. We will also provide exercises and questions to help readers develop their skills and practice the techniques discussed in this chapter. By the end of this chapter, readers will have a thorough understanding of how to provide excellent customer service on the phone and how it can benefit their businesses.

Techniques for answering the phone professionally and promptly

Providing excellent customer service on the phone is an essential aspect of any business. A professional and prompt answer can create a positive first impression and set the tone for the rest of the interaction. In this chapter, we will explore the techniques for answering the phone professionally and promptly, including the importance of phone etiquette, how to handle different types of calls, and ways to improve phone communication skills.

Importance of Phone Etiquette

Phone etiquette is a set of guidelines that govern how to answer the phone, communicate with customers, and handle difficult situations. Good phone etiquette creates a positive experience for the customer and fosters a professional image for the company. Here are some important phone etiquette tips:

Answer promptly - Answering the phone quickly is essential to provide good customer service. Customers should not have to wait for more than three rings before someone answers the phone.

Use a professional greeting - The greeting should include the company name, the name of the person answering the phone, and a friendly tone. For example, "Thank you for calling ABC Company. This is John. How may I assist you?"

Speak clearly and slowly - Speaking clearly and slowly ensures that the customer can understand what is being said. Avoid using technical jargon or slang.

Be polite and courteous - Use polite language, such as "please" and "thank you," and treat the customer with respect. Address them by their name if possible.

Take notes - Take notes during the conversation to ensure that important information is not forgotten.

End the call politely - Thank the customer for calling and offer any necessary follow-up information, such as a reference number or a call-back time.

Handling Different Types of Calls

Different types of calls require different approaches. Here are some examples:

Sales Calls - Sales calls require a friendly and engaging approach. Focus on the customer's needs and explain the benefits of the product or service.

Complaint Calls - Complaint calls require empathy and understanding. Listen to the customer's concerns and offer solutions to resolve the issue.

Technical Calls - Technical calls require a knowledgeable and patient approach. Explain technical information clearly and concisely and be willing to escalate the call if necessary.

Improving Phone Communication Skills

Improving phone communication skills is essential for providing excellent customer service. Here are some tips for improving phone communication skills:

Active Listening - Active listening involves focusing on what the customer is saying and responding appropriately. Avoid interrupting or assuming what the customer wants.

Tone of Voice - The tone of voice conveys the attitude and emotions of the speaker. Use a friendly and professional tone to create a positive experience for the customer.

Empathy - Empathy involves understanding and sharing the customer's feelings. Use phrases such as "I understand how you feel" to show empathy.

Positive Language - Positive language involves using positive words and phrases to create a positive experience for the customer. For example, instead of saying "I don't know," say "I'll find out for you."

Time Management - Time management involves managing the time spent on each call. Avoid keeping customers on hold for extended periods or rushing through calls.

Exercises and Questions

What is phone etiquette and why is it important?

How should you handle a sales call?

What are some ways to improve phone communication skills?

Why is active listening important in phone communication?

How can you show empathy to customers on the phone?

Conclusion

Answering the phone professionally and promptly is an essential aspect of providing excellent customer service. Good phone etiquette, handling different types of calls, and improving phone communication skills are key to creating a positive experience for the customer and fostering a strong relationship with them. In this section, we will discuss techniques for answering the phone professionally and promptly.

Greet the caller warmly and clearly

The first impression counts a lot. When answering the phone, it is important to greet the caller warmly and clearly. This includes identifying oneself and the business. For example, "Thank you for calling XYZ company, this is John speaking, how may I assist you today?" It is essential to use a clear and friendly tone of voice, making sure that the caller feels welcome and appreciated.

Listen attentively and actively

Listening attentively and actively is an essential skill for any customer service representative. Listening to the caller's needs and concerns is important to provide a personalized service experience. Avoid interrupting the caller and allow them to express themselves. By listening actively, you can better understand the caller's needs and respond accordingly.

Speak clearly and concisely

It is important to speak clearly and concisely when answering the phone. Using professional and easy-to-understand language is essential to make the caller feel at ease. Avoid using slang or colloquialisms that may be confusing for the caller. By speaking clearly and concisely, you can provide the information the caller needs promptly and without confusion.

Identify the purpose of the call

Identifying the purpose of the call is essential to provide excellent customer service. Ask the caller what they need and gather any necessary information to address their request. By identifying the purpose of the call, you can respond efficiently and effectively to the caller's needs.

Provide accurate and helpful information

Providing accurate and helpful information is critical to resolving the caller's concerns. If you do not know the answer to the caller's question, let them know that you will find out and get back to them promptly. Provide any relevant information that may help the caller with their request. By providing accurate and helpful information, you can create a positive experience for the caller and enhance their trust in your business.

Close the call professionally

Closing the call professionally is as important as the greeting. Thank the caller for their time and for calling your business. Ask if there is anything else you can assist them with. Inform the caller of any next steps or follow-up that will be taken. Finally, end the call on a positive note, such as "Thank you for calling XYZ company. Have a great day!"

In conclusion, answering the phone professionally and promptly is an essential aspect of providing excellent customer service. By using good phone etiquette, handling different types of calls, and improving phone communication skills, you can create a positive experience for the customer and foster a strong relationship with them.

Strategies for handling phone inquiries and complaints effectively

One of the biggest challenges of providing excellent customer service on the phone is handling inquiries and complaints effectively. Customers who call with an issue or concern expect to be listened to, understood, and helped in a timely manner. Failing to meet these expectations can result in lost business and a negative reputation. However, by following some proven strategies, customer service representatives can handle phone inquiries and complaints with professionalism and effectiveness.

Listen attentively

One of the most important strategies for handling phone inquiries and complaints is to listen attentively. Customers want to feel heard and understood, and the best way to accomplish this is by actively listening. Customer service representatives should let the customer explain their issue or concern without interruption, and then paraphrase it back to ensure understanding. This not only helps to build rapport and trust but also ensures that the representative has a clear understanding of the issue.

Apologize sincerely

When customers call with a complaint, they are often frustrated or angry. One of the most effective ways to diffuse their emotions is to apologize sincerely for the inconvenience or problem. Customer service representatives should avoid making excuses or blaming others and instead take responsibility for the issue. A sincere apology can go a long way toward calming the customer and establishing a positive rapport.

Empathize with the customer

Empathy is another important strategy for handling phone inquiries and complaints. Customers want to feel that the representative understands their situation and is on their side. Customer service representatives should express empathy for the customer's frustration or disappointment, and acknowledge the impact that the issue has had on them. This can help to build trust and rapport and create a positive experience for the customer.

Provide a solution or options
Customers who call with an issue or concern are looking for a resolution. Customer service representatives should be prepared to offer a solution or options for resolving the issue. This may involve providing a refund, replacement, or other compensation, or simply offering an apology and explanation of how the issue will be addressed. Whatever the solution, it should be presented clearly and confidently, and the representative should be prepared to answer any questions or concerns the customer may have.

Follow up promptly
Following up promptly is another important strategy for handling phone inquiries and complaints. Customers want to know that their issue has been resolved and that their business is valued. Customer service representatives should be prepared to follow up with the customer after the issue has been resolved, either by phone or email. This can help to ensure customer satisfaction and loyalty and create a positive experience for the customer.

Example Scenario:

A customer calls a retail store to inquire about a product they purchased online. The product arrived damaged, and the customer wants to know how to get a replacement.

Customer: "Hello, I received my order, but the product is damaged. I need a replacement."

Representative: "I'm sorry to hear that, and I apologize for any inconvenience this has caused. Let me check our inventory to see if we have a replacement in stock."

Customer: "Okay, thank you."

Representative: "I'm sorry, but we don't have any in stock at the moment. However, I can issue a refund for the damaged item or place an order for a replacement as soon as it becomes available. Which would you prefer?"

Customer: "I would like a replacement as soon as possible."

Representative: "Okay, I'll place an order for a replacement right away. You should receive it within 5-7 business days. Is there anything else I can assist you with?"

Customer: "No, that's all. Thank you for your help."

Representative: "You're welcome, and thank you for choosing our store. Please don't hesitate to contact us if you have any further questions or

Tips for speaking clearly and conveying empathy over the phone

Clear and empathetic communication is crucial for providing excellent customer service over the phone. In order to effectively convey empathy and build rapport with customers, representatives must speak clearly, listen actively, and use appropriate language and tone. Here are some tips for achieving clear and empathetic communication over the phone:

Speak Clearly and Slowly: Speaking too fast or too softly can make it difficult for customers to understand what you are saying. To avoid miscommunication, speak clearly and at a moderate pace. Enunciate your words, and use a tone that is friendly, confident, and professional.

Listen Actively: Active listening is the key to understanding customer needs and concerns. It involves paying attention to what the customer is saying, asking clarifying questions, and summarizing what was said to ensure that you have understood the message correctly. Active listening also involves using nonverbal cues, such as nodding or using appropriate vocal responses, to show the customer that you are engaged in the conversation.

Use Empathetic Language: Empathetic language involves acknowledging the customer's feelings and demonstrating that you understand their perspective. Phrases such as "I'm sorry to hear that" or "That must be frustrating for you" can go a long way in showing customers that you care about their concerns. Empathetic language also involves using positive and reassuring language, such as "I'll do my best to help you" or "Let me see what I can do for you."

Avoid Jargon and Technical Terms: Using technical terms or jargon can confuse customers and make it difficult for them to understand what you are saying. When speaking with customers, it is important to use clear and simple language that is easy to understand.

Take Notes: Taking notes during a phone call can help you remember important details and ensure that you are providing accurate information to the customer. Taking notes also shows the customer that you are engaged in the conversation and taking their concerns seriously.

Use Positive Tone and Body Language: Tone and body language can convey a lot of information over the phone. Using a positive and friendly tone can help to build rapport with customers and make them feel more comfortable. Similarly, using appropriate body language, such as smiling or nodding, can help to convey empathy and engagement.

End on a Positive Note: Finally, it is important to end phone calls on a positive note. Thank the customer for calling, express your appreciation for their business, and offer any further assistance if needed. A positive ending can leave a lasting impression and make customers more likely to return in the future.

Overall, clear and empathetic communication is essential for providing excellent customer service over the phone. By speaking clearly, listening actively, using empathetic language, and demonstrating positivity and engagement, representatives can build rapport with customers and create a positive experience that can lead to long-term customer loyalty.

Examples:

Example 1: A customer calls a technical support line because their computer is not working properly.

Representative: "Thank you for calling technical support. My name is John. How may I assist you today?"

Customer: "Hi, my computer won't turn on. Can you help me?"

Representative: "I'm sorry to hear that. Let's see what we can do. Can you check to see if the power cord is plugged in?"

Customer: "Yes, it's plugged in."

Representative: "Okay, let's try something else. Can you hold down the power button for 10 seconds and then try turning it on again?"

Customer: "Okay, let me try that... It worked! Thank you so much."

Representative: "You're welcome. I'm glad I could help. Is there anything else I can assist you with today?"

Customer: "No, that's all. Thank you again for your help."

Representative: "You're welcome, and thank you for choosing our company. Have a great day."

Tips for Speaking Clearly and Conveying Empathy over the Phone:

Speak clearly: When speaking over the phone, it is important to enunciate your words clearly and to speak at a moderate pace. Speaking too quickly or too slowly can make it difficult for the customer to understand you, and may cause frustration or confusion.

Use a friendly tone: Using a friendly tone and sounding upbeat can help put the customer at ease and make them feel more comfortable talking to you. It is important to remember that the customer may be upset or frustrated, so using a friendly tone can help defuse any tension and create a more positive interaction.

Listen actively: When speaking with customers over the phone, it is important to actively listen to their concerns and questions. Make sure to pay attention to what they are saying and respond appropriately. This can help the customer feel heard and understood, and can help to build trust and rapport.

Show empathy: Showing empathy towards the customer can go a long way towards creating a positive interaction. This means acknowledging their feelings and concerns, and demonstrating that you understand their perspective. Empathy can help to build trust and rapport with the customer, and can help to de-escalate any negative emotions they may be experiencing.

Use positive language: Using positive language can help to create a more positive interaction with the customer. Instead of saying "I can't help you with that," try saying "I'm sorry, but I'm not sure how to assist you with that. Let me transfer you to someone who can help." Using positive language can help the customer feel more valued and heard, and can help to create a more positive experience overall.

Repeat key information: When discussing important information with the customer, such as order details or shipping information, it is important to repeat the information back to them to ensure that it is correct. This can help to prevent misunderstandings and ensure that the customer has the information they need.

Use active listening techniques: Active listening techniques, such as repeating key points back to the customer or asking open-ended questions, can help to show that you are actively engaged in the conversation and are interested in helping the customer find a solution to their problem.

Stay calm and patient: When dealing with upset or frustrated customers, it is important to stay calm and patient. This can help to de-escalate the situation and prevent the customer from becoming more upset. Remember that the customer may be upset about something that is outside of your control, and that it is your job to help them find a solution that works for them.

Take ownership of the situation: Taking ownership of the situation and demonstrating that you are committed to finding a solution can help to build trust and rapport with the customer. This means acknowledging the issue and taking responsibility for finding a resolution, even if it means transferring the customer to another representative or escalating the issue to a higher level.

End the call on a positive note: Ending the call on a positive note can help to create a more positive experience for the customer. Thank them for their time and for choosing your company, and wish them a great day. This can help to leave the customer with a positive impression of your company and can increase the likelihood that they will return for future purchases or services.

Exercise: Role-playing common phone-based customer service scenarios

Role-playing exercises are a great way to practice handling common phone-based customer service scenarios. In this exercise, we will provide some examples of scenarios that are commonly encountered in customer service, and suggest ways to role-play these scenarios.

Scenario 1: The customer is angry and upset

The customer may be upset due to a delayed shipment, a defective product, or any other issue that they feel is not being addressed to their satisfaction. In this scenario, the customer service representative should remain calm, listen to the customer's concerns, and offer a solution that meets their needs.

Role-play instructions: One person plays the role of the angry customer, while the other person plays the customer service representative. The customer should express their frustration and anger while the representative should try to empathize with them, and offer a solution that resolves their issue.

Scenario 2: The customer has a question about a product or service

The customer may have a question about a product or service that the company offers. In this scenario, the customer service representative should be knowledgeable about the product or service, and be able to provide accurate and helpful information to the customer.

Role-play instructions: One person plays the role of the customer, while the other person plays the customer service representative. The customer should ask a question about a product or service, and the representative should provide accurate information and be able to answer any follow-up questions that the customer may have.

Scenario 3: The customer is confused about billing or payments

The customer may have a question or concern about their billing or payments, such as a late fee or an incorrect charge. In this scenario, the customer service representative should be able to explain the billing or payment process, and offer a solution that resolves the customer's issue.

Role-play instructions: One person plays the role of the customer, while the other person plays the customer service representative. The customer should express their confusion or concern about their billing or payments, and the representative should be able to explain the process and offer a solution that resolves the customer's issue.

Scenario 4: The customer wants to cancel a service or subscription

The customer may want to cancel a service or subscription that they no longer need or want. In this scenario, the customer service representative should be able to explain the cancellation process, and offer any incentives or alternatives that may encourage the customer to stay.

Role-play instructions: One person plays the role of the customer, while the other person plays the customer service representative. The customer should express their desire to cancel a service or subscription, and the representative should be able to explain the cancellation process and offer any incentives or alternatives that may encourage the customer to stay.

Scenario 5: The customer wants to return a product

The customer may want to return a product that they are not satisfied with, such as a defective or damaged item. In this scenario, the customer service representative should be able to explain the return process, and offer a solution that meets the customer's needs.

Role-play instructions: One person plays the role of the customer, while the other person plays the customer service representative. The customer should express their desire to return a product, and the representative should be able to explain the return process and offer a solution that meets the customer's needs.

Exercise summary:

Role-playing exercises are an effective way to practice handling common phone-based customer service scenarios. By practicing these scenarios, customer service representatives can improve their communication skills, empathy, and problem-solving abilities. These exercises can also help customer service representatives to remain calm and professional in challenging situations, and to provide effective solutions that meet the needs of their customers.

CHAPTER 15: RESPONDING TO CUSTOMER EMAILS AND ONLINE INQUIRIES

In today's digital age, email and online communication have become an essential part of customer service. The convenience of being able to communicate with businesses online has made it easier for customers to reach out for assistance or provide feedback. However, responding to customer emails and online inquiries requires a different approach than handling phone calls or in-person interactions.

In this chapter, we will discuss best practices for responding to customer emails and online inquiries effectively. We will cover topics such as creating a professional email tone, managing customer expectations, addressing complaints, and providing exceptional service through digital channels.

The importance of responding to customer emails and online inquiries promptly cannot be overstated. A study conducted by Forrester Research found that 41% of customers expect an email response within six hours, and 36% of customers expect a response within one hour. Failure to respond to customer inquiries promptly can lead to frustration, negative reviews, and a loss of business.

It is also essential to understand that email and online communication lack nonverbal cues, such as body language and tone of voice. As a result, the message can be easily misinterpreted or misunderstood. Therefore, it is crucial to pay close attention to the language used in emails and online messages.

Furthermore, responding to customer emails and online inquiries requires a different approach than handling phone calls or in-person interactions. When responding to emails or online inquiries, the representative has time to read and reread the message, allowing for a more thoughtful response. However, it is crucial to maintain a sense of urgency in responding to inquiries while also providing thorough and accurate information.

In the following sections, we will provide tips and best practices for responding to customer emails and online inquiries effectively. We will also cover common scenarios that customer service representatives may encounter and provide examples of how to handle these situations professionally and empathetically.

The importance of prompt and personalized email responses

In today's digital age, customers expect prompt and personalized responses to their inquiries and concerns. This is especially true when it comes to email communication. Email has become a primary means of communication for many businesses, and it is crucial to respond promptly and efficiently to customer inquiries to maintain a positive image and reputation. In this chapter, we will discuss the importance of prompt and personalized email responses in customer service and provide practical tips on how to respond to emails effectively.

Why Prompt and Personalized Email Responses Matter:

Prompt and personalized email responses are essential in customer service for several reasons. Firstly, they show the customer that their inquiry or concern is important to the business, and that the business values their time. A prompt response demonstrates that the business is proactive and responsive, which can help to build trust and foster a positive relationship with the customer.

Secondly, personalized email responses can help to differentiate the business from its competitors. When a customer receives a personalized response, it can make them feel valued and appreciated, which can lead to increased loyalty and repeat business. On the other hand, a generic or automated response can make the customer feel unimportant and undervalued, which can lead to a negative perception of the business.

Thirdly, prompt and personalized email responses can help to resolve issues quickly and efficiently. When a customer has a problem or concern, they want a quick resolution, and a prompt response can help to prevent the issue from escalating. Additionally, a personalized response can help to address the customer's specific concerns and provide a more tailored solution.

Tips for Writing Prompt and Personalized Email Responses:

Respond promptly: It is important to respond to customer emails as soon as possible, ideally within 24 hours. A quick response demonstrates that the business values the customer's time and is committed to resolving their issue or concern.

Use a personalized greeting: Address the customer by name and use a friendly and professional tone in the email. This helps to establish a personal connection and makes the customer feel valued.

Acknowledge the customer's concerns: Show empathy and understanding for the customer's issue or concern. This helps to build trust and demonstrates that the business is committed to finding a solution.

Provide a specific solution: Provide a specific solution or course of action to address the customer's concern. This demonstrates that the business is proactive and focused on resolving the issue.

Follow up: Follow up with the customer to ensure that the issue has been resolved and that they are satisfied with the outcome. This demonstrates that the business values the customer's feedback and is committed to providing excellent customer service.

Conclusion:

Prompt and personalized email responses are essential in customer service, and they can have a significant impact on a business's reputation and bottom line. By responding quickly and efficiently to customer inquiries and concerns, businesses can build trust, foster positive relationships, and differentiate themselves from their competitors. By following the tips outlined in this chapter, businesses can provide excellent customer service and achieve long-term success.

Techniques for conveying empathy and resolving issues via email

Email is a powerful communication tool that is widely used in the customer service industry. However, it can be challenging to convey empathy and resolve issues effectively through this medium. Unlike face-to-face or phone conversations, emails lack the benefit of tone of voice, body language, and facial expressions. This can lead to misunderstandings and misinterpretations of the customer's emotions and concerns. In this section, we will discuss techniques for conveying empathy and resolving issues via email.

Use a friendly and empathetic tone
One of the most effective techniques for conveying empathy through email is to use a friendly and empathetic tone. This means using words and phrases that convey your understanding of the customer's situation and your willingness to help. For example, instead of starting with a formal greeting like "Dear Customer," you could start with "Hello, [Customer's Name]."

Additionally, using phrases like "I understand how you feel" or "I'm sorry to hear that you're having trouble" can help to show that you are empathetic and caring.

However, be careful not to sound insincere or robotic in your responses. The key is to strike a balance between being professional and being approachable.

Acknowledge the customer's concerns

Another technique for conveying empathy through email is to acknowledge the customer's concerns. This means taking the time to understand their issue and showing that you are committed to resolving it. One way to do this is to summarize the customer's concerns in your response. For example, "I understand that you're experiencing issues with your product's functionality and that this is causing frustration."

By summarizing the customer's concerns, you are showing that you have taken the time to read their email and understand their situation. This can help to build trust and rapport with the customer, which is crucial for resolving their issue effectively.

Provide clear and concise information

Providing clear and concise information is another key technique for resolving issues via email. This means being specific about what you can do to help the customer and providing them with any necessary information or resources. For example, if a customer is experiencing technical difficulties with a product, you could provide them with step-by-step instructions on how to troubleshoot the issue.

It's also important to be transparent about any limitations or constraints that may impact your ability to resolve the issue. For example, if a customer is requesting a refund for a product that is outside of the return policy timeframe, you could explain the policy and provide any possible alternatives or options.

Personalize your responses

Personalizing your responses is another effective technique for conveying empathy and building rapport with customers. This means addressing the customer by name and tailoring your response to their specific situation. For example, if a customer is inquiring about a product that is out of stock, you could offer to notify them when the product becomes available again.

Additionally, personalizing your responses can help to humanize the customer service experience and make the customer feel valued and heard. This can lead to increased customer satisfaction and loyalty.

Use positive language

Using positive language is another effective technique for resolving issues via email. This means focusing on what you can do to help the customer rather than what you cannot do. For example, instead of saying "I cannot issue a refund," you could say "I can offer you a store credit for your next purchase."

By using positive language, you are showing the customer that you are committed to finding a solution and are willing to work with them to resolve their issue.

Overall, these techniques for conveying empathy and resolving issues via email can help to improve customer satisfaction, build trust and rapport with customers, and ultimately drive business success. By using a friendly and empathetic tone, acknowledging the customer's concerns, providing personalized solutions, and using positive language, customer service representatives can effectively communicate with customers and ensure their needs are met.

However, it is important to note that these techniques should be used in conjunction with other best practices for customer service, such as timely responses and thorough follow-up. Responding to emails in a timely manner shows customers that their concerns are a priority and helps to prevent further frustration or dissatisfaction. Additionally, following up with customers after their issue has been resolved can further improve customer satisfaction and foster loyalty.

To further improve the effectiveness of email communication, it may also be beneficial for companies to provide customer service representatives with training and resources on effective email etiquette and best practices. This can include tips on tone, formatting, and language, as well as guidance on how to handle more complex or sensitive customer issues.

Finally, it is important to regularly review and analyze customer feedback to identify areas for improvement and refine customer service strategies. This can include gathering feedback through surveys, monitoring customer service metrics, and actively seeking out customer feedback and suggestions.

In conclusion, effectively resolving customer issues via email requires a combination of empathy, personalized solutions, positive language, timely responses, and thorough follow-up. By prioritizing the customer experience and investing in ongoing training and analysis, businesses can build strong customer relationships and drive long-term success.

Best practices for formatting and structuring customer service emails

When it comes to providing customer service via email, the content of your message is important, but so is the way in which it is presented. Proper formatting and structure can greatly improve the readability and effectiveness of your emails, and ultimately lead to greater customer satisfaction. In this section, we will discuss some best practices for formatting and structuring customer service emails.

Use a Clear and Concise Subject Line

The subject line of your email is the first thing the customer will see, and it should accurately reflect the content of the message. A clear and concise subject line will help the customer to quickly identify the purpose of the email, and whether or not it requires immediate attention. Avoid using vague or generic subject lines, such as "Regarding Your Order," as this can lead to confusion and delays in response time.

Start with a Greeting

Starting your email with a friendly greeting can help to establish a positive tone and build rapport with the customer. Use the customer's name if possible, and avoid using overly formal language. A simple "Hello [Customer Name]," or "Hi [Customer Name]," is often sufficient.

Provide Context and Details

When addressing the customer's issue, it is important to provide context and details that help to clarify the situation. This can include information such as the customer's order number, the date of purchase, and a brief description of the issue. By providing this information upfront, you can help to streamline the conversation and avoid confusion.

Use Bullet Points or Numbered Lists

When providing instructions or outlining steps for the customer to follow, using bullet points or numbered lists can make the information more accessible and easier to follow. This can be especially helpful for complex issues that require multiple steps to resolve.

Keep Paragraphs Short and to the Point

Long paragraphs can be overwhelming and difficult to read, especially when dealing with complex issues. Keep your paragraphs short and focused on one main point. This will help to improve readability and make it easier for the customer to understand the message.

Use White Space to Improve Readability

Using white space, such as line breaks and paragraph breaks, can help to improve the overall readability of your email. This can make the email look less cluttered and easier on the eyes. Be sure to use white space strategically, however, as too much can also be overwhelming.

End with a Call to Action
When concluding your email, it is important to provide the customer with a clear call to action. This can include instructions for what the customer should do next, such as contacting a specific department or following up with additional information. Be sure to provide clear and specific instructions, and thank the customer for their business and for reaching out.

Overall, by following these best practices for formatting and structuring customer service emails, you can greatly improve the effectiveness and readability of your messages, and ultimately provide better customer service.

Exercise: Analyzing a real customer service email and developing a response

Analyzing a real customer service email and developing a response can be a useful exercise for students in the customer service field. It provides an opportunity to apply the best practices and techniques discussed in the textbook section on formatting and structuring customer service emails.

Here is an example of a customer service email:

Dear Customer Service,

I recently ordered a product from your website, and I am very disappointed with the quality of the item. The stitching is coming apart, and the fabric is very thin. I would like to return the item and receive a full refund.

Please let me know how I can go about returning the product and receiving a refund.

Sincerely,
Jane

To develop an effective response to this email, there are several steps that should be followed. First, it is important to acknowledge the customer's complaint and apologize for any inconvenience or frustration that they may have experienced. This shows that the company takes the customer's concerns seriously and is committed to resolving the issue.

Second, the response should provide a clear and detailed explanation of the company's return and refund policy. This should include any relevant deadlines, requirements, and procedures for returning the product and receiving a refund.

Third, the response should offer a solution that is in line with the customer's request. In this case, the solution would be to provide a full refund for the product.

Here is an example of a response to the customer's email:

Dear Jane,

Thank you for reaching out to us regarding your recent purchase from our website. We are sorry to hear that the product did not meet your expectations, and we apologize for any inconvenience that this may have caused.

We would be happy to assist you with returning the item and receiving a full refund. Please follow the instructions on our website for returning the product. Once we receive the item and verify its condition, we will process a full refund to your original form of payment.

Please let us know if you have any further questions or concerns. We appreciate your business and value your feedback.

Sincerely,
Customer Service

This response follows the best practices for formatting and structuring customer service emails discussed in the textbook section. It begins with a polite greeting and an acknowledgement of the customer's complaint, followed by a clear and detailed explanation of the company's return and refund policy. The response ends with a solution that meets the customer's request and an invitation for further communication.

Overall, analyzing a real customer service email and developing a response can be a useful exercise for students in the customer service field. It helps to reinforce the importance of following best practices and techniques for formatting and structuring customer service emails, and it provides an opportunity to apply these skills in a real-world scenario.

CHAPTER 16: ENSURING EFFICIENT AND ACCURATE SHIPPING AND RECEIVING

Efficient and accurate shipping and receiving are critical components of any successful business. These processes ensure that products are delivered to customers on time and in good condition, which in turn can lead to increased customer satisfaction and repeat business. In this chapter, we will explore best practices for ensuring efficient and accurate shipping and receiving, including proper inventory management, streamlined order processing, and effective communication between all parties involved.

Inventory Management

Effective inventory management is crucial for ensuring that the right products are available to ship to customers when they are needed. It involves keeping track of stock levels, monitoring demand, and ordering new products as needed. One of the most important aspects of inventory management is accurate record keeping, which allows businesses to track product availability and make informed decisions about when to order more inventory.

Inventory management systems can be used to automate many of these processes, including tracking stock levels, reordering products, and generating reports to help businesses make informed decisions about their inventory. These systems can also help businesses avoid overstocking or understocking products, which can lead to increased costs or missed sales opportunities.

Streamlined Order Processing

Another critical component of efficient shipping and receiving is streamlined order processing. This involves taking orders from customers, processing them efficiently, and fulfilling them accurately and on time. One of the keys to successful order processing is ensuring that all parties involved in the process are communicating effectively and that everyone is aware of their roles and responsibilities.

One way to streamline order processing is to use technology such as electronic order forms and automated order processing systems. These systems can help to reduce errors and improve efficiency by automating many of the steps involved in processing orders, including verifying customer information, checking inventory levels, and processing payment information.

Effective Communication

Effective communication is essential for ensuring that all parties involved in shipping and receiving are aware of what is happening at each stage of the process. This includes communication between sales teams, warehouse staff, and shipping and receiving teams.

One way to improve communication is to use a centralized system that allows all parties involved in the process to track the status of orders and shipments in real time. This can help to ensure that everyone is aware of what is happening at each stage of the process and can quickly identify and resolve any issues that arise.

Analyzing Real-World Examples

To reinforce the concepts discussed in this chapter, it can be helpful to analyze real-world examples of shipping and receiving processes. For example, consider the following customer complaint email:

"Dear Customer Service,

I recently received my order and was disappointed to find that one of the items was missing. I ordered two shirts, but only received one in the package. Can you please let me know when I can expect the missing shirt to be shipped to me?

Thank you,
Jane"

To respond to this email, the customer service representative should first acknowledge the customer's concern and apologize for the inconvenience. They should then ask for more information about the order, including the order number and the item that was missing. Finally, they should provide an estimated date for when the missing item will be shipped, as well as any other relevant information about the order.

Sample response:

"Dear Jane,

Thank you for bringing this to our attention. We are sorry for any inconvenience caused by the missing shirt in your recent order. Can you please provide us with your order number and the item that was missing so that we can investigate the matter further?

In the meantime, we will be shipping the missing shirt to you as soon as possible. We apologize for any delay and appreciate your patience.

Best regards,
Customer Service"

Conclusion

Efficient and accurate shipping and receiving are critical components of any successful business. By following best practices for inventory management, streamlined order processing, and effective communication, businesses can ensure that products are delivered to customers on time, in good condition, and with minimal errors.

One key takeaway from this chapter is that investing in technology and automation can help businesses streamline their shipping and receiving processes. This includes using barcode scanners, RFID technology, and other tools to track inventory, automate order fulfillment, and reduce errors. Additionally, businesses can leverage transportation management systems to optimize shipping routes, reduce shipping costs, and improve delivery times.

Another important aspect of efficient shipping and receiving is effective communication between all parties involved, including suppliers, manufacturers, distributors, and customers. By establishing clear communication channels and using standardized terminology, businesses can reduce misunderstandings, resolve issues quickly, and ensure that all parties are working towards the same goals.

Finally, it is crucial for businesses to regularly assess their shipping and receiving processes and make adjustments as needed. This can involve conducting regular audits to identify areas for improvement, soliciting feedback from customers and employees, and implementing continuous improvement processes to ensure that the shipping and receiving processes are always evolving and improving.

By following these best practices and taking a proactive approach to shipping and receiving, businesses can improve customer satisfaction, reduce costs, and gain a competitive advantage in their industry.

The importance of timely and accurate shipping and receiving

Shipping and receiving are critical components of any business that deals with physical goods. Timely and accurate shipping and receiving play a vital role in customer satisfaction, inventory management, and overall business success. In this section, we will discuss the importance of timely and accurate shipping and receiving and explore the best practices businesses can adopt to ensure efficient and effective shipping and receiving operations.

Importance of Timely and Accurate Shipping and Receiving

Customer Satisfaction
In today's fast-paced business environment, customers expect prompt delivery of their orders. Late deliveries, lost shipments, or damaged products can lead to dissatisfied customers and negative reviews. On the other hand, timely and accurate shipping and receiving can enhance customer satisfaction and loyalty, leading to repeat business and positive word-of-mouth referrals.

Inventory Management
Efficient shipping and receiving processes are critical to effective inventory management. Accurate inventory records are essential to avoid stockouts, overstocking, or mismanaged stock. When shipments are received in a timely manner and entered into the inventory management system promptly, businesses can make informed decisions about ordering, forecasting, and demand planning.

Cost Reduction
Inefficient shipping and receiving processes can result in unnecessary costs. For example, if a shipment is lost, damaged, or delayed, businesses may have to bear the costs of reshipping or replacing the products. Additionally, poor inventory management can lead to overstocking, which ties up capital and storage space, and can result in obsolescence or wastage.

Competitive Advantage
Timely and accurate shipping and receiving can give businesses a competitive advantage over their peers. Businesses that can deliver products faster and with greater accuracy than their competitors can attract and retain customers and gain market share.

Best Practices for Timely and Accurate Shipping and Receiving

Plan and Forecast

Effective planning and forecasting are critical to ensure timely and accurate shipping and receiving. Businesses should use historical data, market trends, and demand forecasting techniques to determine inventory levels and anticipate customer demand. This can help businesses to avoid stockouts or overstocking, which can result in lost sales or unnecessary costs.

Efficient Order Processing

Efficient order processing is critical to ensuring timely and accurate shipping and receiving. Automated order processing systems can reduce errors and improve efficiency. In addition, businesses can use tools such as barcoding, scanning, and RFID technology to streamline the order processing process.

Effective Communication

Effective communication is essential to ensure accurate shipping and receiving. Businesses should establish clear communication channels between shipping and receiving departments, suppliers, and customers. This can help to avoid misunderstandings, delays, and errors.

Use Technology

Technology can play a critical role in efficient shipping and receiving. Businesses can use software solutions for inventory management, order processing, and logistics planning. Additionally, businesses can use technology such as GPS tracking, real-time updates, and automated alerts to ensure accurate and timely deliveries.

Conclusion

Timely and accurate shipping and receiving are critical to the success of any business that deals with physical goods. Efficient shipping and receiving processes can lead to satisfied customers, effective inventory management, cost reduction, and competitive advantage. By adopting best practices such as planning and forecasting, efficient order processing, effective communication, and the use of technology, businesses can ensure efficient and effective shipping and receiving operations.

Techniques for tracking and monitoring orders and shipments

Tracking and monitoring orders and shipments is a crucial component of successful shipping and receiving operations. It enables businesses to ensure timely and accurate deliveries, while also providing valuable insights into the supply chain process. In this section, we will discuss various techniques for tracking and monitoring orders and shipments, including order tracking software, RFID technology, and GPS tracking systems.

Order Tracking Software

Order tracking software is a computer program that allows businesses to track orders and shipments from start to finish. It provides real-time visibility into the status of orders, allowing businesses to identify any potential delays or issues before they become major problems. Order tracking software can also automate many of the manual tasks associated with tracking and monitoring orders, freeing up employees to focus on more important tasks.

One popular order tracking software is ShipStation, which is designed specifically for ecommerce businesses. ShipStation allows businesses to manage and track orders from multiple sales channels, including marketplaces like Amazon and eBay. It also integrates with major carriers like USPS, UPS, and FedEx, allowing businesses to track shipments and print shipping labels directly from the software.

RFID Technology

Radio-frequency identification (RFID) technology is a wireless communication technology that uses radio waves to identify and track objects. It has been used in shipping and receiving operations for many years, and is becoming increasingly popular due to its ability to provide real-time visibility into the supply chain process.

RFID tags are attached to products, pallets, or containers, and contain information such as product details, shipping information, and tracking data. RFID readers are used to scan the tags and transmit the data to a central database, where it can be accessed by employees in real-time. This enables businesses to track shipments and monitor inventory levels more accurately, reducing the risk of stockouts and other supply chain disruptions.

GPS Tracking Systems

Global Positioning System (GPS) tracking systems are another technology that can be used to track and monitor shipments. GPS trackers are small devices that can be attached to products or vehicles, and use satellite signals to determine their location in real-time. This information is transmitted to a central database, where it can be accessed by employees to track shipments and monitor delivery times.

GPS tracking systems are particularly useful for businesses that transport goods over long distances, as they provide real-time visibility into the location and status of shipments. They can also help businesses to optimize their delivery routes and improve overall efficiency, by identifying areas where delivery times could be improved.

Conclusion

Tracking and monitoring orders and shipments is a critical component of successful shipping and receiving operations. By using order tracking software, RFID technology, and GPS tracking systems, businesses can ensure timely and accurate deliveries, while also gaining valuable insights into the supply chain process. These technologies are becoming increasingly important in today's fast-paced business environment, and businesses that fail to adopt them risk falling behind their competitors.

Strategies for resolving shipping and receiving issues proactively

Effective shipping and receiving is essential for ensuring that goods are delivered on time and in good condition. However, problems can arise in the shipping and receiving process, such as delays, damaged goods, and lost packages. These issues can cause frustration for customers and result in lost business. In this section, we will explore strategies for resolving shipping and receiving issues proactively to ensure customer satisfaction.

Set Clear Expectations

One of the most effective strategies for resolving shipping and receiving issues is to set clear expectations with customers. This can be done by providing accurate and detailed information about shipping times, delivery dates, and expected delivery times. By providing customers with this information upfront, businesses can help to manage their expectations and reduce the likelihood of issues arising.

For example, businesses can use tracking software to provide customers with real-time updates on their orders. This can include information on when the package was shipped, when it arrived at the carrier's facility, and when it is out for delivery. By keeping customers informed throughout the shipping process, businesses can reduce the likelihood of customer complaints and negative reviews.

Implement Quality Control Measures

Another strategy for resolving shipping and receiving issues is to implement quality control measures. Quality control measures can help to identify potential issues before they occur, allowing businesses to take corrective action and prevent problems from arising.

For example, businesses can implement inspection procedures to ensure that products are packaged correctly and that they are not damaged during shipping. This can include checking the packaging for defects, ensuring that products are securely packed, and checking for any signs of damage during transit. By implementing these quality control measures, businesses can reduce the likelihood of damaged goods and lost packages.

Maintain Open Communication

Maintaining open communication with customers is another key strategy for resolving shipping and receiving issues proactively. By keeping customers informed of any issues that may arise, businesses can help to manage their expectations and reduce the likelihood of negative feedback.

For example, if there is a delay in shipping or if a package is lost, businesses should notify the customer as soon as possible. This can be done via email or phone and should include an explanation of the issue and an estimated timeframe for resolution. By maintaining open communication with customers, businesses can demonstrate that they value their customers and are committed to providing excellent service.

Provide Excellent Customer Service

Providing excellent customer service is another important strategy for resolving shipping and receiving issues proactively. This includes responding promptly to customer inquiries and complaints, and going above and beyond to resolve any issues that may arise.

For example, if a customer receives a damaged product, businesses should offer a replacement or a refund. If there is a delay in shipping, businesses can offer expedited shipping at no additional cost. By providing excellent customer service, businesses can demonstrate that they value their customers and are committed to resolving any issues that may arise.

Continuous Improvement

Finally, businesses should continuously evaluate their shipping and receiving processes to identify areas for improvement. This can include reviewing customer feedback, analyzing shipping data, and implementing new technologies and systems to improve efficiency and accuracy.

For example, businesses can use data analytics to identify trends in shipping and receiving issues and take corrective action to prevent these issues from arising in the future. They can also implement new technologies, such as automated inventory management systems, to improve accuracy and reduce the likelihood of errors.

Conclusion

In conclusion, resolving shipping and receiving issues proactively is essential for ensuring customer satisfaction and maintaining a positive reputation. By setting clear expectations, implementing quality control measures, maintaining open communication, providing excellent customer service, and continuously improving processes, businesses can ensure that goods are delivered on time and in good condition. By taking a proactive approach to shipping and receiving, businesses can reduce the likelihood of issues arising and demonstrate their commitment to providing excellent service to their customers.

To summarize, businesses should take the following steps to proactively resolve shipping and receiving issues:

Set clear expectations: Customers should be informed of expected delivery times, shipping methods, and any potential delays. This can be done through order confirmations and tracking updates.

Implement quality control measures: This includes checking products for accuracy and quality before shipment, as well as conducting regular audits of shipping and receiving processes to identify and address any potential issues.

Maintain open communication: Businesses should keep customers informed of any changes or delays in the shipping process, and promptly address any concerns or complaints that arise.

Provide excellent customer service: This includes being responsive to customer inquiries and complaints, and taking appropriate steps to resolve any issues that arise.

Continuously improve processes: Regularly reviewing and improving shipping and receiving processes can help identify areas for improvement and prevent issues from arising in the future.

By following these strategies, businesses can proactively address shipping and receiving issues and ensure that they are delivering high-quality products to their customers. In addition to improving customer satisfaction and reputation, these efforts can also lead to cost savings and increased efficiency in the shipping and receiving process.

It is important to note that even with proactive measures in place, issues may still arise. In these cases, it is important to have a plan in place for quickly and effectively resolving issues. This may include offering refunds or replacements, providing discounts or incentives for future purchases, or taking other steps to address customer concerns.

Overall, proactive resolution of shipping and receiving issues is essential for any business that wants to provide high-quality products and excellent customer service. By setting clear expectations, implementing quality control measures, maintaining open communication, providing excellent customer service, and continuously improving processes, businesses can ensure that they are delivering products on time and in good condition, while also building a strong reputation for quality and reliability.

Exercise: Analyzing a real shipping or receiving problem and developing a plan for addressing it

Learning Objectives:

Identify a real shipping or receiving problem and analyze its root cause(s)
Develop a plan for addressing the problem using proactive strategies
Introduction:
In the previous sections, we discussed techniques for tracking and monitoring orders and shipments, as well as strategies for resolving shipping and receiving issues proactively. In this exercise, we will apply these concepts to a real-world shipping or receiving problem and develop a plan for addressing it. By doing so, we will gain practical experience in applying the knowledge we have learned and develop critical thinking skills that are essential in the customer service field.

Step 1: Identify a Real Shipping or Receiving Problem
To begin, identify a real shipping or receiving problem that you or your organization has experienced. This could be a problem with delayed shipments, damaged goods, missing items, or any other issue that has affected the delivery of goods. Once you have identified a problem, describe it in detail, including when it occurred, the impact it had on customers or the business, and any other relevant information.

Example:
Problem: Delayed Shipments
When: Over the past month
Impact: Customers have been receiving their orders later than expected, resulting in frustration and negative reviews. The business has also been losing money due to shipping refunds and reduced customer loyalty.

Step 2: Analyze the Root Cause(s) of the Problem
Once you have identified the problem, it is important to analyze its root cause(s). This involves identifying the underlying factors that have contributed to the problem,

such as poor communication, inadequate quality control measures, or inefficient processes. By identifying the root cause(s), you can develop a plan that addresses the source of the problem, rather than just its symptoms.

Example:
Root Cause: Inefficient Processes
Analysis: Upon further investigation, it was found that the business was using outdated shipping software that was prone to errors and delays. Additionally, the warehouse was not organized in a way that allowed for efficient order fulfillment, leading to delays and errors in picking and packing orders.

Step 3: Develop a Plan for Addressing the Problem Using Proactive Strategies
Based on your analysis of the root cause(s), develop a plan for addressing the problem using proactive strategies. This involves implementing measures that prevent the problem from occurring in the first place, rather than just reacting to it after it has already happened. Some strategies to consider include setting clear expectations, implementing quality control measures, maintaining open communication, providing excellent customer service, and continuously improving processes.

Example:
Plan:

✧ Update shipping software to a modern and reliable system that reduces errors and delays.
✧ Reorganize the warehouse to optimize order fulfillment and reduce errors in picking and packing.
✧ Implement quality control measures, such as double-checking orders before shipping, to ensure accuracy and reduce errors.
✧ Provide training to employees on the new software and warehouse organization to ensure they are properly equipped to handle orders efficiently.
✧ Maintain open communication with customers by providing regular updates on their orders and being responsive to any concerns or questions they may have.
✧ Continuously monitor and improve processes to ensure that they are efficient and effective.

Step 4: Implement and Monitor the Plan
Once you have developed your plan, it is important to implement it and monitor its effectiveness. This involves ensuring that all necessary changes are made, and that employees are properly trained and equipped to carry out the plan. Additionally, it involves tracking key performance indicators (KPIs), such as delivery times and customer satisfaction ratings, to evaluate the success of the plan and make adjustments as necessary.

Example:
Implementation:

- ✧ Research and select a modern and reliable shipping software system.
- ✧ Develop a new warehouse layout and implement changes to optimize order fulfillment and shipping processes.
- ✧ Provide additional training and resources for employees to ensure proper handling of packages and efficient shipping practices.
- ✧ Establish clear communication channels with shipping carriers to provide real-time updates on shipment statuses and potential delays.
- ✧ Implement a system for tracking and monitoring packages in real-time, including providing customers with access to shipment tracking information.
- ✧ Regularly review and assess the effectiveness of the new shipping and receiving processes, making adjustments as needed.

Exercise Questions:

Describe a shipping or receiving problem that you have encountered in your professional or personal life. How did the problem impact your experience?

Analyze the problem using the five strategies discussed in this section: setting clear expectations, implementing quality control measures, maintaining open communication, providing excellent customer service, and continuously improving processes. Which strategies could have prevented or mitigated the problem?

Develop a plan for addressing the problem using the strategies discussed in this section. What specific actions would you take to resolve the issue and prevent it from happening again in the future?

Discuss the potential challenges and obstacles that you may encounter when implementing your plan. How would you address these challenges?

How would you measure the success of your plan? What metrics or indicators would you use to evaluate the effectiveness of your solution?

CHAPTER 17: PROVIDING EXCELLENT DELIVERY AND INSTALLATION SERVICES

Providing excellent delivery and installation services is critical for businesses in today's highly competitive marketplace. Customers have come to expect a seamless and hassle-free delivery and installation experience, and businesses that fail to meet these expectations risk losing customers and damaging their reputation. In this chapter, we will discuss the key strategies and best practices for providing excellent delivery and installation services, including the importance of planning, communication, and quality control.

Section 1: Planning for Delivery and Installation

The key to providing excellent delivery and installation services is careful planning. Before a product is delivered or installed, businesses should take the time to assess the customer's needs and develop a comprehensive plan for the delivery and installation process. This plan should include details such as:

- ✧ Delivery and installation schedule
- ✧ Delivery and installation location
- ✧ Required equipment and tools
- ✧ Staffing needs
- ✧ Safety protocols

By taking the time to develop a comprehensive plan, businesses can ensure that the delivery and installation process runs smoothly and that the customer's needs are met.

Exercise: Developing a Delivery and Installation Plan

Research a real-world scenario where a business failed to provide excellent delivery and installation services, and develop a plan for how the business could have improved the delivery and installation process. Consider factors such as planning, communication, and quality control.

Section 2: Communication with Customers

Effective communication is essential for providing excellent delivery and installation services. Businesses should keep customers informed throughout the delivery and installation process, providing regular updates on the status of the delivery and installation and addressing any concerns or questions the customer may have.

To ensure effective communication, businesses should:

✧ Provide clear and detailed delivery and installation instructions
✧ Use tracking systems to keep customers informed of delivery and installation status
✧ Provide a point of contact for customers to address any concerns or questions
✧ Follow up with customers after delivery and installation to ensure satisfaction
✧ By communicating effectively with customers, businesses can build trust and demonstrate their commitment to providing excellent service.

Exercise: Improving Communication with Customers

Research a real-world scenario where a business failed to communicate effectively with customers during the delivery and installation process, and develop a plan for how the business could have improved communication. Consider factors such as clear instructions, tracking systems, and follow-up procedures.

Section 3: Quality Control

Finally, businesses must implement quality control measures to ensure that delivery and installation services meet customer expectations. Quality control should begin with the selection of a reliable delivery and installation team and continue through the entire delivery and installation process.

To ensure quality control, businesses should:

✧ Train staff on proper delivery and installation procedures
✧ Conduct regular safety inspections
✧ Monitor delivery and installation performance

✧   Collect feedback from customers and use it to improve the delivery and installation process

By implementing quality control measures, businesses can identify and address issues before they become problems, ensuring that customers receive excellent delivery and installation services.

Exercise: Implementing Quality Control Measures

Research a real-world scenario where a business experienced quality control issues during the delivery and installation process, and develop a plan for how the business could have implemented quality control measures to prevent these issues. Consider factors such as staff training, safety inspections, and customer feedback.

Conclusion:

Providing excellent delivery and installation services is critical for businesses that want to succeed in today's competitive marketplace. By planning carefully, communicating effectively, and implementing quality control measures, businesses can ensure that customers receive the seamless and hassle-free delivery and installation experience they expect. The exercises in this chapter provide students with the opportunity to analyze real-world scenarios and develop plans for addressing delivery and installation issues, helping them prepare for success in the customer service field.

Techniques for scheduling and coordinating deliveries and installations

Delivering products and services to customers is a crucial part of any business. Providing excellent delivery and installation services can help companies gain a competitive advantage, enhance customer satisfaction, and increase customer loyalty. However, coordinating deliveries and installations can be a complex and challenging task. It requires efficient scheduling, effective communication, and collaboration among various stakeholders involved in the process. This chapter will discuss techniques for scheduling and coordinating deliveries and installations, including effective planning, efficient routing, real-time tracking, and proactive communication.

Effective Planning:

Planning is the foundation of successful deliveries and installations. Companies need to develop a comprehensive plan that outlines the scope of work, delivery schedule, installation requirements, and customer expectations. The plan should also include contingency measures to address any unforeseen challenges that may arise during the process. Effective planning involves gathering information about the customer's location, site conditions, access requirements, and product specifications. This information helps companies to determine the appropriate delivery and installation methods and equipment needed to complete the job.

Efficient Routing:

Routing is another critical aspect of delivering products and services to customers. Efficient routing involves determining the most efficient route to deliver products and services, minimizing travel time and distance, and optimizing resources. Companies can use various routing software tools to plan routes and optimize schedules. These tools help companies to reduce delivery time, save fuel costs, and minimize the environmental impact of transportation.

Real-time Tracking:

Real-time tracking is a valuable tool for coordinating deliveries and installations. Companies can use GPS tracking systems and other tracking technologies to monitor the location and status of deliveries and installations in real-time. This information helps companies to identify potential issues and take proactive measures to address them before they become problems. Real-time tracking also provides customers with updates on the status of their deliveries and installations, increasing transparency and accountability.

Proactive Communication:

Effective communication is critical for coordinating deliveries and installations. Companies need to establish clear communication channels with customers, delivery drivers, and installation teams. They should also provide customers with accurate and timely information about their deliveries and installations, including expected delivery times, installation requirements, and any potential delays or issues. Proactive communication helps to build trust and confidence with customers and reduces the likelihood of misunderstandings or disputes.

Conclusion:

Coordinating deliveries and installations requires efficient planning, effective communication, and collaboration among various stakeholders. By using techniques such as efficient routing, real-time tracking, and proactive communication, companies can provide excellent delivery and installation services that meet customer expectations and enhance their reputation. Delivering products and services to customers is an ongoing process that requires continuous improvement and adaptation to changing circumstances. Companies that prioritize customer satisfaction and invest in their delivery and installation processes are more likely to succeed in today's competitive marketplace.

Examples:

Example 1:
A furniture company that delivers and installs products to customers in different locations has developed an efficient planning system that includes site surveys, equipment assessments, and delivery schedules. The company uses routing software to optimize routes and minimize travel time and distance. The company also uses real-time tracking to monitor the location and status of deliveries and installations, providing customers with updates on their orders. The company communicates with customers via email, text messages, and phone calls to provide them with accurate and timely information about their deliveries and installations. The company's delivery and installation services have received positive feedback from customers, contributing to the company's reputation for quality and reliability.

Example 2:
A plumbing company that provides installation and repair services to customers has implemented a real-time tracking system that allows customers to track the location and status of their service calls. The company uses GPS tracking devices to monitor the location of service trucks and dispatch technicians to the nearest service calls. The company also uses a scheduling system that prioritizes urgent service calls and assigns the appropriate technician based on their expertise and availability.

Implementation:

✧ Research and select a real-time tracking system that is compatible with the company's existing software and hardware.
✧ Train employees on how to use the tracking system and scheduling software to optimize efficiency and accuracy.
✧ Develop a prioritization system that categorizes service calls based on urgency and assigns the appropriate technician based on their expertise and availability.

By implementing a real-time tracking system and scheduling software, the plumbing company is able to provide customers with real-time updates on the status of their service calls. This not only increases customer satisfaction but also improves the efficiency of the company's operations. By prioritizing urgent service calls and assigning the appropriate technician, the company is able to minimize wait times and resolve issues more quickly. This results in happier customers and a more profitable business.

Example 3:
A furniture company that delivers and installs furniture for customers has implemented a scheduling system that allows customers to choose their preferred delivery and installation times. The company also sends a notification to customers on the day of delivery to provide them with a more accurate estimated delivery time. The company has also implemented a system for confirming appointments with customers to ensure that they are available at the scheduled delivery time.

Implementation:

✧ Research and select a scheduling software that is compatible with the company's existing software and hardware.
✧ Train employees on how to use the scheduling software and confirm appointments with customers.
✧ Develop a notification system that sends updates to customers on the day of delivery to provide them with an accurate estimated delivery time.

By implementing a scheduling system that allows customers to choose their preferred delivery and installation times, the furniture company is able to provide a more personalized experience for its customers. By sending notifications and confirming appointments with customers, the company is able to reduce the number of missed appointments and improve customer satisfaction. This results in a more positive reputation for the company and an increase in repeat business.

Strategies for communicating effectively with customers during the process

Strategies for communicating effectively with customers during the delivery and installation process are crucial for ensuring a positive customer experience. Effective communication can help to manage customer expectations, provide transparency, and build trust. In this section, we will discuss several strategies for communicating effectively with customers during the delivery and installation process.

Provide clear and timely communication: One of the most important strategies for communicating effectively with customers is to provide clear and timely communication. This means keeping customers informed about the status of their delivery or installation at every step of the process. The communication should be clear, concise, and free of technical jargon. Customers should be informed about the expected delivery or installation time and any potential delays. This can be done through phone calls, text messages, or emails. Providing customers with regular updates can help to build trust and ensure that they feel informed and in control throughout the process.

Set expectations upfront: It's important to set expectations upfront with customers regarding the delivery and installation process. This can help to manage customer expectations and prevent misunderstandings. Make sure to communicate any specific requirements or limitations regarding the delivery or installation process. This can include things like the need for a loading dock, the availability of parking, or any specific delivery or installation instructions. By setting expectations upfront, customers can prepare for the delivery or installation process and understand what to expect.

Provide detailed information: Providing detailed information to customers about the delivery or installation process can help to alleviate any concerns they may have. This can include providing information about the delivery or installation timeline, the specific steps involved in the process, and any potential challenges that may arise. Providing detailed information can help to build trust and ensure that customers feel confident in the delivery or installation process.

Be available for questions: It's important to be available to customers for questions or concerns they may have during the delivery or installation process. This can be done through phone, email, or text message. Providing a dedicated customer service line can help to ensure that customers can easily reach out for assistance if they need it. Being available for questions can help to build trust and ensure that customers feel supported throughout the process.

Address issues proactively: Despite best efforts, issues may arise during the delivery or installation process. It's important to address any issues proactively to prevent them from escalating. This can include things like addressing delays, providing compensation for any damages, or taking steps to prevent similar issues from occurring in the future. By addressing issues proactively, customers are more likely to feel valued and satisfied with the overall experience.

Example: A furniture retailer has implemented a communication strategy to ensure effective communication with customers during the delivery and installation process. The retailer sends a text message to customers the day before the scheduled delivery or installation date to confirm the appointment and provide a specific time window. On the day of the delivery or installation, the retailer sends another text message to customers with the name and photo of the delivery or installation team and a link to track the status of the delivery or installation. If any issues arise during the process, the retailer has a dedicated customer service line for customers to reach out for assistance. The retailer also follows up with customers after the delivery or installation to ensure satisfaction and address any issues proactively.

Exercises:

What are some potential challenges that may arise during the delivery or installation process, and how can they be addressed proactively?

Why is it important to provide clear and timely communication to customers during the delivery and installation process?

What are some strategies for setting expectations upfront with customers regarding the delivery and installation process?

How can providing detailed information to customers about the delivery and installation process help to build trust and ensure customer satisfaction?

What are some ways that customers can reach out for assistance during the delivery and installation process, and why is it important to provide multiple options for communication?

Exercises:

Brainstorm potential challenges that may arise during the delivery or installation process, such as inclement weather, equipment failure, or unexpected delays. Develop a plan for addressing each potential challenge proactively to minimize negative impacts on the customer experience.

Write a script for a hypothetical scenario where a customer is experiencing a delay or issue with their delivery or installation. Use clear and concise language to communicate the issue and provide a timeline for resolution, while maintaining a professional and empathetic tone.

Role-play a scenario where a customer is frustrated with the delivery or installation process. Practice active listening and responding with empathy and solutions to address the customer's concerns.

Develop a set of guidelines for communicating with customers during the delivery and installation process. Include tips for active listening, using positive language, providing regular updates, and setting realistic expectations.

Create a customer satisfaction survey to gather feedback on the delivery and installation process. Use the results to identify areas for improvement and implement changes to enhance the customer experience.

Research and analyze case studies of companies that have successfully implemented strategies for effective communication during the delivery and installation process. Evaluate the impact of these strategies on customer satisfaction and identify key takeaways for your own organization.

Conduct a focus group with customers to gather feedback on their experience with the delivery and installation process. Use the insights gained to inform changes to processes and communication strategies.

Develop a training program for delivery and installation personnel on effective communication strategies, including active listening, empathy, and conflict resolution.

Analyze customer data to identify patterns and trends in common issues or challenges during the delivery and installation process. Use this information to develop targeted solutions and proactively address potential issues.

Develop a crisis communication plan for addressing major issues that may arise during the delivery and installation process, such as product recalls or safety concerns. Ensure that the plan includes clear and concise communication to customers, stakeholders, and the media.

Discussion Questions:

How does effective communication during the delivery and installation process impact overall customer satisfaction?

What are some common challenges that companies face when communicating with customers during the delivery and installation process, and how can these be addressed proactively?

How can technology be leveraged to enhance communication with customers during the delivery and installation process?

What are some strategies for setting realistic expectations with customers regarding the delivery and installation process, while also ensuring customer satisfaction?

How can organizations ensure that all personnel involved in the delivery and installation process are trained on effective communication strategies and equipped to handle challenging customer interactions?

How can organizations balance the need for clear and timely communication with customers with the challenges of managing multiple orders and installations simultaneously?

The importance of ensuring quality and safety during delivery and installation

Delivering and installing products can be a complex process that requires careful planning and execution to ensure customer satisfaction. In addition to ensuring timely delivery, it is also essential to ensure the quality and safety of the products being delivered and installed. Failure to do so can result in negative customer experiences, potential liability issues, and damage to a company's reputation. This section will explore the importance of ensuring quality and safety during delivery and installation and provide strategies for achieving this goal.

The Importance of Ensuring Quality:

One of the most critical aspects of delivery and installation is ensuring the quality of the products being delivered. Customers expect products that are free from defects and perform as advertised. Failure to meet these expectations can result in customer dissatisfaction and potentially damage a company's reputation. To ensure quality, companies must have processes in place to inspect and verify products before they leave the warehouse or factory. This includes checking for defects, damage, and ensuring that all parts and accessories are included.

In addition to product inspections, companies must also ensure that their delivery and installation teams are properly trained and equipped to handle the products being delivered. This includes providing proper tools and equipment to prevent damage during the delivery process. For example, when delivering large appliances, such as refrigerators or washing machines, companies may need to provide dollies or lift gates to safely move the products. Failure to provide these tools can result in damage to the product or property and potentially cause injuries to delivery personnel or customers.

The Importance of Ensuring Safety:

Ensuring safety during delivery and installation is also critical. Failure to do so can result in injuries to delivery personnel or customers and potentially lead to costly liability issues. To ensure safety, companies must have safety protocols in place that address potential hazards, such as heavy lifting, awkward product shapes, and the use of power tools.

Companies must also provide proper training to their delivery and installation teams on how to handle and install products safely. This includes training on proper lifting techniques, the use of safety equipment, and the proper installation of products. For example, when installing large appliances, such as gas stoves, companies must ensure that their installation teams are trained on how to properly install gas lines to prevent leaks and potential fire hazards.

Strategies for Ensuring Quality and Safety:

To ensure quality and safety during delivery and installation, companies must have processes and procedures in place that address potential issues proactively. Some strategies for achieving this goal include:

Implementing regular product inspections: Regular product inspections can help identify defects or damage before products are delivered. This can prevent potential safety hazards and ensure customer satisfaction.

Providing proper training and equipment to delivery and installation teams: Providing proper training and equipment to delivery and installation teams can help prevent injuries and damage during the delivery and installation process.

Implementing safety protocols: Implementing safety protocols can help prevent potential safety hazards and liability issues. This includes addressing potential hazards such as heavy lifting, awkward product shapes, and the use of power tools.

Providing clear and concise installation instructions: Providing clear and concise installation instructions can help ensure that products are installed correctly, preventing potential safety hazards and ensuring customer satisfaction.

Offering post-installation support: Offering post-installation support can help address any issues that may arise after installation, ensuring customer satisfaction and preventing potential safety hazards.

Conclusion:

Ensuring quality and safety during delivery and installation is critical to maintaining customer satisfaction and preventing potential liability issues. By implementing processes and procedures that address potential issues proactively, companies can ensure that their products are delivered and installed safely and correctly, meeting customer expectations and preserving their reputation.

Exercise: Analyzing a real delivery or installation problem and developing a plan for addressing it

As with any service industry, problems can arise during the delivery or installation process. It is important for businesses to identify potential issues and develop a plan for addressing them proactively. In this exercise, we will analyze a real delivery or installation problem and develop a plan for addressing it.

Step 1: Identify the Problem

The first step in addressing any problem is to identify it. In this case, let's say that a furniture company has received several complaints from customers about the quality of their furniture upon delivery. Customers have reported scratches, dents, and other damages to their furniture.

Step 2: Analyze the Cause

Once the problem has been identified, the next step is to analyze the cause. In this case, the cause of the problem could be one of several factors, such as:

Poor handling during transport: The furniture may have been mishandled during transport, leading to scratches and dents.

Poor quality control: The furniture may have passed through a poor quality control process, allowing damaged products to be shipped out.

Inadequate packaging: The furniture may not have been adequately packaged, leading to damage during transport.

Step 3: Develop a Plan for Addressing the Problem

After analyzing the cause of the problem, the next step is to develop a plan for addressing it. In this case, the furniture company could implement the following strategies:

Improve handling during transport: The company could implement better handling procedures during transport, such as providing training for delivery personnel on how to properly handle furniture.

Improve quality control: The company could improve its quality control process to ensure that damaged products are not shipped out to customers.

Enhance packaging: The company could improve its packaging process to ensure that furniture is adequately protected during transport.

Implement a customer satisfaction guarantee: The company could implement a customer satisfaction guarantee that promises to replace or refund damaged products.

Enhance communication with customers: The company could improve communication with customers during the delivery process, providing updates on the status of their delivery and setting clear expectations for the quality of the product upon arrival.

Step 4: Implement the Plan

The final step is to implement the plan. This may involve training employees on new handling procedures, improving quality control processes, upgrading packaging materials, or implementing new communication protocols with customers. It is important to monitor the effectiveness of the plan and make adjustments as necessary.

Conclusion

In this exercise, we analyzed a real delivery or installation problem and developed a plan for addressing it. By identifying the problem, analyzing the cause, and developing a plan, businesses can proactively address issues and improve the quality of their service. It is important to continually monitor and improve delivery and installation processes to ensure customer satisfaction and safety.

CHAPTER 18: DEVELOPING A CULTURE OF CUSTOMER SERVICE EXCELLENCE

Customer service is a critical component of any successful business. It involves providing a positive experience for customers at every touchpoint, from initial contact to post-sale support. In today's competitive marketplace, customers have high expectations for the quality of service they receive, and businesses that fail to meet these expectations risk losing customers and damaging their reputation.

Developing a culture of customer service excellence is essential for businesses that want to succeed in today's marketplace. This involves creating a work environment where employees are empowered to provide exceptional service, and where customer satisfaction is a top priority.

In this chapter, we will explore the concept of customer service excellence and discuss strategies for developing a culture of customer service excellence within an organization. We will also examine the benefits of providing excellent customer service, as well as the potential pitfalls of failing to do so.

Key Topics:

- ✧ Defining Customer Service Excellence
- ✧ The Benefits of Providing Excellent Customer Service
- ✧ The Pitfalls of Failing to Provide Excellent Customer Service
- ✧ Developing a Culture of Customer Service Excellence
- ✧ Strategies for Empowering Employees to Provide Exceptional Service
- ✧ Measuring and Improving Customer Satisfaction
- ✧ Best Practices for Providing Excellent Customer Service
- ✧ Throughout this chapter, we will use real-world examples to illustrate

key concepts and provide practical advice for businesses looking to improve their customer service. We will also provide exercises and questions to help students develop their understanding of the material and apply it to their own experiences.

By the end of this chapter, students should have a comprehensive understanding of what it takes to develop a culture of customer service excellence and be equipped with the knowledge and skills to apply these concepts in a variety of organizational settings.

The importance of company-wide commitment to customer service

The importance of customer service cannot be overstated in today's business world. It has become increasingly important for companies to provide exceptional customer service to remain competitive in the market. In fact, customer service has become one of the primary factors that determine a customer's choice of brand or business. It is important for companies to create a culture of customer service excellence that is ingrained in the company's values, practices, and policies. This chapter will discuss the importance of a company-wide commitment to customer service and how it can benefit businesses in the long run.

Understanding the Importance of Customer Service

Customer service is a vital aspect of any business, regardless of its size or industry. Companies that prioritize customer service are often more successful than those that do not. Customer service is important because it helps businesses to retain their existing customers and attract new ones. When customers are satisfied with the service they receive from a company, they are more likely to remain loyal and continue to do business with that company. Additionally, satisfied customers are more likely to refer the company to others, thereby increasing the company's customer base.

Creating a Company-wide Culture of Customer Service

Creating a culture of customer service excellence requires a company-wide commitment to putting the customer first. This means that every employee, from the CEO to the front-line staff, must understand and prioritize the customer's needs. Companies that successfully create a culture of customer service excellence have a clear set of customer service standards and guidelines that are communicated throughout the organization. They also provide ongoing training and support to help employees develop the skills they need to deliver exceptional customer service.

Benefits of a Company-wide Commitment to Customer Service

There are several benefits to creating a company-wide commitment to customer service. One of the main benefits is increased customer satisfaction. When every employee in the organization is committed to providing excellent customer service, customers are more likely to have positive experiences with the company. This can lead to increased customer loyalty and repeat business.

Another benefit of a company-wide commitment to customer service is improved employee morale. When employees feel valued and supported in their efforts to provide excellent customer service, they are more likely to be engaged and motivated in their work. This can lead to increased productivity and better overall job performance.

A third benefit of a company-wide commitment to customer service is improved brand reputation. Companies that provide excellent customer service are more likely to be viewed positively by customers and the wider community. This can lead to increased brand recognition and a stronger market position.

Challenges of Implementing a Company-wide Commitment to Customer Service

Implementing a company-wide commitment to customer service can be challenging, especially in organizations with a large workforce or complex structures. One of the main challenges is getting buy-in from all employees, including those in management positions. It can also be difficult to ensure that customer service standards are consistently applied across the organization, especially in companies with multiple locations or franchises.

Strategies for Implementing a Company-wide Commitment to Customer Service

There are several strategies that companies can use to implement a company-wide commitment to customer service. The first step is to establish a clear set of customer service standards and guidelines that are communicated to all employees. This should include regular training and support to help employees develop the skills they need to deliver exceptional customer service.

Another strategy is to provide incentives for employees who excel in customer service. This can include bonuses, promotions, or recognition programs. These incentives can motivate employees to prioritize customer service and make it a central part of their job responsibilities.

Finally, it is important to measure the effectiveness of the company's customer service efforts on an ongoing basis. This can be done through customer satisfaction surveys, employee feedback, and other performance metrics. By tracking and analyzing these metrics, companies can identify areas where they need to improve and make necessary changes to enhance their customer service practices.

It is crucial for companies to understand that a strong commitment to customer service cannot be achieved overnight. It requires a significant amount of effort and investment in terms of time, money, and resources. However, the benefits of such a commitment can be immense, leading to increased customer loyalty, positive word-of-mouth marketing, and ultimately, increased profits.

Moreover, companies that prioritize customer service not only benefit their bottom line, but they also create a positive work culture that fosters employee satisfaction and engagement. When employees feel empowered to provide excellent customer service, they are more likely to take pride in their work and feel a sense of fulfillment in their roles.

In summary, a company-wide commitment to customer service is essential for creating a positive and successful business environment. This commitment involves setting clear expectations and standards for customer service, providing employees with the necessary training and resources, incentivizing exceptional performance, and regularly measuring and improving customer service practices. By prioritizing customer service, companies can create a loyal customer base, increase profits, and foster a positive work culture.

Techniques for training and coaching employees in customer service skills

Providing excellent customer service is not an innate ability that everyone is born with. It is a skill that can be developed and honed over time through proper training and coaching. In fact, studies have shown that companies that invest in their employees' customer service skills tend to have higher levels of customer satisfaction, retention, and loyalty. In this section, we will discuss some techniques for training and coaching employees in customer service skills.

Provide comprehensive training

The first step in training employees in customer service skills is to provide them with comprehensive training that covers all aspects of the job. This includes not only the technical skills required to perform their job duties but also the soft skills required to interact effectively with customers. Some of the key topics that should be covered in customer service training include:

✧ Active listening skills: Employees should be trained to actively listen to customers and understand their needs and concerns.

✧ Empathy: Employees should be trained to understand and empathize with customers, even if they are upset or angry.

✧ Communication skills: Employees should be trained to communicate clearly and effectively with customers, using language that is easy to understand and avoiding technical jargon.

✧ Problem-solving skills: Employees should be trained to identify and solve customer problems quickly and effectively.

Conflict resolution skills: Employees should be trained to resolve conflicts with customers in a professional and courteous manner.

Provide ongoing coaching and feedback

Training is just the first step in developing employees' customer service skills. To ensure that employees continue to improve, it is important to provide ongoing coaching and feedback. This can be done through regular performance evaluations, one-on-one coaching sessions, and feedback from customers.

During coaching sessions, managers should provide specific feedback on employees' strengths and areas for improvement. They should also provide guidance on how to improve in areas where employees are struggling. For example, if an employee is having difficulty communicating effectively with customers, a manager might provide tips on how to simplify language and avoid technical jargon.

Use role-playing exercises

Role-playing exercises can be an effective way to help employees develop their customer service skills. In these exercises, employees play the role of a customer and a manager or trainer plays the role of an employee. The exercise can be designed to simulate a real-life customer service situation, such as a customer complaint or a request for information.

During the exercise, the manager or trainer can provide feedback on the employee's performance, highlighting areas where they did well and areas where they can improve. Role-playing exercises can help employees develop their active listening, empathy, and problem-solving skills, as well as their ability to communicate effectively with customers.

Provide incentives for excellent customer service

Incentives can be a powerful motivator for employees to provide excellent customer service. These incentives can take many forms, such as bonuses, promotions, or recognition programs. For example, a company might offer a bonus to employees who receive high customer satisfaction scores, or promote employees who consistently provide excellent customer service.

Incentives can help employees feel valued and appreciated, which can improve morale and motivation. They can also help reinforce the importance of customer service and make it a central part of employees' job responsibilities.

Encourage a customer-focused culture

Finally, it is important to encourage a customer-focused culture throughout the organization. This means not only training and coaching employees in customer service skills but also creating a company culture that prioritizes customer satisfaction and loyalty.

This can be done through a variety of means, such as setting customer service goals and metrics, celebrating customer service successes, and incorporating customer feedback into business decisions. By encouraging a customer-focused culture, companies can ensure that customer service is a top priority for everyone in the organization.

Conclusion

Training and coaching employees in customer service skills is essential for any company looking to improve its customer experience and increase customer loyalty. By providing employees with the necessary tools and knowledge to deliver excellent customer service, companies can create a positive impression on their customers, which can lead to increased sales, repeat business, and positive word-of-mouth.

Effective training and coaching techniques involve a combination of classroom instruction, on-the-job training, and ongoing feedback and support. Companies can also use technology to enhance the training experience and provide employees with convenient access to training materials and resources.

Furthermore, it is important to make customer service a company-wide priority by creating a customer-focused culture. This involves setting customer service goals and metrics, celebrating customer service successes, and incorporating customer feedback into business decisions. By doing so, companies can ensure that customer service is not just the responsibility of frontline employees but a core value of the entire organization.

In conclusion, companies that invest in training and coaching employees in customer service skills and create a customer-focused culture will reap the benefits of increased customer loyalty, improved brand reputation, and ultimately, increased profitability.

Strategies for measuring and evaluating customer service performance

Measuring and evaluating customer service performance is critical to the success of any organization. Without a clear understanding of how well the company is performing in terms of customer service, it is impossible to make improvements and ensure that customers are satisfied. In this section, we will explore the different strategies that companies can use to measure and evaluate their customer service performance.

Customer Feedback

One of the most important strategies for measuring and evaluating customer service performance is through customer feedback. Customer feedback can come in many forms, such as surveys, reviews, and social media comments. By collecting and analyzing this feedback, companies can gain valuable insights into what their customers think about their products and services.

Customer surveys are a common way for companies to collect feedback from their customers. These surveys can be conducted in many different ways, such as online, by phone, or in-person. Surveys can cover a wide range of topics, such as the customer's satisfaction with the product or service, their experience with customer service, and their likelihood of recommending the company to others.

Reviews are another important source of customer feedback. Online review platforms like Yelp, Google Reviews, and Facebook Reviews allow customers to share their experiences with others. Companies can use these reviews to identify areas where they need to improve their customer service.

Social media is also an important source of customer feedback. Customers can use social media platforms like Twitter and Facebook to share their experiences with a company's products and services. Companies can use social media listening tools to monitor what customers are saying about them and respond to any negative feedback.

Employee Feedback

Another strategy for measuring and evaluating customer service performance is through employee feedback. Employees who interact with customers on a regular basis can provide valuable insights into the customer experience. By collecting feedback from employees, companies can identify areas where they need to improve their customer service.

One way to collect employee feedback is through surveys. Employee surveys can cover topics such as the quality of training and coaching they receive, their satisfaction with their job, and their suggestions for improving customer service.

Mystery Shopping

Mystery shopping is another important strategy for measuring and evaluating customer service performance. Mystery shopping involves hiring individuals to pose as customers and evaluate the customer service they receive. Mystery shoppers can evaluate a wide range of customer service factors, such as the friendliness of employees, the cleanliness of the store, and the speed of service.

Mystery shopping can provide companies with valuable insights into their customer service performance. By identifying areas where they are falling short, companies can make improvements to their customer service.

Performance Metrics

Performance metrics are another important strategy for measuring and evaluating customer service performance. Performance metrics are quantifiable measures of customer service performance. Some common performance metrics include:

- ✧ Average response time: This measures the time it takes for customer service representatives to respond to customer inquiries.
- ✧ Customer satisfaction: This measures the level of satisfaction customers have with the company's products and services.
- ✧ First-call resolution rate: This measures the percentage of customer inquiries that are resolved on the first call.
- ✧ Net promoter score: This measures the likelihood that customers will recommend the company to others.

By tracking and analyzing these performance metrics, companies can identify areas where they need to improve their customer service performance.

Conclusion

Measuring and evaluating customer service performance is critical to the success of any organization. By collecting and analyzing customer feedback, employee feedback, and performance metrics, companies can identify areas where they need to improve their customer service. Mystery shopping is another important strategy for measuring customer service performance. By making improvements based on the insights gained from these strategies, companies can provide better customer service and increase customer satisfaction.

Exercise: Developing a customer service training plan for a specific team or department

Developing a customer service training plan is an essential task for any organization seeking to improve its customer service performance. This process involves identifying the specific needs of the team or department, designing a training program that meets those needs, and implementing and evaluating the program over time.

Step 1: Identify the specific needs of the team or department

The first step in developing a customer service training plan is to identify the specific needs of the team or department. This can be done through a variety of means, such as surveys, focus groups, and interviews with team members, managers, and customers. By gathering feedback from these stakeholders, you can identify the areas where the team or department is excelling in customer service and the areas where improvement is needed.

Step 2: Design a training program that meets those needs

Once you have identified the specific needs of the team or department, you can design a training program that meets those needs. This program should include a mix of classroom and hands-on training, with a focus on developing the specific customer service skills that are needed.

For example, if the team or department is struggling with communication skills, the training program might include modules on active listening, empathy, and effective communication techniques. If the team or department is struggling with problem-solving skills, the training program might include modules on root cause analysis, decision making, and creative problem solving.

In addition to developing the specific customer service skills needed, the training program should also focus on developing a customer-focused culture within the team or department. This can be done through modules on the importance of customer service, the impact of customer service on the business, and the role of the team or department in delivering exceptional customer service.

Step 3: Implement and evaluate the program over time

Once the training program has been designed, it should be implemented and evaluated over time. This evaluation should include both qualitative and quantitative measures, such as customer satisfaction surveys, employee feedback, and performance metrics.

By tracking and analyzing these metrics over time, you can identify the areas where the training program is succeeding and the areas where improvement is needed. This can help you to continually refine and improve the training program, ensuring that it remains effective and relevant over time.

Exercise:

Let's consider an example of developing a customer service training plan for a specific team or department. In this case, we will focus on a customer service team within a retail organization.

Step 1: Identify the specific needs of the team or department

To identify the specific needs of the customer service team, we might start by surveying team members to get their feedback on areas where they feel they need additional training or support. We might also review customer feedback to identify areas where customers have expressed dissatisfaction with the team's performance.

Based on this feedback, we might identify the following areas as priorities for the customer service training plan:

✧ Communication skills: Many team members feel that they struggle to communicate effectively with customers, leading to frustration and misunderstandings.
✧ Product knowledge: Some team members lack in-depth knowledge of the products they are selling, which can make it difficult to answer customer questions and provide effective recommendations.
✧ Problem-solving skills: The team has struggled to effectively resolve customer complaints and issues, leading to negative feedback and customer churn.
✧ Step 2: Design a training program that meets those needs

Based on the identified needs of the customer service team, we might design a training program that includes the following modules:

✧ Communication skills: This module would focus on developing effective communication skills, such as active listening, empathy, and clear and concise language. It might include role-playing exercises and feedback sessions to help team members improve their communication skills.
✧ Product knowledge: This module would focus on developing in-depth product knowledge, including features, benefits, and recommended use cases. It might include product training sessions, product demos, and quizzes to test knowledge retention.
✧ Problem-solving skills: This module would teach team members how to solve customer problems effectively and efficiently. It might include case studies, group discussions, and role-playing exercises to help team members develop critical thinking and problem-solving skills.

✧ Handling difficult customers: This module would teach team members how to handle difficult customers, including de-escalating tense situations, managing emotional responses, and finding effective solutions to problems. It might include role-playing exercises and case studies to help team members develop confidence and practical skills in handling challenging situations.

✧ Time management: This module would focus on time management skills, including setting priorities, managing workload, and staying organized. It might include time management exercises and tools, as well as coaching and feedback to help team members develop effective time management habits.

Step 3: Implement the training program

Once the training program has been designed, it's time to implement it. Here are some tips for implementing the training program:

✧ Schedule training sessions at a time when all team members can attend, and provide adequate notice so that everyone can plan accordingly.

✧ Provide clear instructions and expectations for the training program, including the goals, objectives, and expectations for participation.

✧ Make the training interactive and engaging, using a variety of methods such as group discussions, role-playing exercises, and quizzes to keep team members engaged and interested.

✧ Provide feedback and coaching throughout the training program, offering praise for progress and constructive feedback to help team members improve their skills.

✧ Encourage team members to apply what they learn in the training program to their daily work, and provide opportunities for them to practice and refine their skills.

✧ Evaluate the training program to measure its effectiveness and identify areas for improvement.

Step 4: Follow up and reinforce training

Training should not be a one-time event, but rather an ongoing process that requires follow-up and reinforcement. Here are some tips for reinforcing and building on the training program:

✧ Provide ongoing coaching and feedback to help team members continue to improve their skills.

✧ Offer additional training modules or refreshers as needed to address new challenges or areas for improvement.

✧ Incorporate training into the team's regular activities, such as team meetings or one-on-one coaching sessions.

✧ Recognize and reward team members who demonstrate exceptional customer service skills, and encourage others to learn from their example.
✧ Monitor and measure the impact of the training program over time, and make adjustments as needed to ensure continued success.

Exercise: Developing a customer service training plan for a specific team or department

Now that we have reviewed the key steps in developing a customer service training plan, let's apply these steps to a specific scenario. Suppose you are a customer service manager for a retail company, and you have identified that your sales team needs training in handling difficult customers. How might you develop a training plan to address this need?

Step 1: Identify the training need

In this scenario, the identified training need is to help the sales team handle difficult customers more effectively. This might include skills such as de-escalating tense situations, managing emotional responses, and finding effective solutions to problems.

Step 2: Design a training program that meets those needs

Based on the identified needs of the sales team, we might design a training program that includes the following modules:

✧ Understanding customer needs: This module would focus on developing a deeper understanding of customer needs and expectations, and how to meet those needs effectively. It might include case studies and group discussions to help team members develop empathy and customer-focused skills.
✧ De-escalating tense situations: This module would focus on teaching team members how to de-escalate tense situations, such as when a customer is angry or upset. It might include role-playing exercises and case studies to help team members develop practical skills and confidence.
✧ Managing emotional responses: This module would focus on teaching team members how to manage their own emotional responses, such as frustration or anxiety, during challenging customer interactions. It might include techniques such as deep breathing, mindfulness, and positive self-talk to help team members stay calm and composed.
✧ Conflict resolution: This module would focus on teaching team members how to effectively resolve conflicts with customers, colleagues, or supervisors. It might include techniques such as active listening, negotiation, and compromise, as well

as role-playing exercises and case studies to help team members develop practical skills.

- ✧ Time management: This module would focus on teaching team members how to manage their time effectively, prioritize tasks, and meet customer service goals within set timeframes. It might include time-management tools and techniques, such as the Eisenhower matrix or Pomodoro technique, as well as group discussions and feedback sessions to help team members develop time-management skills.
- ✧ Multicultural sensitivity: This module would focus on developing sensitivity to cultural differences and diversity in the customer base. It might include training on cultural competence, unconscious bias, and effective communication in cross-cultural contexts.
- ✧ Technology training: This module would focus on training team members on any relevant technology, such as customer relationship management (CRM) software, social media platforms, or chatbots. It might include hands-on training sessions, instructional videos, and assessments to ensure team members have the necessary technical skills.

Step 3: Implement the training program

Once the training program has been designed, it can be implemented by scheduling training sessions, assigning trainers or facilitators, and providing necessary resources such as training materials and technology. It is important to establish a timeline and communicate the training plan clearly to all team members to ensure that everyone is aware of the training requirements and expectations.

Step 4: Evaluate the training program

After the training program has been implemented, it is important to evaluate its effectiveness in meeting the identified training needs and improving customer service performance. Evaluation might include conducting pre- and post-training assessments, soliciting feedback from trainees, and analyzing customer service metrics such as customer satisfaction scores or response times.

By following these steps, a customer service team can develop and implement an effective training program that improves team members' skills and performance, ultimately leading to improved customer satisfaction and loyalty.

CHAPTER 19: CASE STUDIES IN EXCEPTIONAL CUSTOMER SERVICE

In today's competitive business landscape, providing exceptional customer service is no longer optional, but rather a necessity for companies that want to succeed. Customers have a wide range of choices, and they are more likely to choose companies that provide exceptional customer service. The quality of customer service can significantly impact a company's reputation, customer loyalty, and profitability.

This chapter focuses on exceptional customer service, which refers to customer service that goes beyond meeting customers' basic needs and expectations. Exceptional customer service involves creating a positive emotional connection with customers and providing an experience that exceeds their expectations.

The chapter presents case studies of companies that have achieved exceptional customer service and examines the strategies and practices that have contributed to their success. The case studies provide real-world examples of how companies have transformed their customer service from average to exceptional.

The chapter is divided into sections that focus on different aspects of exceptional customer service. The sections include:

Understanding the importance of exceptional customer service: This section provides an overview of the importance of exceptional customer service in today's business environment. It highlights the benefits of providing exceptional customer service, including customer loyalty, increased profitability, and positive word-of-mouth marketing.

Creating a customer-focused culture: This section examines how companies can create a customer-focused culture that prioritizes exceptional customer service. It discusses the importance of aligning company values with customer needs and expectations and providing employees with the necessary training and support to deliver exceptional customer service.

Understanding customer needs and expectations: This section explores how companies can understand customer needs and expectations and use that knowledge to provide exceptional customer service. It discusses the importance of listening to customers, collecting customer feedback, and using customer data to inform business decisions.

Developing customer service strategies and practices: This section examines the strategies and practices that companies can use to provide exceptional customer service. It includes case studies of companies that have developed innovative customer service strategies and practices, such as personalized customer experiences, 24/7 customer support, and proactive issue resolution.

Measuring and evaluating customer service performance: This section discusses how companies can measure and evaluate their customer service performance to identify areas for improvement and ensure that they are meeting customer needs and expectations. It includes case studies of companies that have developed effective customer service metrics and measurement tools.

Overall, this chapter provides a comprehensive overview of exceptional customer service and presents case studies that illustrate how companies have achieved exceptional customer service. By studying these case studies and applying the strategies and practices presented in the chapter, students can develop the skills and knowledge needed to provide exceptional customer service in their future careers.

Examining real-life examples of companies with exceptional customer service

Exceptional customer service is a critical factor in the success of any business. It not only helps retain customers but also attracts new ones. Exceptional customer service involves going above and beyond to meet the needs of customers and ensure their satisfaction. Companies that provide exceptional customer service understand the importance of creating a positive customer experience, and they prioritize it in their business strategy.

In this chapter, we will examine real-life examples of companies that have excelled in providing exceptional customer service. We will explore the strategies they used, the challenges they faced, and the lessons we can learn from their experiences.

Case Study 1: Zappos

Zappos is an online shoe and clothing retailer that has gained a reputation for providing exceptional customer service. Zappos' mission is to "deliver happiness" to its customers, and it has achieved this through its customer-centric business model.

One of the key strategies that Zappos uses is to empower its employees to go above and beyond to meet the needs of customers. Zappos' employees are encouraged to take their time with customers and ensure that they find the perfect product. Zappos also has a generous return policy, which allows customers to return items for up to a year after purchase, with free shipping both ways.

Another way Zappos provides exceptional customer service is through its customer service team. Zappos' customer service representatives are available 24/7 and are empowered to make decisions that will benefit the customer. This includes offering discounts, free shipping, and even sending flowers to customers who are going through a tough time.

Zappos' commitment to exceptional customer service has paid off. The company has a high customer retention rate, and many of its customers become advocates for the brand. Zappos has also been recognized for its exceptional customer service, winning numerous awards, including the JD Power Customer Service Champions award.

Case Study 2: Ritz-Carlton

Ritz-Carlton is a luxury hotel chain that is known for its exceptional customer service. Ritz-Carlton's motto is "We are Ladies and Gentlemen serving Ladies and Gentlemen", which emphasizes the importance of treating both guests and employees with respect and dignity.

Ritz-Carlton's approach to customer service is centered on creating personalized experiences for guests. Each guest is assigned a personal concierge, who is responsible for ensuring that their stay is tailored to their needs and preferences. Ritz-Carlton also uses technology to enhance the guest experience, including a mobile app that allows guests to communicate with hotel staff and make requests.

Another way Ritz-Carlton provides exceptional customer service is through its employee training programs. Ritz-Carlton employees undergo extensive training in customer service, with a focus on anticipating guests' needs and exceeding their expectations. Ritz-Carlton also has a "wow stories" program, which encourages employees to share stories of exceptional customer service, and rewards them for doing so.

Ritz-Carlton's commitment to exceptional customer service has led to high levels of customer loyalty and repeat business. The company has also been recognized for its customer service, winning numerous awards, including the Forbes Travel Guide Five-Star Award.

Case Study 3: Nordstrom

Nordstrom is a department store chain that is known for its exceptional customer service. Nordstrom's approach to customer service is centered on creating a personalized shopping experience for each customer. Nordstrom's employees are trained to provide individualized attention to each customer, with a focus on building relationships and earning their trust.

One of the key strategies that Nordstrom uses is to empower its employees to make decisions that benefit the customer. Nordstrom's employees are given the authority to make decisions on things like refunds, exchanges, and discounts, without needing to consult with a manager. This enables Nordstrom's employees to respond quickly to customers' needs and requests, which in turn leads to a higher level of customer satisfaction.

In addition to empowering its employees, Nordstrom also invests heavily in customer feedback and data analysis. The company regularly surveys its customers to gather feedback on their shopping experiences, and uses this data to make improvements to its customer service offerings. Nordstrom also tracks customer behavior and purchase patterns, which enables the company to offer personalized recommendations and promotions to each customer.

Another company that is known for its exceptional customer service is Zappos, an online shoe and clothing retailer. Like Nordstrom, Zappos emphasizes the importance of building strong relationships with its customers. Zappos' employees are trained to go above and beyond in order to provide exceptional customer service, and the company encourages employees to think creatively in order to find solutions to customers' problems.

One of the ways that Zappos achieves this is through its unique company culture. Zappos places a strong emphasis on employee happiness and well-being, and the company offers a number of perks and benefits to its employees, such as free lunches, on-site fitness classes, and opportunities for professional development. By taking care of its employees, Zappos is able to create a positive work environment that translates into exceptional customer service.

Another company that is often cited for its exceptional customer service is The Ritz-Carlton, a luxury hotel chain. The Ritz-Carlton's approach to customer service is centered on anticipating customers' needs and exceeding their expectations. The company places a strong emphasis on employee training and empowerment, and each employee is given the authority to spend up to $2,000 in order to resolve a customer complaint or issue.

In addition to empowering its employees, The Ritz-Carlton also places a strong emphasis on personalization. The company uses data and analytics to understand each customer's preferences and history, which enables its employees to provide personalized recommendations and experiences. The Ritz-Carlton also invests heavily in employee training, and the company has developed a comprehensive training program called "The Ritz-Carlton Gold Standards," which teaches employees how to provide exceptional customer service at every touchpoint.

These examples demonstrate that exceptional customer service is not just about meeting customers' basic needs, but about going above and beyond in order to create memorable experiences. Companies that prioritize customer service by empowering their employees, gathering customer feedback, and investing in training and development are able to create strong relationships with their customers and build a loyal customer base. By examining these examples and learning from their strategies, companies can improve their own customer service offerings and stand out in today's competitive business landscape.

Analyzing the strategies and techniques used by these companies

Analyzing the strategies and techniques used by companies with exceptional customer service can provide valuable insights into how to build and maintain a customer-centric culture. In this section, we will examine some of the key strategies and techniques used by companies with exceptional customer service, including Nordstrom, Zappos, and Ritz-Carlton.

Nordstrom is a department store chain that is known for its exceptional customer service. Nordstrom's approach to customer service is centered on creating a personalized shopping experience for each customer. Nordstrom's employees are trained to provide individualized attention to each customer, with a focus on building relationships and earning their trust.

One of the key strategies that Nordstrom uses is to empower its employees to make decisions that benefit the customer. Nordstrom's employees are given the authority to make decisions on things like refunds, exchanges, and discounts, without needing approval from a manager. This allows Nordstrom's employees to quickly resolve customer issues, without creating unnecessary delays.

Another key strategy used by Nordstrom is to provide ongoing training and development opportunities for its employees. Nordstrom's employees receive extensive training on product knowledge, customer service, and sales techniques. This ensures that Nordstrom's employees are equipped with the knowledge and skills necessary to provide exceptional customer service.

Zappos is an online retailer that is known for its exceptional customer service. Zappos' approach to customer service is centered on providing a personalized and memorable shopping experience for each customer. Zappos' employees are trained to go above and beyond for their customers, with a focus on creating emotional connections.

One of the key strategies that Zappos uses is to invest heavily in employee training and development. Zappos' employees receive extensive training on customer service, communication skills, and company culture. This ensures that Zappos' employees are aligned with the company's values and are able to provide exceptional customer service.

Another key strategy used by Zappos is to empower its employees to make decisions that benefit the customer. Zappos' employees are given the authority to make decisions on things like refunds, exchanges, and discounts, without needing approval from a manager. This allows Zappos' employees to quickly resolve customer issues, without creating unnecessary delays.

Ritz-Carlton is a luxury hotel chain that is known for its exceptional customer service. Ritz-Carlton's approach to customer service is centered on creating personalized experiences for each guest. Ritz-Carlton's employees are trained to anticipate and fulfill the needs of their guests, with a focus on creating lasting memories.

One of the key strategies that Ritz-Carlton uses is to empower its employees to make decisions that benefit the guest. Ritz-Carlton's employees are given the authority to make decisions on things like room upgrades, complimentary services, and personalized amenities, without needing approval from a manager. This allows Ritz-Carlton's employees to quickly resolve guest issues, without creating unnecessary delays.

Another key strategy used by Ritz-Carlton is to create a strong organizational culture that is focused on customer service. Ritz-Carlton's employees are trained to uphold the company's values and to provide exceptional customer service at all times. This ensures that Ritz-Carlton's guests receive consistent and exceptional service, regardless of which employee they interact with.

In conclusion, companies with exceptional customer service share some common strategies and techniques, such as empowering employees to make decisions that benefit the customer, investing in employee training and development, and creating a customer-centric organizational culture. By analyzing these strategies and techniques, organizations can learn valuable lessons on how to build and maintain a culture that prioritizes customer service.

Identifying opportunities for improvement in your own customer service approach

Providing exceptional customer service is not just the responsibility of the customer service team. Every employee in a company has a role to play in ensuring that customers have a positive experience with the brand. Whether you are in sales, marketing, or human resources, your interactions with customers can leave a lasting impression on their perception of the company. This section will provide guidance on how to identify opportunities for improvement in your own customer service approach, regardless of your role in the organization.

Seek Feedback
One of the best ways to identify opportunities for improvement in your customer service approach is to seek feedback from customers. This can be done through surveys, focus groups, or simply by asking customers for their opinions. When gathering feedback, it is important to ask open-ended questions that allow customers to provide detailed responses. This can help you identify specific areas of your customer service approach that may need improvement.

Analyze Customer Complaints
Another way to identify opportunities for improvement is to analyze customer complaints. By examining the types of complaints that customers are making, you can identify patterns and trends that may indicate areas of weakness in your customer service approach. For example, if customers are frequently complaining about long wait times on the phone, this may indicate that your call center is understaffed or that your processes need to be reevaluated.

Review Customer Service Metrics
Customer service metrics can provide valuable insights into the effectiveness of your customer service approach. Metrics like customer satisfaction scores, response times, and first-contact resolution rates can help you identify areas of strength and weakness. If you notice that certain metrics are consistently falling below expectations, this may indicate that changes need to be made.

Conduct Employee Training

Investing in employee training can also help identify opportunities for improvement in your customer service approach. By providing employees with the tools and skills they need to provide exceptional customer service, you can ensure that every customer interaction is positive. This can include training on communication skills, conflict resolution, and empathy.

Benchmark Against Competitors

Analyzing your competitors' customer service approaches can provide valuable insights into how your own approach compares. By identifying areas where your competitors excel, you can develop strategies to improve your own customer service approach. This can include analyzing their customer service metrics, reviewing their online reviews, and even conducting mystery shopping exercises.

Continuously Evaluate and Improve

Finally, it is important to continuously evaluate and improve your customer service approach. This requires a commitment to ongoing monitoring and analysis of customer feedback and metrics. By regularly reviewing your approach, you can identify areas for improvement and make the necessary changes to ensure that your customers are receiving exceptional service.

In conclusion, providing exceptional customer service is a key component of building a successful business. By identifying opportunities for improvement in your own customer service approach, you can ensure that your customers have a positive experience with your brand. This can be achieved by seeking feedback, analyzing customer complaints and service metrics, conducting employee training, benchmarking against competitors, and continuously evaluating and improving your approach.

Exercise: Analyzing a real case study and developing a plan for implementing similar strategies

Analyzing a real case study and developing a plan for implementing similar strategies is an excellent way to put the knowledge gained in this chapter into practice. In this exercise, we will examine a case study of a company with exceptional customer service and develop a plan for implementing similar strategies in your own organization.

Case Study: Zappos

Zappos is an online shoe and clothing retailer that is well-known for its exceptional customer service. The company's approach to customer service is centered on creating a positive emotional connection with its customers. Zappos employees are trained to go above and beyond in order to create a memorable experience for each customer.

One of the key strategies that Zappos uses is to empower its employees to make decisions that benefit the customer. Zappos employees are given the authority to make decisions on things like refunds, exchanges, and discounts without needing approval from a supervisor. This approach creates a culture of trust and empowerment within the organization, which translates into exceptional customer service.

Another strategy that Zappos uses is to prioritize employee happiness. The company offers its employees a range of benefits, including health insurance, 401(k) matching, and free lunches. Additionally, the company encourages employees to have fun and be themselves at work, which creates a positive and supportive work environment.

Zappos also places a strong emphasis on building relationships with customers. The company's customer service representatives are trained to engage in friendly conversations with customers, rather than simply providing transactional service. This approach helps to build trust and loyalty with customers, which in turn leads to repeat business and positive word-of-mouth advertising.

Plan for Implementing Similar Strategies

Based on the case study of Zappos, there are several strategies that organizations can implement to improve their customer service approach. The following plan outlines steps for implementing these strategies:

Empower Employees: The first step in implementing a customer service strategy similar to Zappos is to empower employees to make decisions that benefit the customer. This involves training employees on how to make decisions and providing them with the authority to do so. It is important to establish clear guidelines and boundaries to ensure that employees are making decisions that align with the company's values and goals.

Prioritize Employee Happiness: The second step is to prioritize employee happiness. This involves offering competitive salaries and benefits, as well as creating a positive work environment that encourages employee engagement and creativity. It is important to regularly solicit employee feedback to identify areas for improvement and make necessary changes.

Build Relationships with Customers: The third step is to build relationships with customers. This involves training customer service representatives to engage in friendly conversations with customers, listen to their needs and concerns, and provide personalized service. It is also important to follow up with customers after their purchase to ensure that they are satisfied and to address any concerns or issues.

Measure Success: The final step is to measure the success of the customer service strategy. This involves establishing clear metrics for success, such as customer satisfaction ratings and repeat business. It is important to regularly track and analyze these metrics to identify areas for improvement and make necessary changes.

Exercise Questions:

What are some strategies used by Zappos to create exceptional customer service?
How can organizations implement similar strategies in their own customer service approach?
Why is it important to prioritize employee happiness in the context of customer service?
How can organizations measure the success of their customer service strategy?

PART 3 OF THE CUSTOMER SERVICE TRAINING COURSE, WHICH COULD BE TITLED "CUSTOMER SERVICE MASTERY":

In Parts 1 and 2 of this customer service training course, we covered the foundational principles of customer service and the strategies and techniques used by successful companies such as Nordstrom and Zappos. In Part 3, we will build on that knowledge and explore advanced concepts in customer service mastery.

Creating a Culture of Customer Service

In order to achieve mastery in customer service, it is important to create a culture that values it. This chapter will explore how organizations can create a culture of customer service, including:

✦ The role of leadership in setting the tone for customer service
✦ How to align employee goals with customer service goals
✦ The importance of training and ongoing education for employees
✦ Creating a system of rewards and recognition for exceptional customer service
✦ Measuring the success of a customer service culture
✦ Case Study: Ritz-Carlton

The Ritz-Carlton hotel chain is known for its exceptional customer service. In this case study, we will examine the strategies used by the Ritz-Carlton to create a culture of customer service and explore how other organizations can implement similar strategies.

Handling Difficult Customers

One of the biggest challenges in customer service is dealing with difficult customers. This chapter will explore strategies for handling difficult customers, including:

✧ Active listening and empathy
✧ De-escalation techniques
✧ Setting boundaries and managing expectations
✧ Problem-solving and conflict resolution
✧ Knowing when to escalate a situation to a supervisor or manager

Case Study: Comcast

Comcast is a telecommunications company that has received criticism for its customer service practices. In this case study, we will examine a specific incident in which a Comcast customer service representative was recorded berating a customer and explore what could have been done differently to handle the situation.

Managing Customer Feedback

Customer feedback is essential for improving customer service, but managing that feedback can be challenging. This chapter will explore strategies for managing customer feedback, including:

✧ Collecting feedback through surveys and other methods
✧ Analyzing feedback to identify trends and areas for improvement
✧ Responding to customer feedback in a timely and effective manner
✧ Incorporating customer feedback into product and service development
✧ Using customer feedback to improve the customer experience
✧ Case Study: Airbnb

Airbnb is an online platform that allows people to rent out their homes or apartments to travelers. In this case study, we will examine how Airbnb uses customer feedback to improve its platform and explore how other organizations can use similar strategies.

Continuous Improvement in Customer Service

Customer service is an ongoing process, and organizations must continually strive to improve. This chapter will explore strategies for continuous improvement in customer service, including:

✧ Measuring the success of customer service initiatives
✧ Identifying areas for improvement and setting goals
✧ Experimenting with new strategies and techniques
✧ Incorporating customer feedback into the improvement process
✧ Celebrating successes and recognizing areas for improvement
✧ Case Study: Amazon

Amazon is an online retailer that is known for its exceptional customer service. In this case study, we will examine how Amazon continually improves its customer service and explore how other organizations can learn from Amazon's approach.

Conclusion

Customer service mastery is a continuous journey, but with the right strategies and techniques, organizations can create a culture of exceptional customer service. By aligning employee goals with customer service goals, handling difficult customers with empathy and problem-solving, managing customer feedback effectively, and continuously striving for improvement, organizations can deliver a superior customer experience and build a loyal customer base.

CHAPTER 20: BUILDING AND MAINTAINING CUSTOMER RELATIONSHIPS

In the modern business landscape, the importance of building and maintaining customer relationships cannot be overstated. Research has consistently shown that customer retention is a key driver of business success, and that acquiring new customers can be several times more expensive than retaining existing ones (Reichheld & Sasser, 1990). Furthermore, satisfied customers are more likely to refer new business, leading to increased revenue and a larger customer base. This chapter will examine the importance of building and maintaining customer relationships and explore strategies for doing so effectively.

Understanding Customer Needs

Before businesses can build and maintain strong relationships with their customers, they must first understand their customers' needs. This involves more than simply offering high-quality products or services. It requires a deep understanding of the customer's wants, needs, and preferences, as well as the ability to anticipate their future needs. To gain this understanding, businesses must engage in ongoing dialogue with their customers through various channels, such as surveys, focus groups, and social media. Businesses can also use data analytics to gain insights into customer behavior and preferences, enabling them to tailor their offerings to meet their customers' needs.

Communication and Relationship Building

Effective communication is a critical component of building and maintaining strong customer relationships. Businesses must establish clear and effective channels of communication with their customers, such as email, social media, or chatbots, and be responsive to their customers' inquiries and concerns. They must also use positive and empathetic language, active listening, and prompt follow-up to build trust and rapport with their customers.

One of the most effective ways to build strong relationships with customers is through personalization. Personalization involves tailoring the customer's experience to their specific needs and preferences, such as recommending products or services based on their past purchases or browsing history. This can help businesses create a sense of loyalty and trust with their customers and lead to increased revenue through repeat business.

Resolving Customer Issues

Even the most attentive and customer-centric businesses will encounter issues or complaints from time to time. It is critical that businesses handle these issues with care and efficiency to maintain strong relationships with their customers. The first step in resolving customer issues is to acknowledge the problem and take responsibility for it. This involves listening to the customer's concerns, apologizing for any inconvenience caused, and working to find a satisfactory resolution. Businesses should also be transparent about their policies and procedures for handling customer complaints, as this can help build trust and credibility with their customers.

Creating Customer Loyalty Programs

Customer loyalty programs can be a powerful tool for building and maintaining strong relationships with customers. These programs typically involve offering incentives, such as discounts, rewards points, or exclusive offers, to customers who make repeat purchases or refer new business. Loyalty programs can help businesses create a sense of community and loyalty among their customer base, as well as encourage repeat business and referrals.

Measuring Customer Satisfaction

To effectively build and maintain customer relationships, businesses must have a way to measure customer satisfaction. This involves collecting feedback from customers through various channels, such as surveys, social media, or online reviews. Businesses can use this feedback to identify areas for improvement and make changes to their products or services to better meet their customers' needs. It is important for businesses to act on customer feedback in a timely manner, as this can demonstrate a commitment to customer satisfaction and lead to increased loyalty and repeat business.

Conclusion

Building and maintaining strong customer relationships is essential for businesses to succeed in today's competitive landscape. This requires a deep understanding of customer needs, effective communication and relationship building, resolving customer issues with care, creating customer loyalty programs, and measuring customer satisfaction. By prioritizing these strategies, businesses can create a loyal customer base that is not only more likely to make repeat purchases but also to refer others to the company. In this chapter, we explored the key concepts and techniques involved in building and maintaining strong customer relationships.

First, we examined the importance of understanding customer needs and preferences. We explored the various methods businesses can use to gain insights into customer behavior and preferences, including surveys, feedback forms, social media monitoring, and data analysis tools. By gathering and analyzing customer data, businesses can identify areas for improvement, develop targeted marketing strategies, and tailor their products and services to meet the needs of their target audience.

We then discussed the importance of effective communication and relationship building. Strong relationships are built on trust, respect, and open communication. We explored the key communication skills that customer service representatives should possess, including active listening, empathy, and clear and concise communication. We also examined the importance of building rapport with customers, which can help to establish a sense of trust and create a positive customer experience.

In addition, we discussed the importance of resolving customer issues with care. Even the best businesses encounter issues and problems from time to time. It's essential that businesses have effective processes in place to deal with customer complaints and concerns. We explored the key steps involved in resolving customer issues, including listening to the customer, apologizing for the problem, offering a solution, and following up to ensure customer satisfaction.

We then discussed the importance of creating customer loyalty programs. Customer loyalty programs can be an effective way to incentivize customers to return to your business and make repeat purchases. We explored the various types of loyalty programs, including points-based programs, tiered programs, and cashback programs, and examined the key elements that make these programs effective.

Finally, we explored the importance of measuring customer satisfaction. Measuring customer satisfaction is essential for understanding how well your business is meeting customer needs and expectations. We explored the various methods businesses can use to measure customer satisfaction, including customer surveys, net promoter scores (NPS), and customer feedback forms. By regularly measuring customer satisfaction, businesses can identify areas for improvement, track progress, and make data-driven decisions to improve customer relationships.

In conclusion, building and maintaining strong customer relationships is critical for businesses to succeed in today's competitive landscape. By prioritizing strategies such as understanding customer needs, effective communication, resolving customer issues with care, creating customer loyalty programs, and measuring customer satisfaction, businesses can create a loyal customer base that will drive growth and success over the long term.

Strategies for building and maintaining strong relationships with customers

As we have discussed, building and maintaining strong relationships with customers is essential for businesses to succeed in today's competitive marketplace. But how can businesses do this effectively? In this section, we will explore some of the most effective strategies for building and maintaining strong relationships with customers.

Understand your customers' needs
To build strong relationships with your customers, you need to understand their needs. This means taking the time to get to know your customers, listening to their concerns and feedback, and using this information to improve your products and services. By understanding your customers' needs, you can tailor your offerings to better meet their needs, which will help to build loyalty and trust.

Provide exceptional customer service
Providing exceptional customer service is one of the most effective ways to build and maintain strong relationships with your customers. This means being responsive to customer inquiries and concerns, providing prompt and efficient service, and going above and beyond to meet their needs. By providing exceptional customer service, you can create a positive customer experience that will keep customers coming back.

Communicate effectively
Effective communication is key to building strong relationships with your customers. This means being clear and concise in your communications, listening carefully to customer feedback, and responding promptly and appropriately to their inquiries and concerns. By communicating effectively, you can build trust and credibility with your customers, which will help to strengthen your relationships over time.

Resolve issues with care

No business is perfect, and there will inevitably be times when you need to resolve issues with customers. When this happens, it is important to do so with care and attention. This means taking the time to listen to the customer's concerns, acknowledging their frustration, and working with them to find a resolution that meets their needs. By resolving issues with care, you can turn a potentially negative experience into a positive one, which will help to build loyalty and trust with your customers.

Create customer loyalty programs

Customer loyalty programs are an effective way to build and maintain strong relationships with your customers. By offering incentives and rewards for repeat business, you can encourage customers to keep coming back to your business. This can include discounts, free products or services, and other special offers. By creating customer loyalty programs, you can build a loyal customer base that will help to sustain your business over time.

Measure customer satisfaction

Finally, it is important to measure customer satisfaction to ensure that you are meeting your customers' needs effectively. This means soliciting feedback from customers on a regular basis, using surveys and other tools to measure their satisfaction with your products and services. By measuring customer satisfaction, you can identify areas for improvement and make changes to your business that will help to strengthen your relationships with your customers over time.

Exercises:

Why is it important for businesses to understand their customers' needs?

What are some strategies for providing exceptional customer service?

How can businesses communicate effectively with their customers?

Why is it important to resolve issues with care?

What are some effective strategies for creating customer loyalty programs?

How can businesses measure customer satisfaction effectively?

The role of effective communication and follow-up in building relationships

The role of effective communication and follow-up in building strong customer relationships cannot be overstated. In fact, it is one of the most important components of any successful customer relationship strategy. Effective communication is critical for building trust, addressing concerns and issues, and creating a positive customer experience.

Effective communication involves not only what is said but also how it is said. It is important to use clear, concise language and to actively listen to the customer. This means paying attention to what they are saying, asking clarifying questions, and responding in a way that is appropriate for the situation. Additionally, the tone and demeanor of the communication can make a big difference in how the customer perceives the interaction. A positive and empathetic tone can go a long way in building trust and creating a positive customer experience.

Following up with customers is also crucial for building strong relationships. It shows that the business values the customer and their feedback, and is willing to take action to address their concerns. Follow-up can take many forms, such as a phone call, email, or even a handwritten note. It is important to follow up in a timely manner, and to ensure that the issue or concern has been fully addressed.

For example, imagine a customer calls a business with a complaint about a product they purchased. The customer service representative listens to the customer's concerns, acknowledges their frustration, and promises to investigate the issue further. The representative follows up with the customer the next day to let them know that the issue has been resolved, and offers a discount on their next purchase as a gesture of goodwill. This level of communication and follow-up can turn a negative experience into a positive one, and can even create a loyal customer.

Effective communication and follow-up are not only important for addressing customer complaints, but also for building relationships with customers over time. Regular communication with customers can help businesses understand their needs and preferences, and can allow for opportunities to upsell or cross-sell products or services. For example, a business might send out a survey to customers to gather feedback on their experiences, and then use that feedback to make improvements or to tailor their offerings to better meet customer needs.

In addition to direct communication with customers, businesses can also leverage social media and other digital channels to engage with customers and build relationships. These channels can be used to share updates and news, to respond to customer inquiries and comments, and to offer special promotions or discounts.

However, it is important to use these channels effectively and to ensure that communication is consistent with the brand's values and messaging.

Overall, effective communication and follow-up are critical for building strong customer relationships. By using clear, empathetic communication and following up in a timely manner, businesses can build trust, create a positive customer experience, and foster loyalty over time.

Example Exercises:

Describe the importance of effective communication in building customer relationships, and provide examples of how businesses can use effective communication to create a positive customer experience.

Discuss the benefits of following up with customers, and provide examples of how businesses can follow up with customers to address concerns and build relationships.

Evaluate the role of social media and other digital channels in building customer relationships, and describe the best practices for using these channels effectively.

Imagine you are a customer service representative for a retail store. A customer has called with a complaint about a product they purchased. Describe how you would use effective communication and follow-up to address the customer's concerns and build a positive relationship with them.

Create a sample survey that businesses can use to gather feedback from customers, and describe how the feedback can be used to improve customer relationships and tailor offerings to better meet customer needs.

Techniques for addressing customer needs and concerns proactively

In today's business landscape, it is important for businesses to not only address customer needs and concerns, but also to do so proactively. By anticipating customer needs and concerns before they become major issues, businesses can build stronger relationships with their customers and ensure customer satisfaction.

There are several techniques that businesses can use to address customer needs and concerns proactively, including effective communication, active listening, empathy, and personalization.

Effective Communication

Effective communication is one of the most important techniques for addressing customer needs and concerns proactively. By communicating with customers in a clear and concise manner, businesses can avoid misunderstandings and ensure that customers have the information they need to make informed decisions.

Businesses should ensure that they have clear communication channels in place, such as phone lines, email addresses, and social media accounts, and that they respond to customer inquiries and concerns in a timely manner. It is important for businesses to use language that is easy to understand and avoid using jargon or technical terms that customers may not be familiar with.

Active Listening

Active listening is another technique that businesses can use to address customer needs and concerns proactively. By actively listening to customers and paying attention to their concerns, businesses can identify potential issues before they become major problems.

Businesses should encourage their employees to practice active listening by asking open-ended questions, paraphrasing customer concerns to ensure understanding, and providing feedback to customers to show that they are being heard. By practicing active listening, businesses can not only identify potential issues but also build stronger relationships with their customers by demonstrating that they care about their concerns.

Empathy

Empathy is an important skill for businesses to cultivate when addressing customer needs and concerns proactively. By putting themselves in their customers' shoes and understanding their perspectives, businesses can better anticipate customer needs and concerns and provide more personalized service.

Businesses can demonstrate empathy by acknowledging customer concerns and validating their feelings. They can also offer solutions that are tailored to the customer's specific needs and preferences. By showing empathy, businesses can build trust and loyalty with their customers, which can lead to long-term relationships.

Personalization

Personalization is another technique that businesses can use to address customer needs and concerns proactively. By personalizing their service to meet the unique needs and preferences of each customer, businesses can demonstrate that they value their customers and are willing to go the extra mile to meet their needs.

Businesses can personalize their service in a variety of ways, such as by using customer data to tailor product recommendations or by offering personalized promotions and discounts. By personalizing their service, businesses can create a more positive customer experience and build stronger relationships with their customers.

Conclusion

In today's competitive business landscape, addressing customer needs and concerns proactively is essential for building strong relationships with customers and ensuring customer satisfaction. By using techniques such as effective communication, active listening, empathy, and personalization, businesses can anticipate customer needs and concerns and provide more personalized service. By building stronger relationships with their customers, businesses can create loyal customers who will continue to do business with them for years to come.

Exercise: Analyzing a real customer relationship problem and developing a plan for improving it

Building and maintaining strong relationships with customers is a crucial aspect of business success, and it requires constant effort and attention. One of the ways to strengthen customer relationships is to proactively address their needs and concerns. However, even with the best intentions and efforts, customer relationship problems can arise. In this section, we will explore an exercise that involves analyzing a real customer relationship problem and developing a plan for improving it. This exercise will help students develop critical thinking and problem-solving skills, which are essential for success in the customer service field.

Analyzing a real customer relationship problem:
The first step in addressing a customer relationship problem is to identify the problem and its underlying causes. This requires careful analysis of the customer's feedback and interaction with the business. For this exercise, students should be provided with a real-life customer complaint or negative feedback that the business has received.

Once students have a clear understanding of the problem, they should conduct a root cause analysis to identify the underlying causes of the problem. This may involve reviewing customer feedback, talking to the employees involved in the interaction with the customer, and analyzing the company's policies and procedures. Students should use tools like fishbone diagrams or process flowcharts to help them visualize the causes of the problem.

✧ Developing a plan for improving customer relationships:
After identifying the underlying causes of the problem, the next step is to develop a plan for improving customer relationships. This plan should address the root causes of the problem and be focused on improving the customer experience. The following are some techniques that can be used to develop an effective plan:

✧ Apologize and acknowledge the problem:
The first step in improving a customer relationship is to apologize and acknowledge the problem. This shows the customer that their feedback is being taken seriously, and the business is committed to improving their experience. In the plan, students should outline how the business will apologize and acknowledge the problem to the customer.

✧ Address the root causes of the problem:
To prevent similar problems from occurring in the future, it is essential to address the root causes of the problem. This may involve changes to company policies, procedures, or employee training. Students should identify the specific changes that need to be made and outline how these changes will be implemented.

✧ Provide compensation or make amends:
In some cases, it may be necessary to provide compensation or make amends to the customer to restore their trust in the business. This may involve offering a refund, a discount, or a free product or service. In the plan, students should outline how the business will provide compensation or make amends to the customer.

✧ Follow up with the customer:
Following up with the customer is essential to ensure that their needs have been met and that they are satisfied with the resolution of the problem. Students should outline how the business will follow up with the customer, such as through a phone call or email.

Conclusion:
The exercise of analyzing a real customer relationship problem and developing a plan for improving it is an effective way to teach students critical thinking and problem-solving skills. By using real-life examples, students can learn how to identify the underlying causes of customer problems, develop effective solutions, and improve customer relationships. This exercise can be adapted to different business settings and industries, making it a valuable tool for students seeking a bachelor's degree in customer service or related fields.

CHAPTER 21: HANDLING DIFFICULT CUSTOMERS AND SITUATIONS

As customer service professionals, one of the most challenging aspects of our job is dealing with difficult customers and situations. Customers can become upset or angry for a variety of reasons, such as a product defect, a delay in service, or a perceived lack of attention or care from the service provider. It is our job as customer service representatives to handle these situations with professionalism, empathy, and a willingness to find a solution that satisfies the customer and preserves the reputation of the company.

In this chapter, we will explore various techniques for handling difficult customers and situations. We will discuss the importance of active listening, empathy, and clear communication, as well as the benefits of conflict resolution and problem-solving skills. We will also examine the different types of difficult customers, such as the aggressive customer, the indecisive customer, and the overly demanding customer, and provide strategies for dealing with each type.

Through case studies, role-playing exercises, and real-world examples, students will learn how to identify the root causes of difficult customer behavior and develop effective strategies for resolving conflicts and managing emotions. They will also learn how to handle common difficult situations, such as complaints, returns, and refunds, and how to effectively communicate with customers through phone, email, and in-person interactions.

By the end of this chapter, students will have a deeper understanding of the importance of effective communication and conflict resolution in customer service, and be equipped with practical tools and strategies for handling difficult customers and situations with confidence and professionalism. They will also gain an appreciation for the value of building long-term customer relationships based on trust, respect, and mutual understanding.

Techniques for handling challenging customer situations with empathy and professionalism

In any customer service role, it's almost inevitable that you will encounter challenging customers and situations. These can range from irate customers who are dissatisfied with a product or service, to those who are difficult to understand or communicate with due to language barriers or other factors. Regardless of the situation, it's important to handle these interactions with empathy and professionalism to de-escalate the situation and maintain a positive customer relationship.

Techniques for handling challenging customer situations with empathy and professionalism:

Listen actively: One of the most important things you can do when dealing with a challenging customer is to actively listen to what they are saying. This means giving them your full attention, avoiding interruptions, and showing that you understand their perspective. Active listening helps you understand the customer's needs and concerns, which can help you find a solution that works for both parties.

Show empathy: Demonstrating empathy means recognizing and acknowledging the customer's emotions and feelings. This can be as simple as saying, "I'm sorry you're experiencing this frustration," or "I understand why you're upset." By acknowledging the customer's emotions, you can help them feel heard and understood, which can go a long way toward resolving the issue.

Stay calm and professional: Even if the customer is yelling or being rude, it's important to remain calm and professional. Responding in a defensive or hostile manner can escalate the situation and make it more difficult to resolve. Instead, take a deep breath and respond in a calm, measured tone. This can help defuse the situation and show the customer that you are taking their concerns seriously.

Offer solutions: Once you understand the customer's needs and concerns, it's important to offer solutions that address their specific issues. This might involve finding a replacement product, offering a refund or credit, or suggesting an alternative solution. By offering solutions, you can show the customer that you are committed to resolving the issue and ensuring their satisfaction.

Follow up: After the interaction, it's important to follow up with the customer to ensure that the issue has been resolved to their satisfaction. This can be as simple as sending a follow-up email or making a phone call to check in. Following up shows the customer that you care about their experience and are committed to ensuring their satisfaction.

Examples:

Example 1: A customer contacts a bank to report a fraudulent charge on their account. The customer is frustrated and upset, and demands that the charge be refunded immediately. The customer service representative listens actively, shows empathy by acknowledging the customer's frustration, and offers a solution by initiating a refund and providing information on how to prevent future fraud. The representative also follows up with the customer to ensure that the issue has been resolved to their satisfaction.

Example 2: A customer enters a retail store to return a defective item. The customer is angry and confrontational, accusing the store of selling faulty products. The store employee remains calm and professional, listening actively and acknowledging the customer's frustration. The employee offers a solution by providing a replacement product and apologizing for the inconvenience. The employee also follows up with the customer to ensure that the replacement product is working correctly.

Exercises:

Think of a challenging customer situation that you have encountered in the past. What techniques did you use to handle the situation with empathy and professionalism? What could you have done differently?

Watch a customer service interaction in a public place, such as a restaurant or retail store. Take notes on how the employee handles the situation with empathy and professionalism. What techniques do they use? What could they have done differently?

Imagine a customer contacts your company with a complaint about a product or service. Write out a script for how you would handle the situation with empathy and professionalism. Be sure to include active listening, empathy, offering a solution, and following up to ensure customer satisfaction.

Exercises:

Think of a challenging customer situation that you have encountered in the past. What techniques did you use to handle the situation with empathy and professionalism? What could you have done differently?

One example of a challenging customer situation I encountered was when a customer came into the store I worked at with a defective product that was beyond our return policy timeframe. The customer was upset and demanded a full refund, but our store policy didn't allow for it. To handle the situation with empathy and professionalism, I listened actively to the customer's concerns and tried to understand their perspective. I apologized for the inconvenience and suggested alternative solutions such as a store credit or a partial refund. Eventually, we were able to reach a compromise that satisfied both the customer and the store.

Looking back, I could have handled the situation differently by setting clear expectations for our return policy and suggesting alternative solutions earlier in the interaction. It's important to be empathetic towards customers' concerns, but also to be transparent and fair with them.

Watch a customer service interaction in a public place, such as a restaurant or retail store. Take notes on how the employee handles the situation with empathy and professionalism. What techniques do they use? What could they have done differently?

During a recent visit to a restaurant, I observed a server handling a challenging customer situation with empathy and professionalism. A customer was upset with their meal and demanded a refund. The server listened actively to the customer's concerns and apologized for the mistake. They offered to replace the meal with a different dish or provide a full refund. They also ensured that the customer had a pleasant dining experience by checking on them frequently and offering complimentary dessert.

The server used a variety of techniques to handle the situation with empathy and professionalism, including active listening, empathy, and offering solutions. They also took the initiative to make sure the customer was satisfied with their dining experience. One thing that could have been done differently is to address the issue earlier in the interaction, instead of waiting for the customer to become upset.

Imagine a customer contacts your company with a complaint about a product or service. Write out a script for how you would handle the situation with empathy and professionalism. Be sure to include active listening, empathy, offering a solution, and following up to ensure customer satisfaction.

Example script:

Customer: "I purchased a product from your company and it's not working properly. I'm very disappointed and would like a refund."

Customer Service Representative: "I'm sorry to hear that you're having trouble with our product. That must be frustrating. Can you tell me more about the issue you're experiencing?"

Customer: "The product won't turn on and I've tried everything."

CSR: "I understand how inconvenient that can be. I want to make sure we find a solution that works for you. Have you tried troubleshooting the issue or contacting our technical support team?"

Customer: "No, I haven't. Can you walk me through some troubleshooting steps?"

CSR: "Absolutely. Let me guide you through some troubleshooting steps, and if that doesn't solve the problem, we can discuss other options such as a refund or replacement. Is that okay with you?"

Customer: "Yes, that sounds good."

CSR: "Great. Let's try these steps together. If they don't work, please let me know and we can move on to the next solution. And if there's anything else I can help you with, just let me know."

Customer: "Thank you, I appreciate your help."

CSR: "You're welcome. I'll follow up with you in a few days to make sure everything is working properly. Is there anything else I can assist you with today?"

By using active listening, empathy, and offering solutions, the CSR was able to address the customer's concerns and provide a satisfactory solution. It's important for customer service representatives to remain calm and professional in challenging situations, while also showing empathy and understanding towards the customer's frustrations.

One technique for handling challenging customer situations with empathy and professionalism is to acknowledge the customer's feelings and concerns. This can be done through active listening, where the representative repeats back what the customer has said to show that they are listening and understand their perspective.

Another technique is to offer solutions that meet the customer's needs and preferences. This involves understanding the customer's problem and working collaboratively with them to find a resolution that works for both parties.

In addition, it's important for customer service representatives to remain respectful and professional, even in challenging situations. They should avoid taking the customer's frustration personally and instead focus on finding a solution to the problem at hand.

Exercises:

Think of a challenging customer situation that you have encountered in the past. What techniques did you use to handle the situation with empathy and professionalism? What could you have done differently?

Watch a customer service interaction in a public place, such as a restaurant or retail store. Take notes on how the employee handles the situation with empathy and professionalism. What techniques do they use? What could they have done differently?

Imagine a customer contacts your company with a complaint about a product or service. Write out a script for how you would handle the situation with empathy and professionalism. Be sure to include active listening, empathy, offering solutions, and maintaining a professional demeanor throughout the interaction.

Strategies for defusing anger and resolving conflicts with customers

Handling difficult customer situations requires the ability to defuse anger and resolve conflicts with professionalism and empathy. While some customer interactions may be straightforward and easy to resolve, others can be emotionally charged and require a more nuanced approach. In this section, we will explore strategies for defusing anger and resolving conflicts with customers.

Active Listening

One of the most important strategies for defusing anger and resolving conflicts with customers is active listening. Active listening involves paying close attention to what the customer is saying and making an effort to understand their perspective. By actively listening to the customer, you can show them that you value their concerns and are committed to finding a solution that meets their needs.

Active listening involves several key techniques, including:

Paying attention to the customer's words, tone of voice, and body language.
Asking open-ended questions to gather more information.
Restating the customer's concerns to show that you understand their perspective.

Empathizing with the customer's situation.
By using these techniques, you can demonstrate to the customer that you are taking their concerns seriously and are committed to finding a solution.

Empathy

Another important strategy for defusing anger and resolving conflicts with customers is empathy. Empathy involves putting yourself in the customer's shoes and trying to understand their emotions and perspective. By demonstrating empathy, you can show the customer that you care about their concerns and are committed to finding a solution that meets their needs.

Empathy involves several key techniques, including:

Acknowledging the customer's emotions and concerns.
Using "I" statements to express empathy, such as "I can understand how frustrating that must be for you."
Offering reassurance and support.
By using these techniques, you can show the customer that you are committed to finding a solution that meets their needs and are empathetic to their situation.

Problem-Solving

Another important strategy for defusing anger and resolving conflicts with customers is problem-solving. Problem-solving involves working collaboratively with the customer to identify and address the root cause of their concerns. By engaging in problem-solving, you can demonstrate to the customer that you are committed to finding a solution that meets their needs.

Problem-solving involves several key techniques, including:

Gathering information about the customer's concerns.
Collaboratively identifying potential solutions.
Evaluating the pros and cons of each solution.
Implementing the chosen solution.
By using these techniques, you can show the customer that you are committed to finding a solution that meets their needs and are willing to work collaboratively to identify and address the root cause of their concerns.

De-escalation

Another important strategy for defusing anger and resolving conflicts with customers is de-escalation. De-escalation involves calming the customer down and reducing the emotional intensity of the situation. By de-escalating the situation, you can create a more productive environment for problem-solving and conflict resolution.

De-escalation involves several key techniques, including:

Remaining calm and composed.
Speaking in a calm and measured tone of voice.
Using non-threatening body language.
Acknowledging the customer's emotions and concerns.
Redirecting the conversation to focus on problem-solving.
By using these techniques, you can create a more productive environment for problem-solving and conflict resolution and demonstrate to the customer that you are committed to finding a solution that meets their needs.

Examples and Exercises:

Think of a challenging customer situation that you have encountered in the past. What strategies did you use to defuse anger and resolve conflicts with the customer? What could you have done differently?

Watch a customer service interaction in a public place, such as a restaurant or retail store. Take notes on how the employee defuses anger and resolves conflicts with the customer. What strategies do they use? What could they have done differently?

Imagine a scenario where a customer is angry and confrontational. Write out a script for how you would defuse their anger and resolve the conflict with professionalism and empathy. Be sure to include active listening, empathy, and offering solutions.

Exercises:

Think of a time when a customer was angry and confrontational with you. What strategies did you use to defuse their anger and resolve the conflict? Were these strategies effective? What could you have done differently?

Watch a customer service interaction in a public place and observe how the employee handles an angry or confrontational customer. Take notes on the strategies they use and consider if there are any other strategies that could have been employed.

Imagine a scenario where a customer is upset about a product or service that did not meet their expectations. Write out a script for how you would handle the situation with professionalism and empathy. Be sure to include strategies for defusing anger and resolving the conflict.

Role-play a scenario with a partner where one of you is an angry and confrontational customer and the other is a customer service representative. Practice using strategies for defusing anger and resolving conflicts with professionalism and empathy.

Conclusion:

Defusing anger and resolving conflicts with customers is an essential skill for any customer service representative. By using active listening, empathy, and offering solutions, a CSR can help turn a negative experience into a positive one. It is important to remain calm, patient, and professional in these situations, as this can help to deescalate the situation and build trust with the customer. By practicing these strategies and learning from past experiences, a CSR can become more confident and effective in handling difficult customer situations.

Tips for maintaining composure and professionalism in difficult situations

Dealing with difficult customers can be a challenging task, but maintaining composure and professionalism is crucial to providing good customer service. It is essential to have a positive attitude and good communication skills when interacting with difficult customers. In this section, we will discuss some tips and techniques for maintaining composure and professionalism in difficult situations.

Stay Calm and Focused
One of the most important things to remember when dealing with a difficult customer is to remain calm and focused. It can be easy to get angry or frustrated, but this will only escalate the situation. Take a deep breath and stay focused on the issue at hand. Listen carefully to the customer's concerns and avoid interrupting them.

Use Empathy
Empathy is the ability to understand and share the feelings of another person. It is an important skill in customer service, especially when dealing with difficult customers. When a customer is upset, it is essential to acknowledge their feelings and show that you understand their perspective. This can help to defuse the situation and build trust with the customer.

Stay Positive

Maintaining a positive attitude is crucial in customer service. Even in the most difficult situations, it is important to remain positive and look for solutions. Avoid getting defensive or argumentative and focus on finding a resolution that satisfies the customer.

Be Patient

Patience is a key virtue in customer service. Dealing with difficult customers can be time-consuming, but it is important to take the time to listen to their concerns and find a resolution. Avoid rushing the customer or becoming impatient, as this can only make the situation worse.

Use Active Listening

Active listening is an essential skill in customer service. It involves fully concentrating on what the customer is saying, understanding their perspective, and responding appropriately. Active listening can help to defuse the situation and build trust with the customer.

Remain Professional

It is essential to remain professional in all customer interactions, even in difficult situations. This includes using proper language, maintaining a calm tone of voice, and avoiding any behavior that could be perceived as rude or unprofessional.

Take Responsibility

If the customer has a legitimate complaint, take responsibility for the issue and work to find a solution. Avoid making excuses or blaming others for the problem. By taking responsibility, you can build trust with the customer and demonstrate your commitment to providing good customer service.

Seek Help When Necessary

Sometimes, despite your best efforts, it may be difficult to resolve a customer's issue. In these situations, it is important to seek help from a manager or supervisor. This can help to ensure that the customer's issue is addressed appropriately and that they leave feeling satisfied.

Examples and Exercises:

Think of a challenging customer situation that you have encountered in the past. How did you maintain composure and professionalism in the situation? What could you have done differently?

Watch a customer service interaction in a public place, such as a restaurant or retail store. Take notes on how the employee maintains composure and professionalism in a difficult situation. What techniques do they use? What could they have done differently?

Imagine a customer contacts your company with a complaint about a product or service. Write out a script for how you would maintain composure and professionalism in the situation. Be sure to include tips such as active listening, empathy, staying positive, and taking responsibility.

Exercise: Role-playing common difficult customer scenarios and practicing techniques for handling them

Role-playing is a powerful tool for improving customer service skills. By simulating real-life situations, employees can practice techniques for handling difficult customers in a safe and controlled environment. In this exercise, we will explore common difficult customer scenarios and practice techniques for handling them.

Scenario 1: Dealing with an angry customer

Angry customers can be challenging to deal with, but it's essential to remain calm and professional. Here are some techniques to try:

✧ Listen actively: Let the customer vent their frustrations without interrupting them. Show empathy by nodding and acknowledging their feelings.

✧ Apologize sincerely: Even if the customer's complaint isn't your fault, offer a sincere apology for their experience.

✧ Offer a solution: Work with the customer to find a solution that meets their needs. If necessary, escalate the issue to a supervisor or manager.

In this role-play, one participant will play the role of an angry customer, while the other participant plays the role of the customer service representative. Switch roles after 5-10 minutes.

Scenario 2: Dealing with a confused customer

✧ Sometimes, customers may be confused about a product or service, and it's the customer service representative's job to clarify the situation. Here are some techniques to try:

✧ Use simple language: Avoid technical jargon or industry-specific terms. Explain things in a way that a high school student would understand.

✧ Provide visual aids: If possible, provide visual aids such as diagrams, images, or videos to help explain the product or service.

✧ Ask open-ended questions: Encourage the customer to ask questions and provide them with clear, concise answers.

In this role-play, one participant will play the role of a confused customer, while the other participant plays the role of the customer service representative. Switch roles after 5-10 minutes.

Scenario 3: Dealing with a demanding customer

Demanding customers can be challenging to handle, but it's essential to remain calm and professional. Here are some techniques to try:

✧ Set boundaries: Politely explain what you can and can't do for the customer. Be clear about what is possible and what is not.

✧ Offer alternatives: If you can't meet the customer's demands, offer alternative solutions that might be acceptable to them.

✧ Stand your ground: If the customer becomes aggressive or abusive, it's important to stand your ground and protect your boundaries.

In this role-play, one participant will play the role of a demanding customer, while the other participant plays the role of the customer service representative. Switch roles after 5-10 minutes.

Scenario 4: Dealing with a disinterested customer

Sometimes, customers may be disinterested in the product or service you're offering. Here are some techniques to try:

✧ Be enthusiastic: Show genuine enthusiasm for the product or service. Use positive language and express excitement about the benefits it offers.

✧   Ask questions: Encourage the customer to share their needs and preferences. Ask open-ended questions to engage them in a conversation.
✧   Provide value: Show the customer the value of the product or service. Highlight its features and benefits and explain how it can meet their needs.

In this role-play, one participant will play the role of a disinterested customer, while the other participant plays the role of the customer service representative. Switch roles after 5-10 minutes.

Conclusion:

Role-playing is an effective way to improve customer service skills. By practicing techniques for handling difficult customers, employees can feel more confident and prepared to deal with real-life situations. Encourage employees to role-play regularly, and provide feedback and support to help them improve.

CHAPTER 22: EMPOWERING EMPLOYEES TO PROVIDE EXCELLENT CUSTOMER SERVICE

Providing excellent customer service is an essential component of any successful business. However, it is not enough to simply train employees to be polite and friendly; they must also be empowered to solve problems and make decisions that benefit the customer. In this chapter, we will discuss the importance of empowering employees in customer service and provide strategies for doing so effectively.

Section 1: The Importance of Empowering Employees in Customer Service

In today's highly competitive business environment, companies must differentiate themselves from their competitors by providing exceptional customer service. The key to achieving this is by empowering employees to take ownership of customer issues and providing them with the tools and training they need to solve problems effectively.

Empowering employees in customer service has several benefits. Firstly, it enhances the customer experience. When employees are empowered to take ownership of customer issues, they can resolve them quickly and efficiently, leading to greater customer satisfaction. Secondly, it improves employee engagement and job satisfaction. Empowering employees to make decisions and solve problems gives them a sense of autonomy and responsibility, leading to greater job satisfaction and motivation. Finally, it improves the bottom line. Satisfied customers are more likely to become repeat customers and recommend the company to others, leading to increased revenue and profitability.

Section 2: Strategies for Empowering Employees in Customer Service

Empowering employees in customer service requires a deliberate and systematic approach. Here are some strategies that businesses can use to empower their employees effectively:

Hire the Right People: Hiring the right people is the first step in empowering employees. Look for candidates who are empathetic, have strong communication skills, and can think on their feet. These traits are essential in customer service.

Provide Training and Development: Provide employees with the training and development they need to perform their jobs effectively. This includes technical training, product knowledge, and soft skills training, such as communication and conflict resolution.

Encourage Autonomy: Encourage employees to take ownership of customer issues and make decisions to resolve them. This requires trust and a willingness to delegate authority. By doing so, employees feel valued and respected, leading to greater job satisfaction.

Set Clear Expectations: Set clear expectations for employees in terms of their roles and responsibilities. Provide them with the tools and resources they need to perform their jobs effectively, and establish performance metrics to measure success.

Recognize and Reward Success: Recognize and reward employees who provide excellent customer service. This includes both formal and informal recognition, such as bonuses, promotions, and verbal praise. By doing so, employees feel valued and motivated to continue providing exceptional service.

Section 3: Overcoming Barriers to Empowering Employees in Customer Service

Despite the benefits of empowering employees in customer service, there are some barriers that businesses must overcome. Here are some common barriers and strategies for overcoming them:

Fear of Making Mistakes: Employees may be hesitant to make decisions for fear of making mistakes. To overcome this, provide them with clear guidelines and decision-making frameworks, and encourage them to seek guidance when needed.

Lack of Trust: Employees may not feel trusted to make decisions on behalf of the company. To overcome this, establish a culture of trust and transparency, and delegate decision-making authority to employees.

Lack of Training: Employees may not have the training or resources they need to make decisions effectively. To overcome this, provide them with the training and resources they need to perform their jobs effectively.

Lack of Communication: Employees may not have access to the information they need to make informed decisions. To overcome this, establish clear channels of communication and provide employees with the information they need to perform their jobs effectively.

Conclusion:

Empowering employees in customer service is essential for providing exceptional customer experiences and improving the bottom line. By providing training and resources, setting clear expectations, and creating a culture of empowerment and support, organizations can equip their employees to handle challenging customer interactions with confidence and professionalism.

Through the strategies outlined in this chapter, businesses can develop a workforce that is capable of delivering excellent customer service consistently, leading to increased customer loyalty, positive word-of-mouth, and ultimately, a competitive advantage in the marketplace.

It is important to note that employee empowerment is not a one-time initiative, but rather an ongoing process that requires continuous evaluation and improvement. Organizations must regularly assess the effectiveness of their training programs and support structures and adjust them as needed to ensure that their employees are well-equipped to meet the evolving needs of their customers.

By prioritizing employee empowerment and investing in the development of their customer service teams, organizations can create a culture of excellence and drive long-term success.

The benefits of empowering employees to solve customer problems on their own

Empowering employees is becoming increasingly essential in today's competitive business environment. Organizations that enable their employees to solve customer problems on their own have a competitive edge over their peers. Empowered employees can help a company achieve higher levels of customer satisfaction, loyalty, and retention. In this section, we will explore the benefits of empowering employees to solve customer problems on their own and how it can help businesses achieve success.

Benefits of Empowering Employees to Solve Customer Problems:

Faster Resolution of Customer Issues: When employees are empowered to solve customer problems, they can handle customer issues more efficiently and promptly. Empowered employees have the knowledge, skills, and authority to solve customer problems on their own, which results in faster resolution of issues. Customers appreciate when their problems are resolved quickly, which can lead to higher customer satisfaction and retention rates.

Improved Customer Satisfaction: Empowering employees to solve customer problems can lead to improved customer satisfaction. When employees are authorized to solve customer problems on their own, they can provide personalized solutions that meet the customer's specific needs. Customers appreciate when their problems are solved in a way that is tailored to their unique situation, which can result in higher customer satisfaction rates.

Higher Customer Retention: Empowered employees can help businesses achieve higher customer retention rates. When customers feel that their problems are being handled efficiently and effectively, they are more likely to remain loyal to the company. Loyal customers are essential for long-term business success, and empowering employees to solve customer problems can help achieve that goal.

Increased Employee Satisfaction and Motivation: Empowering employees to solve customer problems can also increase employee satisfaction and motivation. When employees are given the authority and responsibility to handle customer issues, they feel valued and appreciated. Empowered employees are more likely to feel invested in the success of the company and are motivated to provide exceptional customer service.

Enhanced Brand Reputation: Empowering employees to solve customer problems can enhance a company's brand reputation. Customers appreciate when a company goes above and beyond to solve their problems, and they are more likely to share positive experiences with others. Positive word-of-mouth can help enhance a company's reputation and attract new customers.

Challenges in Empowering Employees:

While empowering employees to solve customer problems can provide significant benefits to a company, it is not without its challenges. Some of the challenges that companies may face when implementing an employee empowerment program include:

Lack of Training: Employees need to be trained on how to solve customer problems effectively. Lack of training can lead to inconsistent problem-solving methods, which can result in lower customer satisfaction rates.

Fear of Making Mistakes: Employees may be hesitant to solve customer problems on their own due to the fear of making mistakes. This fear can lead to lower levels of employee empowerment and lower customer satisfaction rates.

Resistance to Change: Empowering employees to solve customer problems may require changes to the company's culture and processes. Resistance to change can make it difficult to implement an employee empowerment program successfully.

Lack of Trust: Employees need to trust that they have the authority and support to solve customer problems effectively. Lack of trust can lead to lower levels of employee empowerment and lower customer satisfaction rates.

Conclusion:

Empowering employees to solve customer problems on their own can provide significant benefits to a company, including faster resolution of customer issues, improved customer satisfaction, higher customer retention rates, increased employee satisfaction and motivation, and enhanced brand reputation. However, implementing an employee empowerment program is not without its challenges, including lack of training, fear of making mistakes, resistance to change, and lack of trust. Companies that successfully implement an employee empowerment program can achieve long-term success by providing exceptional customer service and building a loyal customer base.

Techniques for training and coaching employees to make customer-centric decisions

Empowering employees to make customer-centric decisions is a crucial aspect of delivering excellent customer service. It helps to build customer loyalty, reduce customer churn, and improve the overall customer experience. However, for employees to make customer-centric decisions, they need to be trained and coached on how to do so effectively. This section will discuss some techniques that managers can use to train and coach their employees to make customer-centric decisions.

Role-playing exercises
Role-playing exercises are an effective way to train employees on how to handle different customer situations. During these exercises, employees can practice how to

handle difficult customers, how to manage customer complaints, and how to provide excellent customer service. Role-playing exercises can be conducted in groups or one-on-one, and they can be tailored to specific customer scenarios that employees are likely to encounter.

Coaching and mentoring

Coaching and mentoring are also important techniques for training employees to make customer-centric decisions. Managers can work one-on-one with employees to help them develop their customer service skills and improve their ability to make customer-centric decisions. Coaching and mentoring can be done through regular feedback sessions, where managers provide employees with constructive feedback on their customer service performance.

Ongoing training

Ongoing training is critical to ensure that employees have the knowledge and skills they need to provide excellent customer service consistently. Managers can provide employees with ongoing training on customer service best practices, customer experience, and customer-centric decision-making. This training can be delivered through in-person workshops, e-learning modules, or other training methods.

Providing clear guidelines and policies

To empower employees to make customer-centric decisions, managers should provide clear guidelines and policies on how to handle different customer situations. These guidelines should be easy to understand and apply, and they should align with the company's customer service strategy. When employees have clear guidelines and policies to follow, they are more likely to make customer-centric decisions that align with the company's overall objectives.

Encouraging open communication

Encouraging open communication between employees and managers is essential for empowering employees to make customer-centric decisions. Managers should create an environment where employees feel comfortable sharing their ideas, feedback, and concerns about customer service. This open communication can help managers identify opportunities for improvement and provide employees with the support they need to make customer-centric decisions.

Celebrating successes

Celebrating successes is an effective way to motivate employees to continue making customer-centric decisions. Managers should recognize and reward employees who provide exceptional customer service, handle difficult customer situations effectively, and make customer-centric decisions. These celebrations can be as simple as a public recognition or a small reward, such as a gift card.

In conclusion, training and coaching employees to make customer-centric decisions are critical for delivering excellent customer service. By using techniques such as role-playing exercises, coaching and mentoring, ongoing training, providing clear guidelines and policies, encouraging open communication, and celebrating successes, managers can empower their employees to make customer-centric decisions that align with the company's overall objectives. By doing so, they can build customer loyalty, reduce customer churn, and improve the overall customer experience.

Strategies for creating a culture of ownership and accountability in customer service

In order to provide excellent customer service, it is not enough to simply empower employees to make decisions and solve problems on their own. It is also necessary to create a culture of ownership and accountability, in which employees take pride in their work and feel personally responsible for ensuring that customers are satisfied.

Here are some strategies for creating a culture of ownership and accountability in customer service:

Hire the Right People: The first step in creating a culture of ownership and accountability is to hire the right people. Look for candidates who are passionate about customer service and who take pride in their work. Look for individuals who are willing to take initiative and who are eager to learn.

Define Expectations: Once you have hired the right people, it is important to clearly define expectations. Make sure that employees understand what is expected of them in terms of providing excellent customer service. Communicate your vision and values to employees, and make sure they understand how their work fits into the bigger picture.

Provide Training and Support: In order to create a culture of ownership and accountability, it is important to provide employees with the training and support they need to succeed. This includes not only training on customer service techniques and best practices, but also ongoing coaching and mentoring to help employees continue to grow and develop.

Encourage Feedback and Collaboration: Employees are more likely to take ownership of their work and feel accountable for their results when they feel that their ideas and opinions are valued. Encourage employees to provide feedback and collaborate with their peers to find new and better ways to provide excellent customer service.

Recognize and Reward Success: Finally, it is important to recognize and reward success. When employees go above and beyond to provide excellent customer service, make sure to acknowledge their efforts and reward them accordingly. This can be done through formal recognition programs, bonuses, or even just a simple thank you.

By following these strategies, you can create a culture of ownership and accountability in customer service that will lead to better results for both your customers and your business.

Examples:

Let's take a look at a couple of examples of how these strategies can be put into practice:

Example 1: Zappos

Zappos is a well-known example of a company that has created a culture of ownership and accountability in customer service. The company hires employees who are passionate about customer service and who are willing to go above and beyond to ensure customer satisfaction. Zappos also provides extensive training and support to its employees, including ongoing coaching and mentoring. The company encourages feedback and collaboration through regular team meetings and brainstorming sessions. Finally, Zappos recognizes and rewards success through its "WOW" program, which encourages employees to provide exceptional customer service and rewards them for doing so.

Example 2: Ritz-Carlton

The Ritz-Carlton is another company that is known for its culture of ownership and accountability in customer service. The company hires employees who are passionate about providing excellent service and who take pride in their work. The Ritz-Carlton provides extensive training and support to its employees, including ongoing coaching and mentoring. The company also encourages feedback and collaboration through regular team meetings and brainstorming sessions. Finally, the Ritz-Carlton recognizes and rewards success through its "Guests First" program, which encourages employees to go above and beyond to provide exceptional service and rewards them for doing so.

Exercises:

How can providing training and support help to create a culture of ownership and accountability in customer service?

What are some examples of how companies can recognize and reward employees for providing excellent customer service?

Why is it important to encourage feedback and collaboration in creating a culture of ownership and accountability in customer service?

How can hiring the ight people help to create a culture of ownership and accountability in customer service?

Exercises:

Describe a scenario where an employee took ownership of a customer issue and resolved it successfully. What actions did the employee take, and how did they contribute to the customer's positive experience?

Research a company known for its exceptional customer service. How does this company recognize and reward employees for their contributions to customer satisfaction?

Write an essay discussing the benefits of creating a culture of ownership and accountability in customer service. Provide examples of companies that have successfully implemented this culture and how it has improved their customer satisfaction and bottom line.

Conduct a survey among employees in a customer service role to determine their level of engagement and ownership in their work. Analyze the results and identify areas for improvement in creating a culture of ownership and accountability.

Role-play a scenario where a customer is dissatisfied with a product or service. Have one employee respond in a way that reflects a lack of ownership and accountability, and another employee respond in a way that demonstrates ownership and accountability. Analyze the differences in their approaches and discuss the impact on the customer's experience.

In conclusion, creating a culture of ownership and accountability in customer service is essential for companies looking to provide exceptional customer experiences and improve their bottom line. This culture can be established through a combination of strategies, including hiring the right people, providing training and support, recognizing and rewarding excellent customer service, and encouraging feedback and collaboration. By implementing these strategies and promoting a culture of ownership and accountability, companies can empower their employees to take ownership of customer issues, make customer-centric decisions, and ultimately provide exceptional customer experiences.

Exercise: Developing a plan for empowering employees to make customer-centric decisions

As we have discussed throughout this section, empowering employees to make customer-centric decisions can have a significant impact on the success of a business. In this exercise, we will develop a plan for empowering employees in your hypothetical organization to make customer-centric decisions.

Step 1: Define the goals and objectives of the plan

The first step in developing a plan for empowering employees to make customer-centric decisions is to define the goals and objectives of the plan. Consider the following questions:

What specific business goals do you hope to achieve through empowering employees to make customer-centric decisions?

What are the key performance indicators (KPIs) that will measure the success of the plan?

What are the specific objectives that the plan aims to achieve?

Examples of goals and objectives could include:

- ✧ Increasing customer satisfaction scores by 10% within the next year
- ✧ Reducing customer complaints by 20% within the next six months
- ✧ Increasing employee engagement by 15% within the next year

Step 2: Identify the key stakeholders

In order to successfully implement a plan for empowering employees to make customer-centric decisions, it is important to identify the key stakeholders who will be involved in the process. These stakeholders may include:

✧ Senior management
✧ HR and training staff
✧ Frontline employees
✧ Customers

Step 3: Assess the current state of the organization

Before developing a plan, it is important to assess the current state of the organization. This may involve conducting a survey or focus group with employees and customers, reviewing customer feedback and complaints, and analyzing customer satisfaction scores and other relevant metrics. This will help to identify areas where employees may need additional support or training in order to make customer-centric decisions.

Step 4: Develop a training and support plan

Based on the assessment of the current state of the organization, develop a training and support plan that will help employees make customer-centric decisions. This may include:

✧ Providing training on customer service skills, such as active listening, empathy, and problem-solving
✧ Providing employees with access to customer feedback and other relevant data to help them make informed decisions
✧ Developing a system for coaching and mentoring employees, such as regular one-on-one meetings with managers or peer-to-peer mentoring programs
✧ Providing incentives and rewards for employees who consistently provide excellent customer service
✧ Developing a system for soliciting and incorporating feedback from employees and customers to continuously improve the training and support program

Step 5: Implement and monitor the plan

Once the plan has been developed, it is important to implement and monitor its effectiveness. This may involve:

✧ Communicating the plan to all stakeholders and providing them with the necessary resources to support its implementation
✧ Establishing regular checkpoints to monitor progress towards the goals and objectives of the plan
✧ Adjusting the plan as needed based on feedback and data analysis

Conclusion:

Developing a plan for empowering employees to make customer-centric decisions can help to improve customer satisfaction, reduce customer complaints, and increase employee engagement. By following the steps outlined in this exercise, organizations can create a culture of ownership and accountability in customer service, leading to better outcomes for both customers and employees.

CHAPTER 23: LEVERAGING TECHNOLOGY FOR BETTER CUSTOMER SERVICE

In today's digital age, technology plays a crucial role in every aspect of our lives. From ordering food online to booking a cab through an app, we are heavily dependent on technology to make our lives easier and more convenient. The same applies to customer service, where technology can be leveraged to provide a seamless and personalized experience to customers.

The use of technology in customer service has become a necessity for businesses to stay competitive and meet the ever-growing demands of customers. Technology not only helps in streamlining operations but also enhances the overall customer experience. In this chapter, we will discuss how businesses can leverage technology to improve customer service.

Section 1: Understanding the Role of Technology in Customer Service

In this section, we will explore the different ways in which technology can be used to enhance customer service. We will discuss how technology can be leveraged to:

Automate processes: With the help of technology, businesses can automate various processes, such as appointment scheduling, order tracking, and feedback collection, among others. This not only saves time and resources but also provides a more efficient and error-free experience to customers.

Provide real-time support: Technology allows businesses to provide real-time support to customers through various channels, such as live chat, social media, and chatbots. This helps in resolving customer issues quickly and efficiently, leading to higher customer satisfaction.

Personalize the customer experience: With the help of customer data and analytics, businesses can personalize the customer experience by providing tailored recommendations and offers based on their preferences and behavior.

Provide self-service options: Technology enables businesses to provide self-service options to customers, such as FAQs, knowledge bases, and tutorials. This empowers customers to find solutions to their queries on their own, reducing the load on customer service agents.

Section 2: Implementing Technology for Better Customer Service

In this section, we will discuss the various steps involved in implementing technology for better customer service. We will cover the following topics:

Assessing the business needs: Before implementing any technology, businesses need to assess their specific needs and requirements. This includes evaluating the current customer service processes and identifying the areas that need improvement.

Choosing the right technology: Once the business needs have been identified, the next step is to choose the right technology that aligns with those needs. This includes evaluating various options, such as CRM systems, chatbots, and social media management tools, among others.

Training employees: Implementing new technology requires proper training of employees to ensure they are proficient in using it. This includes providing hands-on training, conducting workshops, and creating user manuals.

Monitoring and optimizing: After implementing technology, it is important to continuously monitor and optimize its performance. This includes tracking metrics, such as customer satisfaction, response time, and resolution rate, and making necessary adjustments to improve the overall customer experience.

Section 3: Challenges and Considerations in Leveraging Technology for Customer Service

In this section, we will discuss the various challenges and considerations businesses need to keep in mind while leveraging technology for customer service. We will cover the following topics:

Balancing technology and human touch: While technology can provide a seamless and efficient experience to customers, it is important to maintain a human touch to create a personal connection with customers.

Privacy and security concerns: With the increasing use of technology in customer service, businesses need to ensure the privacy and security of customer data.

This includes implementing appropriate security measures and complying with data protection regulations.

Cost and resource implications: Implementing technology for customer service can be costly and resource-intensive. Businesses need to carefully evaluate the costs and benefits of technology before investing in it.

Technology has revolutionized the way businesses interact with customers. From online chatbots to social media platforms, companies can now reach customers across multiple channels and provide a personalized experience that meets their needs. In this chapter, we have explored how technology can be leveraged to improve customer service.

We began by discussing the importance of customer-centricity and how technology can be used to create a customer-centric culture. We then delved into the various tools and platforms that businesses can use to interact with customers, such as chatbots, social media, and mobile apps. We also explored how businesses can use data and analytics to gain insights into customer behavior and preferences, which can inform their customer service strategies.

Additionally, we discussed the benefits of automation and how it can help businesses to streamline their customer service processes, reduce costs, and improve efficiency. We also explored the role of artificial intelligence in customer service, including its ability to provide personalized recommendations and responses.

Finally, we discussed the importance of maintaining a human touch in customer service, despite the increasing use of technology. We emphasized the need for businesses to balance the benefits of technology with the importance of human interaction and empathy in providing an exceptional customer experience.

Overall, technology is a powerful tool that can help businesses to improve customer service, but it must be used strategically and in conjunction with a customer-centric mindset. By leveraging technology effectively, businesses can create a more efficient, personalized, and empathetic customer experience, which can lead to increased customer satisfaction and loyalty.

The role of technology in enhancing customer service

Customer service has always been a crucial component of any business. However, with the advancement of technology, customer service has undergone a significant transformation. In today's digital age, businesses are increasingly relying on technology to provide efficient and effective customer service.

This chapter will explore the role of technology in enhancing customer service. We will discuss the different technologies available to businesses and how they can be used to improve customer service. Additionally, we will analyze the benefits and challenges associated with the use of technology in customer service.

Types of Technology Used in Customer Service:

Customer Relationship Management (CRM) Systems
CRM systems are software programs that help businesses manage their customer interactions and relationships. These systems allow businesses to store customer information, track customer interactions, and analyze customer data. By using a CRM system, businesses can provide personalized customer service and build long-term relationships with their customers.

Chatbots
Chatbots are computer programs that use artificial intelligence to converse with customers. These programs can be used to answer basic customer inquiries and provide customer support. Chatbots can be integrated into a company's website or social media platforms, providing customers with 24/7 support.

Social Media
Social media platforms such as Facebook, Twitter, and Instagram have become powerful tools for businesses to interact with their customers. These platforms allow businesses to receive feedback from customers, respond to customer inquiries, and engage with customers on a personal level.

Mobile Apps
Mobile apps have become increasingly popular among businesses as they allow customers to interact with businesses from their mobile devices. Businesses can use mobile apps to provide customer support, offer promotions, and send personalized messages to customers.

Benefits of Using Technology in Customer Service:

Increased Efficiency
By using technology, businesses can automate many of their customer service processes, saving time and resources. For example, chatbots can be used to answer basic customer inquiries, freeing up customer service representatives to focus on more complex issues.

Personalized Customer Service
Technology can be used to provide personalized customer service. For example, CRM systems allow businesses to store customer information, such as purchase history and preferences. This information can be used to provide personalized product recommendations and tailored promotions.

Improved Customer Satisfaction
Technology can be used to improve customer satisfaction by providing faster and more efficient customer service. For example, chatbots can provide instant responses to customer inquiries, reducing wait times and improving customer satisfaction.

Challenges of Using Technology in Customer Service:

Technical Issues
One of the main challenges associated with the use of technology in customer service is technical issues. Software programs and hardware can malfunction, causing customer service disruptions.

Lack of Personalization
While technology can be used to provide personalized customer service, there is a risk that it can feel impersonal. Customers may prefer to interact with a human customer service representative rather than a chatbot or mobile app.

Privacy Concerns
The use of technology in customer service raises privacy concerns. Customers may be hesitant to provide personal information to businesses, particularly if they are unsure how this information will be used.

Conclusion:

The use of technology in customer service has become increasingly prevalent in today's digital age. Businesses can use a range of technologies, such as CRM systems, chatbots, social media, and mobile apps, to enhance customer service. While there are benefits associated with the use of technology, such as increased efficiency, personalized customer service, and improved customer satisfaction, there are also challenges, such as technical issues, lack of personalization, and privacy concerns. As technology continues to evolve, businesses must carefully consider how they can use technology to enhance customer service while also addressing these challenges.

Techniques for using technology to streamline customer interactions and communications

As businesses increasingly move towards digitalization, the role of technology in enhancing customer service has become more significant. One of the main ways that technology can improve customer service is by streamlining customer interactions and communications. This means using technology to make customer interactions smoother, more efficient, and more effective. In this section, we will discuss various techniques that businesses can use to streamline customer interactions and communications using technology.

Using Chatbots to Improve Customer Interactions

Chatbots are computer programs designed to mimic human conversation. They can be used in various applications, including customer service. By using chatbots, businesses can provide 24/7 customer support without the need for human intervention. Chatbots can answer common customer questions, provide information about products and services, and even troubleshoot issues.

One of the key benefits of using chatbots is their speed. They can handle multiple customer queries simultaneously, reducing wait times for customers. Chatbots can also provide customers with personalized experiences. By collecting data about customer interactions, chatbots can learn about customer preferences and provide tailored recommendations.

However, businesses need to be careful when implementing chatbots. If not programmed correctly, chatbots can provide generic, unhelpful responses that frustrate customers. It is essential to design chatbots with a clear understanding of customer needs and to continually monitor and update them to improve their effectiveness.

Using Automated Emails to Improve Communications

Automated emails are pre-written messages that are triggered by specific customer actions or events, such as placing an order or signing up for a newsletter. By using automated emails, businesses can keep customers informed about their orders, send personalized marketing messages, and provide support.

Automated emails can be used to create personalized experiences for customers. By using customer data, businesses can segment customers and provide targeted messages based on their preferences. For example, if a customer has purchased a product in a specific category, the business can send them personalized recommendations for related products.

Using automated emails can also help businesses save time and resources. Rather than manually sending individual emails, businesses can create pre-written messages that are triggered automatically. This frees up staff time to focus on other areas of customer service.

However, it is important to ensure that automated emails are not overused. Customers can quickly become overwhelmed with too many messages, leading to annoyance and unsubscribing. Businesses need to strike a balance between providing helpful information and avoiding spamming customers with excessive messages.

Using Social Media to Improve Customer Interactions
Social media platforms, such as Facebook and Twitter, have become popular channels for businesses to interact with customers. By using social media, businesses can provide quick and personalized responses to customer queries and complaints. Customers can also use social media to share their experiences and provide feedback, providing businesses with valuable insights into customer needs.

Social media can be particularly useful for businesses with a large customer base. Rather than handling customer queries one by one, social media platforms allow businesses to respond to multiple customers simultaneously. Social media can also be used to provide proactive customer service. By monitoring social media mentions, businesses can identify potential issues and address them before they become problems.

However, businesses need to be careful when using social media for customer service. Social media is a public forum, and any responses to customers are visible to other users. Businesses need to ensure that they respond in a timely and professional manner and avoid getting into public arguments with customers. It is also important to monitor social media channels continually to ensure that all customer queries are addressed promptly.

Using Mobile Apps to Improve Customer Experience
Mobile apps have become a popular way for businesses to interact with customers. By using mobile apps, businesses can provide customers with a more personalized experience, offer promotions and discounts, and even provide support.

One of the key benefits of using mobile apps is their convenience. Customers can access information about products and services, make purchases, and contact customer support at any time and from any location. This flexibility allows customers to engage with a business on their own terms, which can lead to higher satisfaction and loyalty.

Mobile apps can also provide businesses with valuable data on customer behavior and preferences. By analyzing this data, businesses can identify trends and make data-driven decisions to improve customer experience. For example, a business may notice that a large number of customers are abandoning their shopping carts during the checkout process. By analyzing the data, the business may identify that the checkout process is too complicated and take steps to simplify it, leading to a reduction in cart abandonment and an increase in sales.

Another way that mobile apps can improve customer experience is by providing personalized recommendations and offers. By analyzing a customer's purchase history and browsing behavior, a business can provide targeted offers and recommendations that are more likely to be of interest to the customer. This can lead to higher engagement and increased sales.

However, businesses need to ensure that their mobile apps are user-friendly and easy to navigate. A poorly designed app can lead to frustration and a negative customer experience. Additionally, businesses need to ensure that their mobile apps are secure, as customers may be hesitant to provide sensitive information if they do not trust the security of the app.

Using Chatbots for Customer Support

Chatbots are another technology that businesses can use to improve customer experience. Chatbots are computer programs designed to simulate conversation with human users, typically through text-based interfaces. Businesses can use chatbots to provide customers with quick and efficient support, 24/7.

One of the key benefits of using chatbots is their speed. Chatbots can provide customers with instant responses to their queries, which can lead to higher satisfaction and loyalty. Additionally, chatbots can handle a large volume of queries simultaneously, which can reduce wait times and improve efficiency.

Chatbots can also be used to provide personalized recommendations and offers, similar to mobile apps. By analyzing a customer's purchase history and browsing behavior, a chatbot can provide targeted recommendations and offers that are more likely to be of interest to the customer. This can lead to higher engagement and increased sales.

However, businesses need to ensure that their chatbots are well-designed and properly trained. A poorly designed or untrained chatbot can lead to frustration and a negative customer experience. Additionally, businesses need to ensure that their chatbots are able to handle complex queries and escalate issues to human support agents if necessary.

Overall, technology can be a powerful tool for businesses looking to improve customer experience. By using social media, mobile apps, and chatbots, businesses can streamline customer interactions and communications, provide personalized recommendations and offers, and offer quick and efficient support. However, businesses need to ensure that they use technology in a way that is secure, user-friendly, and well-designed to avoid negative customer experiences.

The benefits and challenges of using technology in customer service

The use of technology in customer service has become increasingly common in recent years, and for good reason. There are many benefits to using technology to improve customer service, such as increased efficiency, improved communication, and greater personalization. However, there are also some challenges associated with using technology in customer service that businesses need to be aware of. In this section, we will discuss both the benefits and challenges of using technology in customer service.

Benefits of Using Technology in Customer Service

Increased Efficiency: One of the main benefits of using technology in customer service is increased efficiency. Automated systems can handle routine tasks such as scheduling appointments, answering common questions, and routing calls to the appropriate department. This allows customer service representatives to focus on more complex issues that require their expertise, and can help reduce wait times for customers.

Improved Communication: Technology can also improve communication between customers and businesses. For example, chatbots and instant messaging services can allow customers to get quick answers to their questions, while email and social media can provide a way for customers to get in touch with businesses at any time, from anywhere. This can help businesses provide more responsive customer service and improve customer satisfaction.

Greater Personalization: Technology can also help businesses provide more personalized customer service. For example, customer relationship management

(CRM) software can track customer interactions and preferences, allowing businesses to provide targeted offers and recommendations based on their individual needs and interests. This can help businesses build stronger relationships with their customers and improve customer loyalty.

Challenges of Using Technology in Customer Service

Technical Issues: One of the main challenges of using technology in customer service is technical issues. If the technology used to provide customer service fails, customers may become frustrated and lose confidence in the business. It is important for businesses to have backup systems in place and to provide timely support when technical issues arise.

Lack of Personal Touch: Another challenge of using technology in customer service is the lack of personal touch. Customers may feel that they are not being heard or understood when communicating with automated systems or chatbots, and may prefer to speak with a live representative. It is important for businesses to strike a balance between using technology to improve efficiency and providing a human touch to customer interactions.

Security and Privacy Concerns: Finally, businesses need to be aware of security and privacy concerns when using technology in customer service. For example, storing customer data in the cloud can expose it to potential security breaches. Businesses need to take steps to protect customer data and comply with regulations such as the General Data Protection Regulation (GDPR) and the California Consumer Privacy Act (CCPA).

Conclusion

In conclusion, using technology in customer service can bring many benefits to businesses, including increased efficiency, improved communication, and greater personalization. However, there are also some challenges associated with using technology in customer service, such as technical issues, a lack of personal touch, and security and privacy concerns. By being aware of these challenges and taking steps to mitigate them, businesses can provide excellent customer service while taking advantage of the benefits that technology has to offer.

Exercise: Analyzing a real customer service technology problem and developing a plan for addressing it

In this exercise, we will analyze a real customer service technology problem and develop a plan for addressing it. The problem we will be analyzing is the long wait times customers experience when calling customer service.

Step 1: Analyze the Problem

The first step in addressing a customer service technology problem is to analyze the problem. In this case, the problem is long wait times when calling customer service. We need to determine the cause of the problem to develop an effective plan for addressing it.

There are several possible causes of long wait times when calling customer service, including:

✧ Lack of staffing: If there are not enough agents available to take calls, customers will experience long wait times.

✧ Inefficient call routing: If calls are not being routed efficiently, customers may be waiting longer than necessary.

✧ Complex issues: If customers are calling with complex issues that require more time to resolve, this can result in longer wait times.

✧ Inadequate technology: If the technology being used for customer service is outdated or inefficient, this can contribute to longer wait times.

Step 2: Develop a Plan

Once we have identified the cause of the problem, we can develop a plan for addressing it. In this case, we will assume that the cause of the problem is lack of staffing.

Our plan for addressing the problem of long wait times when calling customer service would include the following steps:

✧ Hire additional staff: The first step in addressing the problem of long wait times is to hire additional staff to handle calls.

✧ Implement call queuing: Implementing call queuing can help to ensure that customers are served in the order in which they called, reducing wait times.

✧ Implement call-back options: Implementing call-back options can allow customers to leave a message with their contact information and receive a call back when an agent is available, reducing wait times.

✧ Improve training: Improving the training of customer service agents can help them to resolve issues more efficiently, reducing the time customers spend on hold.

Implement new technology: Implementing new technology, such as automated chatbots or artificial intelligence systems, can help to handle customer inquiries more efficiently, reducing the need for additional staff.

Step 3: Implement the Plan

Once we have developed a plan for addressing the problem, the next step is to implement the plan. This may involve hiring additional staff, purchasing new technology, or implementing new processes. It is important to track progress and make adjustments as needed to ensure that the plan is effective.

Step 4: Evaluate the Results

After implementing the plan, it is important to evaluate the results to determine whether the problem has been effectively addressed. This may involve tracking wait times, customer satisfaction ratings, or other metrics. Based on the results, adjustments may need to be made to the plan to further improve customer service.

Conclusion

Analyzing a real customer service technology problem and developing a plan for addressing it is an important skill for customer service professionals. By identifying the cause of the problem, developing a plan, implementing the plan, and evaluating the results, customer service professionals can improve the customer experience and ensure that customers are served in a timely and efficient manner.

CRM: Maximizing Customer Relationships with Technology

In today's fast-paced business environment, customer relationship management (CRM) has become a crucial aspect of business success. Customers expect personalized interactions and seamless communication when interacting with businesses, and companies that fail to meet these expectations risk losing customers to competitors. RhinoLeg CRM is an AI-powered software that helps businesses manage their customer interactions, marketing campaigns, and sales activities. This section will provide an in-depth analysis of RhinoLeg CRM and its functions, including its sales management, marketing automation, customer service automation, analytics and reporting, mobile app integration, and other key features.

The Importance of Customer Relationship Management in Today's Business Environment

Customer relationship management is the practice of managing a company's interactions with customers to improve customer satisfaction and retention. In today's digital age, customers have more options than ever before, and businesses must work harder to retain their customers. By implementing a customer relationship management strategy, businesses can gain insights into customer behavior and preferences, improve customer satisfaction, and ultimately increase revenue.

The Benefits of Using RhinoLeg CRM for Businesses

RhinoLeg CRM is an all-in-one customer relationship management software that helps businesses manage their customer interactions, marketing campaigns, and sales activities. By using RhinoLeg CRM, businesses can streamline their communication with customers, gain insights into customer behavior and preferences, and improve their sales and marketing activities. Some of the key benefits of using RhinoLeg CRM include:

- Improved customer engagement and satisfaction
- Increased revenue and profitability
- Streamlined communication with customers
- Insights into customer behavior and preferences
- Improved sales and marketing activities
- Improved efficiency and productivity
- RhinoLeg CRM Overview

RhinoLeg CRM is an all-in-one customer relationship management software that helps businesses manage their customer interactions, marketing campaigns, and sales activities. RhinoLeg CRM offers a variety of features and benefits, including sales management, marketing automation, customer service automation, analytics and reporting, mobile app integration, and other key features. Some of the key features and benefits of RhinoLeg CRM are discussed below.

Sales Management

Sales management is an important aspect of customer relationship management, and RhinoLeg CRM offers a variety of features to help businesses manage their sales activities. Some of the key sales management features of RhinoLeg CRM include:

> ✦ Lead generation: RhinoLeg CRM helps businesses generate leads by identifying potential customers based on their behavior and preferences.
> ✦ Sales pipeline management: RhinoLeg CRM helps businesses manage their entire sales process, from lead generation to closing deals.
> ✦ Lead routing: RhinoLeg CRM helps businesses route leads to the appropriate sales team member based on their behavior and preferences.
> ✦ Customer segmentation: RhinoLeg CRM helps businesses segment their customers based on behavior and preferences, allowing for targeted marketing and sales activities.

Knowledge management is also an important aspect of sales management, and RhinoLeg CRM offers features to help businesses manage their knowledge base. By providing access to relevant information and training materials, businesses can improve their sales team's performance and ultimately increase revenue.

Marketing Automation

Marketing automation is another important aspect of customer relationship management, and RhinoLeg CRM offers a variety of features to help businesses create and manage targeted marketing campaigns. Some of the key marketing automation features of RhinoLeg CRM include:

> ✦ Lead nurturing: RhinoLeg CRM helps businesses nurture leads by providing personalized content and communication based on their behavior and preferences.
> ✦ Multi-channel communication: RhinoLeg CRM helps businesses communicate with customers across multiple channels, including email, social media, and SMS.
> ✦ Social media engagement: RhinoLeg CRM helps businesses engage with customers on social media by monitoring conversations and responding to comments and messages.
> ✦ Marketing attribution: RhinoLeg CRM helps businesses track the effectiveness of their marketing campaigns and attribute sales to specific marketing activities.

✧   Marketing automation is an effective way to increase customer engagement and conversion rates, and RhinoLeg CRM's marketing automation features can help businesses achieve these goals.

Customer Service Automation

RhinoLeg CRM's customer service automation features allow businesses to provide efficient and personalized customer support. One of the key features of customer service automation is customer satisfaction surveys. These surveys can be sent to customers after an interaction with a business, giving them the opportunity to provide feedback and rate their experience. This information can be used to improve customer service processes and identify areas for improvement.

RhinoLeg CRM's ticket management feature allows businesses to organize and prioritize customer inquiries, complaints, and other issues. This helps ensure that every customer inquiry is addressed in a timely and efficient manner. Customer journey tracking is another important feature of RhinoLeg CRM's customer service automation. This feature allows businesses to track customer interactions across multiple touchpoints, including phone, email, social media, and chat. By understanding the customer's journey, businesses can provide more personalized and efficient support.

Analytics and Reporting

RhinoLeg CRM's analytics and reporting features help businesses gain insights into customer behavior and preferences. These features allow businesses to track and analyze customer interactions, sales data, and marketing campaigns. Forecasting and trend analysis features can help businesses predict future sales trends and make informed decisions about marketing strategies.

Data visualization is another important feature of RhinoLeg CRM's analytics and reporting capabilities. By using charts, graphs, and other visual aids, businesses can better understand their data and make informed decisions. Machine learning-based lead generation is another innovative feature of RhinoLeg CRM. This feature uses artificial intelligence to analyze customer data and identify potential leads.

Mobile App Integration

RhinoLeg CRM's mobile app integration feature allows businesses to manage customer interactions on-the-go. This is particularly important for businesses with a mobile workforce, such as sales teams or field service technicians. By using the

RhinoLeg CRM mobile app, employees can access customer data, update records, and respond to customer inquiries from anywhere, at any time.

Other Key Features

In addition to its sales management, marketing automation, customer service automation, analytics and reporting, and mobile app integration features, RhinoLeg CRM offers a range of other key features. These features include document automation, integration with social media advertising platforms, website analytics tools, partner relationship management, social listening, gamification, predictive analytics, sales coaching, business process automation, and artificial intelligence-powered chatbots.

Document automation features allow businesses to automate the creation of documents such as proposals, contracts, and invoices, saving time and increasing efficiency. Integration with social media advertising platforms allows businesses to track and analyze the effectiveness of social media advertising campaigns. Website analytics tools allow businesses to track website traffic and visitor behavior, helping to optimize the user experience.

Partner relationship management is an important feature for businesses that work with a network of partners or affiliates. Social listening features allow businesses to monitor social media platforms for mentions of their brand, products, or services. Gamification features can be used to increase employee engagement and motivation by adding elements of competition and reward to tasks and activities. Predictive analytics features can help businesses identify trends and patterns in customer behavior, allowing them to make more informed decisions.

Sales coaching features provide employees with training and support to improve their sales skills and performance. Business process automation features allow businesses to automate repetitive tasks and streamline workflows, increasing efficiency and reducing errors. Finally, artificial intelligence-powered chatbots can be used to provide automated customer support, answering common questions and resolving issues without the need for human intervention.

Conclusion

RhinoLeg CRM is a powerful customer relationship management software that offers a range of features to help businesses streamline their customer management and communication processes. From sales management to marketing automation, customer service automation to analytics and reporting, RhinoLeg CRM provides businesses with the tools they need to understand their customers, personalize interactions, and increase engagement and conversion rates.

By implementing RhinoLeg CRM as part of their customer relationship management strategy, businesses can improve their efficiency, reduce costs, and increase their bottom line. The software's user-friendly interface, mobile app integration, and artificial intelligence-powered chatbots make it easy for businesses of all sizes to manage their customer interactions and communication effectively.

RhinoLeg CRM's marketing automation features help businesses create and manage targeted marketing campaigns, increasing customer engagement and conversion rates. The software's customer service automation features help businesses provide efficient and personalized customer support, improving customer satisfaction and loyalty. The analytics and reporting features help businesses gain insights into customer behavior and preferences, allowing them to make data-driven decisions.

In addition to these key features, RhinoLeg CRM also offers document automation, integration with social media advertising platforms, website analytics tools, partner relationship management, social listening, gamification, predictive analytics, sales coaching, and business process automation. These features help businesses optimize their customer management and communication processes and stay ahead of their competition.

In conclusion, RhinoLeg CRM is an essential tool for businesses looking to streamline their customer management and communication processes, improve efficiency, and increase customer engagement and conversion rates. By implementing RhinoLeg CRM as part of their customer relationship management strategy, businesses can gain a competitive advantage in today's digital age.

CHAPTER 24: MEASURING AND EVALUATING CUSTOMER SERVICE PERFORMANCE

In today's highly competitive business environment, customer service is a key factor in attracting and retaining customers. Providing excellent customer service can help businesses differentiate themselves from their competitors and build a loyal customer base. However, providing excellent customer service is not enough; businesses must also measure and evaluate their customer service performance to ensure that they are meeting their customers' expectations.

This chapter will provide an in-depth analysis of measuring and evaluating customer service performance, including the importance of customer service metrics, methods for measuring customer service performance, and strategies for improving customer service performance.

Importance of Customer Service Metrics

Customer service metrics are key performance indicators (KPIs) that businesses use to measure their customer service performance. These metrics provide businesses with valuable insights into their customers' experiences and perceptions, enabling them to identify areas for improvement and make data-driven decisions.

Examples of customer service metrics include:

First Contact Resolution (FCR) - measures the percentage of customer issues that are resolved on the first contact with customer service.

Average Handle Time (AHT) - measures the average time it takes for a customer service representative to handle a customer inquiry or issue.

Net Promoter Score (NPS) - measures the likelihood that a customer will recommend a business to others.

Customer Satisfaction Score (CSAT) - measures the level of satisfaction that customers have with a business's products or services.

Customer Effort Score (CES) - measures the ease of which a customer is able to resolve their issue or inquiry.

Measuring Customer Service Performance

Measuring customer service performance involves collecting and analyzing data from various sources, including customer feedback, call center metrics, and social media analytics. Businesses can use this data to identify trends and patterns in their customer service performance, and to make data-driven decisions to improve their customer service.

One method for measuring customer service performance is through customer feedback surveys. These surveys can be conducted through various channels, including email, phone, and social media. They can be used to gather feedback on specific customer service interactions or to gather general feedback on a business's overall customer service performance.

Another method for measuring customer service performance is through call center metrics. These metrics provide businesses with valuable insights into the efficiency and effectiveness of their call center operations, including average handle time, call abandonment rate, and service level.

Social media analytics is another valuable tool for measuring customer service performance. Businesses can monitor social media channels for customer feedback and complaints, and use this data to identify trends and patterns in their customer service performance.

Improving Customer Service Performance

Improving customer service performance requires a systematic approach that involves identifying areas for improvement, developing strategies to address these areas, and monitoring and measuring the results of these strategies.

One strategy for improving customer service performance is through employee training and development. By providing customer service representatives with the skills and knowledge they need to effectively handle customer inquiries and issues, businesses can improve their customer service performance and build customer loyalty.

Another strategy for improving customer service performance is through process improvement. By analyzing and streamlining their customer service processes, businesses can reduce wait times, eliminate bottlenecks, and improve overall efficiency.

Finally, businesses can use customer feedback to drive improvements in their customer service performance. By listening to their customers' feedback and addressing their concerns and complaints, businesses can build customer loyalty and improve their overall customer service performance.

Conclusion

Measuring and evaluating customer service performance is a critical component of a successful customer service strategy. By using customer service metrics, measuring customer service performance, and developing strategies to improve customer service, businesses can differentiate themselves from their competitors and build a loyal customer base.

The importance of measuring and evaluating customer service performance

Customer service is the cornerstone of any successful business. In today's competitive business environment, providing exceptional customer service is not only important but also essential for the long-term success of any organization. Customer service performance is a critical aspect of any business operation, and measuring and evaluating that performance is essential to ensure that the business is meeting its customer service goals.

The purpose of this chapter is to explore the importance of measuring and evaluating customer service performance, the various methods that can be used to measure and evaluate performance, and the benefits that businesses can gain from doing so. We will discuss how businesses can use this information to improve their customer service performance and ultimately achieve their long-term business goals.

Why Measure and Evaluate Customer Service Performance?

Measuring and evaluating customer service performance is essential for several reasons. Firstly, it provides businesses with insights into how well they are meeting the needs of their customers. By measuring and evaluating customer service performance, businesses can identify areas where they are performing well and areas where they need to improve.

Secondly, measuring and evaluating customer service performance is essential for benchmarking. Benchmarking allows businesses to compare their customer service performance to that of their competitors, enabling them to identify areas where they need to improve to remain competitive.

Thirdly, measuring and evaluating customer service performance is essential for accountability. It provides businesses with a means of tracking and evaluating the performance of their customer service teams, ensuring that they are meeting the needs of their customers.

Methods of Measuring and Evaluating Customer Service Performance

There are several methods that businesses can use to measure and evaluate customer service performance. These methods include:

Customer feedback surveys: This is one of the most common methods of measuring customer service performance. Customer feedback surveys allow businesses to gather information directly from their customers about their experiences with their products or services. Businesses can use this information to identify areas where they need to improve their customer service.

Mystery shopping: This is a method of measuring customer service performance by having individuals pose as customers to evaluate the quality of service they receive. Mystery shopping allows businesses to identify areas where they need to improve their customer service.

Net Promoter Score (NPS): This is a method of measuring customer loyalty by asking customers how likely they are to recommend the business to others. NPS provides businesses with insights into customer loyalty and satisfaction.

Customer retention rates: This is a measure of the percentage of customers who return to do business with the company. High customer retention rates indicate that a business is providing exceptional customer service.

Benefits of Measuring and Evaluating Customer Service Performance

There are several benefits that businesses can gain from measuring and evaluating customer service performance. These benefits include:

Improving customer satisfaction: Measuring and evaluating customer service performance enables businesses to identify areas where they need to improve their customer service. By addressing these areas, businesses can improve customer satisfaction and loyalty.

Increasing customer retention: Providing exceptional customer service can help businesses retain customers. Measuring and evaluating customer service performance can help businesses identify areas where they need to improve their customer service, ultimately leading to increased customer retention.

Gaining a competitive advantage: Measuring and evaluating customer service performance allows businesses to identify areas where they need to improve their customer service. By improving their customer service, businesses can gain a competitive advantage over their competitors.

Conclusion

In conclusion, measuring and evaluating customer service performance is essential for the long-term success of any business. By using methods such as customer feedback surveys, mystery shopping, NPS, and customer retention rates, businesses can gain insights into how well they are meeting the needs of their customers. Measuring and evaluating customer service performance enables businesses to identify areas where they need to improve their customer service, ultimately leading to increased customer satisfaction, retention, and a competitive advantage over their competitors.

Techniques for gathering and analyzing customer feedback and satisfaction data

In today's highly competitive marketplace, customer satisfaction is critical for business success. Companies that are able to measure and evaluate customer service performance are better equipped to identify opportunities for improvement and make informed decisions about how to allocate resources. Gathering and analyzing customer feedback and satisfaction data is an essential part of this process.

There are several techniques that companies can use to gather and analyze customer feedback and satisfaction data. In this section, we will discuss some of the most common methods, including surveys, focus groups, customer service metrics, and social media monitoring.

Surveys

Surveys are one of the most popular methods of gathering customer feedback and satisfaction data. They are relatively easy to administer and can provide a wealth of information about customer preferences, opinions, and behaviors. Surveys can be conducted in several ways, including online, by mail, or by phone.

Online surveys are the most common type of survey used today. They are convenient and cost-effective, and can be distributed quickly to a large audience. Online surveys can be customized to include a variety of questions, such as open-ended questions, multiple choice questions, and rating scales. They can also be targeted to specific customer segments or demographics, which allows businesses to obtain more focused feedback.

Mail and phone surveys are less common than online surveys, but can be useful in certain situations. Mail surveys are often used for customer satisfaction surveys or when a company needs to gather feedback from customers who may not have regular access to the internet. Phone surveys can be effective for gathering immediate feedback from customers who have recently interacted with a company.

Focus Groups

Focus groups are another popular method of gathering customer feedback and satisfaction data. They involve bringing together a small group of customers to discuss their experiences with a company's products or services. Focus groups are typically conducted in person, but can also be conducted online.

Focus groups are useful because they allow companies to obtain in-depth feedback from customers. Participants are encouraged to share their opinions and ideas, and can provide valuable insights into how a company can improve its products or services. Focus groups can also be used to test new products or services before they are released to the market.

Customer Service Metrics

Customer service metrics are quantitative measures that are used to evaluate customer service performance. They can provide valuable information about how well a company is meeting its customers' needs, and can be used to identify areas for improvement.

Some of the most common customer service metrics include:

First response time: the amount of time it takes for a customer service representative to respond to a customer's inquiry.
Average handle time: the amount of time it takes for a customer service representative to resolve a customer's issue.

Customer satisfaction score: a rating given by customers to indicate their level of satisfaction with a company's products or services.

Net promoter score: a rating given by customers to indicate how likely they are to recommend a company's products or services to others.

Social Media Monitoring

Social media monitoring involves tracking and analyzing customer conversations on social media platforms like Twitter, Facebook, and Instagram. Social media monitoring can provide valuable insights into how customers perceive a company's products or services, and can be used to identify potential issues or opportunities for improvement.

Social media monitoring can be a useful tool for businesses of all sizes. Small businesses can use social media monitoring to identify and respond to customer complaints or feedback, while larger businesses can use it to track sentiment over time and identify trends.

Conclusion

Gathering and analyzing customer feedback and satisfaction data is critical for businesses that want to improve their customer service performance. Surveys, focus groups, customer service metrics, and social media monitoring are all effective methods for obtaining customer feedback and satisfaction data. By analyzing this data, businesses can identify areas for improvement and make informed decisions about how to allocate resources.

Strategies for using performance metrics to drive continuous improvement

Measuring and evaluating customer service performance is an essential aspect of delivering high-quality customer service. However, merely collecting data on customer satisfaction and feedback is not enough. The true value of measuring and evaluating customer service performance lies in the ability to use this data to drive continuous improvement in the organization. In this section, we will discuss the strategies for using performance metrics to drive continuous improvement.

Set Measurable Goals
The first step in using performance metrics to drive continuous improvement is to set measurable goals. These goals should be specific, measurable, achievable, relevant, and time-bound (SMART). The organization's goals should align with its overall mission and vision and support the customer service strategy.

For example, if the goal is to improve customer satisfaction, the organization can set a goal to increase its Net Promoter Score (NPS) by a specific percentage over a particular period. By setting measurable goals, the organization can track progress and identify areas for improvement.

Focus on Key Performance Indicators (KPIs)

Key Performance Indicators (KPIs) are the metrics used to track progress toward achieving the organization's goals. KPIs can vary depending on the organization's goals, but they should focus on measuring customer satisfaction, efficiency, and effectiveness.

Some common KPIs for customer service include:

- ✧ Average response time
- ✧ First contact resolution rate
- ✧ Customer satisfaction score (CSAT)
- ✧ Net Promoter Score (NPS)
- ✧ Customer retention rate

By focusing on KPIs, the organization can identify areas for improvement and prioritize its efforts accordingly.

Analyze Data and Identify Trends

Once the organization has collected data on its KPIs, it is essential to analyze this data and identify trends. By analyzing the data, the organization can identify patterns and correlations that may not be immediately apparent. For example, the organization may discover that customer satisfaction is highest when customers interact with a specific customer service representative.

By identifying trends, the organization can make informed decisions about where to focus its improvement efforts.

Develop and Implement Action Plans

Based on the analysis of the data and identified trends, the organization can develop and implement action plans to address areas for improvement. These action plans should be specific, measurable, achievable, relevant, and time-bound (SMART).

For example, if the organization has identified that its first contact resolution rate is low, it can develop an action plan to improve training for customer service representatives, implement new tools to assist with issue resolution, and track progress toward the goal of increasing the first contact resolution rate.

Monitor Progress and Make Adjustments

Once the organization has implemented its action plans, it is essential to monitor progress toward achieving its goals and make adjustments as necessary. This monitoring should be ongoing, and the organization should regularly review its KPIs and adjust its strategies based on the data.

For example, if the organization has implemented a new training program for customer service representatives, it should regularly review its first contact resolution rate to determine if the training has been effective. If the rate has not improved, the organization may need to adjust the training program or implement additional measures to achieve its goal.

Conclusion

Using performance metrics to drive continuous improvement is essential for delivering high-quality customer service. By setting measurable goals, focusing on key performance indicators, analyzing data and identifying trends, developing and implementing action plans, and monitoring progress and making adjustments, organizations can improve their customer service performance continuously. These strategies allow organizations to stay competitive, meet customer expectations, and deliver an exceptional customer experience.

Exercise: Developing a plan for measuring and evaluating customer service performance

Measuring and evaluating customer service performance is essential for businesses to improve their customer experience and ensure customer satisfaction. In this exercise, you will develop a plan for measuring and evaluating customer service performance for a hypothetical business.

Step 1: Identify Your Business Goals

The first step in developing a plan for measuring and evaluating customer service performance is to identify your business goals. What are you trying to achieve with your customer service? Do you want to improve customer satisfaction, increase customer loyalty, or reduce customer complaints? Your goals should be specific, measurable, achievable, relevant, and time-bound (SMART).

Step 2: Identify Your Key Performance Indicators (KPIs)

Once you have identified your business goals, the next step is to identify your key performance indicators (KPIs). KPIs are metrics that you use to measure the performance of your customer service. They help you determine whether you are meeting your business goals and provide you with insight into how you can improve your customer service.

Some common KPIs for customer service include:

✧ Customer satisfaction score (CSAT): This measures how satisfied your customers are with your products or services. You can measure CSAT through surveys or feedback forms.

✧ Net Promoter Score (NPS): This measures the likelihood that your customers will recommend your products or services to others. You can measure NPS through surveys or feedback forms.

✧ First Contact Resolution (FCR): This measures the percentage of customer inquiries or complaints that are resolved during the first contact with a customer service representative.

✧ Average Handle Time (AHT): This measures the average time it takes for a customer service representative to handle a customer inquiry or complaint.

✧ Depending on your business goals, you may choose to track different KPIs. For example, if your goal is to reduce customer complaints, you may choose to focus on FCR and AHT.

Step 3: Determine Your Data Collection Methods

Once you have identified your KPIs, the next step is to determine your data collection methods. How will you collect data on your KPIs? Will you use surveys, feedback forms, or analytics tools?

If you are using surveys or feedback forms, you will need to determine the frequency and distribution of your surveys. For example, you may choose to send out surveys after each customer interaction or on a quarterly basis.

If you are using analytics tools, you will need to ensure that you have the necessary software and systems in place to collect and analyze data on your KPIs.

Step 4: Develop Your Reporting and Analysis Plan

Once you have collected your data, the next step is to develop your reporting and analysis plan. How will you analyze your data? Will you use dashboards or reports? Who will be responsible for analyzing the data and identifying areas for improvement?

Your reporting and analysis plan should provide you with actionable insights into how you can improve your customer service. For example, if you find that your CSAT score is low, you may need to improve your product quality or customer support.

Step 5: Implement Your Plan

The final step is to implement your plan. Ensure that you have the necessary resources and systems in place to collect and analyze data on your KPIs. Train your employees on your reporting and analysis plan and ensure that they understand their role in improving customer service.

Conclusion

Measuring and evaluating customer service performance is critical for businesses to improve their customer experience and ensure customer satisfaction. By identifying your business goals, selecting the right KPIs, and developing a plan for data collection and analysis, you can gain insights into how you can improve your customer service and drive continuous improvement.

CHAPTER 25: CREATING A CULTURE OF CONTINUOUS IMPROVEMENT IN CUSTOMER SERVICE

In today's highly competitive business world, creating a culture of continuous improvement in customer service is essential for any company that wants to succeed. By constantly striving to improve the customer experience, businesses can increase customer loyalty, improve customer retention rates, and ultimately, increase profitability.

Creating a culture of continuous improvement in customer service requires a proactive approach to customer service. It involves identifying areas of improvement, setting performance goals, measuring performance against those goals, and taking action to make necessary improvements.

This chapter will provide an overview of the key concepts involved in creating a culture of continuous improvement in customer service. We will explore the benefits of creating such a culture, the key steps involved in the process, and some best practices that companies can adopt to achieve success.

Benefits of Creating a Culture of Continuous Improvement in Customer Service

Creating a culture of continuous improvement in customer service offers numerous benefits for businesses. These benefits include:

Increased customer loyalty: When businesses consistently deliver exceptional customer service, customers are more likely to remain loyal to the company.

Improved customer retention rates: By providing exceptional customer service, businesses can reduce customer churn rates and retain more customers over time.

Increased profitability: Businesses that consistently provide excellent customer service are more likely to experience increased revenue and profits.

Improved employee engagement: Creating a culture of continuous improvement in customer service can also improve employee engagement, as employees are more likely to feel motivated and engaged when they see their efforts making a positive impact on the customer experience.

Key Steps in Creating a Culture of Continuous Improvement in Customer Service

Creating a culture of continuous improvement in customer service involves several key steps. These steps include:

Setting performance goals: The first step in creating a culture of continuous improvement in customer service is to set performance goals. These goals should be specific, measurable, achievable, relevant, and time-bound (SMART).

Measuring performance: Once performance goals have been established, the next step is to measure performance against those goals. This can be done through customer feedback surveys, customer satisfaction scores, or other metrics.

Identifying areas for improvement: Based on the results of performance measurements, businesses can identify areas for improvement. These areas may include specific customer touchpoints, employee training needs, or internal processes.

Taking action: Once areas for improvement have been identified, the next step is to take action to make necessary improvements. This may involve implementing new processes or procedures, providing additional employee training, or making changes to the customer experience.

Best Practices for Creating a Culture of Continuous Improvement in Customer Service

To successfully create a culture of continuous improvement in customer service, companies should adopt some best practices. These include:

Communicating performance goals: It is important to communicate performance goals to all employees and stakeholders to ensure that everyone is working toward the same objectives.

Encouraging employee feedback: Employees should be encouraged to provide feedback on the customer experience and suggest areas for improvement.

Providing regular training: Regular training should be provided to employees to ensure that they have the necessary skills and knowledge to deliver exceptional customer service.

Celebrating successes: When performance goals are achieved, it is important to celebrate successes and recognize employees who have contributed to the achievement.

Conclusion

Creating a culture of continuous improvement in customer service is essential for businesses that want to succeed in today's competitive market. By setting performance goals, measuring performance, identifying areas for improvement, and taking action, companies can improve the customer experience and increase profitability. By adopting best practices such as communicating performance goals, encouraging employee feedback, providing regular training, and celebrating successes, companies can create a culture of continuous improvement in customer service that drives success and growth.

The role of continuous improvement in customer service excellence

In today's business world, customer service has become a vital component of any organization's success. Companies that focus on creating a culture of continuous improvement in customer service are more likely to achieve high levels of customer satisfaction and loyalty, which, in turn, can lead to increased revenue and profitability. Continuous improvement in customer service involves a systematic approach to identifying, analyzing, and improving customer service processes and practices.

This chapter will explore the role of continuous improvement in customer service excellence. We will examine the benefits of continuous improvement, the key principles and tools of continuous improvement, and the steps that organizations can take to create a culture of continuous improvement in customer service.

Benefits of Continuous Improvement:

Continuous improvement in customer service can provide numerous benefits for organizations. Some of the key benefits include:

Increased customer satisfaction: By continuously improving customer service processes and practices, organizations can identify and address areas where they are falling short of customer expectations. This can lead to increased customer satisfaction and loyalty.

Improved efficiency and productivity: By identifying and eliminating waste and inefficiencies in customer service processes, organizations can improve their efficiency and productivity, which can result in cost savings.

Increased revenue and profitability: By providing excellent customer service, organizations can differentiate themselves from their competitors and attract more customers. This can lead to increased revenue and profitability.

Improved employee engagement and morale: By involving employees in the continuous improvement process, organizations can improve employee engagement and morale, which can lead to higher levels of job satisfaction and lower turnover rates.

Key Principles and Tools of Continuous Improvement:

There are several key principles and tools that organizations can use to achieve continuous improvement in customer service. Some of the key principles and tools include:

Customer focus: Continuous improvement in customer service starts with a focus on the customer. Organizations should be dedicated to understanding the needs and expectations of their customers and delivering service that exceeds those expectations.

Process orientation: Continuous improvement requires a process-oriented approach. Organizations must understand the customer service processes that are in place and identify areas where improvements can be made.

Data-driven decision-making: To achieve continuous improvement, organizations must use data to make informed decisions. This requires collecting and analyzing customer feedback, performance metrics, and other data points to identify areas for improvement.

Employee involvement: Continuous improvement requires the involvement of all employees. Organizations must engage employees at all levels in the continuous improvement process and provide them with the tools and resources they need to contribute to the process.

Steps for Creating a Culture of Continuous Improvement in Customer Service:

Creating a culture of continuous improvement in customer service requires a deliberate and sustained effort. The following steps can help organizations create a culture of continuous improvement in customer service:

Define the customer service vision: The first step in creating a culture of continuous improvement in customer service is to define the customer service vision. This should include a clear understanding of the organization's values, goals, and objectives related to customer service.

Collect and analyze customer feedback: Organizations must collect and analyze customer feedback to identify areas where improvements can be made. This can include surveys, focus groups, social media monitoring, and other feedback mechanisms.

Develop and implement improvement plans: Based on the feedback collected, organizations should develop and implement improvement plans. This can include process improvements, training programs, and other initiatives to address areas for improvement.

Monitor and measure progress: Organizations must monitor and measure progress towards their customer service goals. This requires tracking performance metrics, analyzing data, and making adjustments as needed.

Recognizing and rewarding success is an essential part of any continuous improvement program. When employees know that their hard work is appreciated and valued, they are more likely to stay motivated and engaged in the process.

There are several ways to recognize and reward success in the context of customer service excellence. One effective strategy is to provide incentives and bonuses for employees who meet or exceed performance targets. For example, a call center might offer bonuses to agents who achieve high customer satisfaction ratings or resolve a high percentage of calls on the first attempt.

Another effective strategy is to provide regular feedback and coaching to employees. This can help to identify areas where improvement is needed and provide guidance on how to improve. When employees see that their efforts are being recognized and that they are receiving constructive feedback, they are more likely to stay engaged in the continuous improvement process.

In addition to incentives and coaching, organizations can also recognize success through public recognition and celebration. For example, a retail store might celebrate a team's achievement of high customer satisfaction ratings by holding a company-wide celebration or giving the team a public shout-out in a company newsletter.

It is also important to recognize the contributions of employees who are not directly involved in customer service. For example, a company might recognize the contributions of a software development team that creates tools and systems to support customer service excellence. By recognizing the contributions of all employees, organizations can create a culture of continuous improvement that is embraced by everyone.

In conclusion, recognizing and rewarding success is an essential part of the continuous improvement process. By providing incentives, coaching, feedback, public recognition, and celebration, organizations can motivate employees to stay engaged in the process and help to achieve customer service excellence.

Techniques for identifying areas for improvement and implementing change

Identifying areas for improvement and implementing change is an essential part of the continuous improvement process in customer service. It requires a systematic approach that involves identifying areas of weakness, developing solutions, and implementing changes. In this section, we will discuss some techniques for identifying areas for improvement and implementing change.

Customer feedback: One of the best ways to identify areas for improvement in customer service is to ask customers for feedback. This can be done through surveys, focus groups, or one-on-one interviews. Customer feedback can provide valuable insights into areas of weakness and help organizations develop targeted solutions to address them.

For example, a hotel might survey its guests to determine their level of satisfaction with the check-in process. If the survey results reveal that many guests are dissatisfied with the time it takes to check-in, the hotel can develop solutions such as adding more check-in staff, streamlining the check-in process, or introducing self-check-in kiosks.

Employee feedback: Another valuable source of information for identifying areas for improvement is employee feedback. Employees who work in customer service roles can provide valuable insights into the customer experience and areas where improvements can be made. This feedback can be obtained through regular meetings, surveys, or suggestion boxes.

For example, a call center might hold regular meetings with its customer service representatives to discuss customer feedback and areas for improvement. The representatives might suggest changes such as improving the call routing system or providing additional training on handling difficult customers.

Process mapping: Process mapping is a technique that involves visually representing a process to identify areas for improvement. This can be done by creating a flowchart that shows each step of the process and the inputs and outputs at each step. Process mapping can help organizations identify areas where processes are inefficient or where there are bottlenecks that slow down the process.

For example, a retail store might create a process map of its checkout process to identify areas where customers experience long wait times. The process map might reveal that the bottleneck is caused by the need for manual price checks or an outdated point-of-sale system. This information can be used to develop solutions such as upgrading the point-of-sale system or providing additional training to staff to eliminate the need for manual price checks.

Benchmarking: Benchmarking is a technique that involves comparing an organization's performance to that of its peers in the industry. This can be done by gathering data on key performance metrics such as customer satisfaction, response time, and first-call resolution rate. Benchmarking can help organizations identify areas where they are lagging behind their competitors and develop strategies to catch up.

For example, a bank might benchmark its customer satisfaction scores against those of other banks in the region. If the bank's scores are lower than its competitors, it can develop strategies such as improving the onboarding process for new customers or introducing new products and services to improve customer satisfaction.

Root cause analysis: Root cause analysis is a technique that involves identifying the underlying cause of a problem or issue. This can be done by asking "why" questions to get to the root cause of the issue. Root cause analysis can help organizations identify the underlying cause of a problem and develop targeted solutions to address it.

For example, a restaurant might use root cause analysis to identify the cause of a high rate of customer complaints about cold food. The restaurant might ask "why" questions such as "Why is the food cold?" and "Why are the plates not heated?" The root cause might be that the kitchen does not have a system for heating plates before serving food. The restaurant can then develop a solution such as introducing a plate-warming system to address the root cause of the problem.

Exercise:

Choose a business in your local area and conduct a customer feedback survey to identify areas for improvement in customer service. Once you have collected the data, use techniques such as root cause analysis to identify the underlying causes of any issues identified by the customers. Then, develop an action plan for implementing changes to address these issues.

To begin, choose a business in your local area that you would like to focus on. This could be a restaurant, retail store, bank, or any other type of business that provides customer service. Next, create a customer feedback survey to gather information about customers' experiences with the business. The survey should include questions about the quality of service, the friendliness of staff, the speed of service, and any other factors that are important to customers.

Once you have collected the data from the survey, analyze it to identify any areas where the business is falling short of customer expectations. Use techniques such as root cause analysis to identify the underlying causes of any issues that have been identified. For example, if customers have complained about long wait times, you might ask "Why are customers waiting so long?" and "Why is the staff not able to serve customers more quickly?" The root cause might be that there are not enough staff members working during peak hours.

Once you have identified the underlying causes of any issues, develop an action plan for addressing them. This might involve hiring additional staff, changing procedures to improve efficiency, or providing additional training to employees to improve their customer service skills. Be sure to set specific goals and timelines for implementing the changes and monitoring progress.

In addition to implementing changes to address specific issues, it is also important to establish a culture of continuous improvement within the organization. Encourage employees to provide feedback on a regular basis and to share ideas for improving customer service. Recognize and reward employees who contribute to the process and help to achieve customer service excellence.

Exercise questions:

What is the first step in identifying areas for improvement in customer service?

What is root cause analysis and how can it be used to identify underlying causes of customer service issues?

What are some techniques for addressing customer service issues identified through a feedback survey?

How can organizations establish a culture of continuous improvement in customer service?

The benefits of a customer-centric culture of continuous improvement

A customer-centric culture of continuous improvement offers many benefits to organizations, including increased customer loyalty, higher levels of employee engagement, improved business performance, and increased profitability.

One of the main benefits of a customer-centric culture is increased customer loyalty. When organizations prioritize the needs and wants of their customers and continually work to improve the customer experience, customers are more likely to remain loyal to the company. This can lead to repeat business and positive word-of-mouth referrals, which can ultimately drive revenue growth.

A customer-centric culture can also lead to higher levels of employee engagement. When employees feel empowered to make decisions that positively impact the customer experience, they are more likely to feel invested in the success of the organization. This can lead to increased motivation, job satisfaction, and productivity, which can ultimately improve business performance.

In addition, a customer-centric culture can help organizations improve their business performance by identifying areas for improvement and implementing changes to address customer needs and wants. This can lead to increased efficiency, streamlined processes, and cost savings, which can ultimately improve profitability.

Overall, a customer-centric culture of continuous improvement can help organizations build stronger relationships with their customers, increase employee engagement, improve business performance, and ultimately achieve long-term success.

Exercise: Developing a plan for implementing a continuous improvement program in customer service

A continuous improvement program is an essential element for achieving customer service excellence. Developing a plan for implementing such a program requires careful planning, execution, and evaluation. This exercise will guide you through the steps involved in creating a comprehensive continuous improvement plan for customer service.

Step 1: Identify the areas for improvement

The first step in developing a continuous improvement plan is to identify the areas that need improvement. This can be done through customer feedback surveys, employee feedback, and other forms of data collection. Analyze the data to identify the most significant areas for improvement. Common areas for improvement include:

- ✧ Response time to customer inquiries
- ✧ Accuracy of information provided to customers
- ✧ Consistency in service delivery
- ✧ Customer satisfaction levels
- ✧ Employee satisfaction levels

Step 2: Establish goals and objectives

Once you have identified the areas for improvement, the next step is to establish goals and objectives for the continuous improvement program. These goals and objectives should be specific, measurable, achievable, relevant, and time-bound (SMART). For example, a goal could be to reduce response time to customer inquiries from 24 hours to 12 hours within six months.

Step 3: Develop a plan of action

The next step is to develop a plan of action for achieving the established goals and objectives. The plan of action should outline the steps that need to be taken, who is responsible for each step, and the timeline for completion. The plan of action should also include a budget for any necessary resources, such as training or technology upgrades.

Step 4: Implement the plan

With the plan of action in place, it's time to put it into action. This involves communicating the plan to all employees, providing any necessary training, and implementing any changes to processes or procedures. The implementation phase should be carefully monitored to ensure that the plan is being followed and that progress is being made towards the established goals and objectives.

Step 5: Monitor and evaluate progress

The final step in implementing a continuous improvement program is to monitor and evaluate progress towards the established goals and objectives. This involves regularly collecting and analyzing data to track progress and make any necessary adjustments to the plan of action. Feedback from employees and customers should also be collected and incorporated into the evaluation process.

Conclusion:

Developing a plan for implementing a continuous improvement program in customer service requires careful planning, execution, and evaluation. By following the steps outlined above, you can create a comprehensive plan that will help you identify areas for improvement, establish goals and objectives, develop a plan of action, implement the plan, and monitor and evaluate progress towards achieving customer service excellence. Continuous improvement is an ongoing process, and it requires a commitment from all employees to ensure that the program is successful. By creating a customer-centric culture of continuous improvement, you can ensure that your organization is always striving to provide the best possible customer service.

APPENDIX/GLOSSARY:

Key customer service terms and definitions

A/B testing: A method used in marketing and website design to compare two versions of a webpage, email, or other marketing material to determine which one performs better. The two versions are randomly shown to different groups of people, and the results are analyzed to determine which version leads to better engagement, conversion, or other desired outcomes.

Call center: A call center is a centralized facility or department within an organization that is responsible for receiving and transmitting large volumes of telephone-based inquiries, requests, and support calls.

Chatbots: Computer programs designed to simulate conversation with human users, often used in customer service to answer basic questions or provide assistance. Chatbots use natural language processing and artificial intelligence to understand user input and provide relevant responses. They can be integrated into messaging platforms, websites, and mobile apps.

Continuous improvement: Continuous improvement is an ongoing effort to improve products, services, and processes through incremental and breakthrough improvements. It involves a systematic approach to identifying and eliminating waste, reducing defects, improving efficiency, and enhancing quality.

CRM: Customer relationship management (CRM) is a strategy for managing interactions with customers and potential customers. It involves the use of technology to organize, automate, and synchronize sales, marketing, customer service, and technical support processes.

Customer-centric culture: A customer-centric culture is a business culture that places a strong emphasis on meeting the needs and expectations of customers. It involves prioritizing customer satisfaction and creating a customer-focused approach throughout the organization, from front-line employees to senior management. In a customer-centric culture, customer feedback is valued and used to drive continuous improvement.

Customer effort score (CES): A metric used to measure the ease of a customer's experience with a company's product or service. CES is typically measured using a survey question that asks customers how easy or difficult it was to complete a specific task or interact with a company's customer service team.

Customer experience (CX): The overall perception a customer has of a company based on all interactions with the brand throughout the customer journey. CX encompasses every touchpoint with the company, from the initial marketing message to the after-sales support.

Customer journey mapping: The process of visualizing and analyzing all of the touchpoints a customer has with a company, from initial awareness to post-purchase support. The goal of customer journey mapping is to identify pain points and opportunities for improvement in the customer experience.

Customer lifetime value (CLV): The estimated monetary value a customer brings to a company over the duration of their relationship with the business. CLV takes into account the customer's purchase history, the frequency of purchases, and the likelihood of future purchases.

Customer segmentation: The process of dividing customers into smaller groups based on shared characteristics such as demographics, behaviors, and preferences. This enables companies to tailor their products, services, and marketing messages to specific customer segments.

Digital customer service: The use of digital channels such as chat, email, social media, and self-service portals to provide customer support. Digital customer service allows customers to interact with a company on their own terms, at their own pace, and via their preferred communication channel.

Emotional intelligence: The ability to recognize and manage one's own emotions, as well as the emotions of others. In the context of customer service, emotional intelligence is essential for understanding and empathizing with customers, defusing difficult situations, and building strong relationships.

Empathy: The ability to understand and share the feelings of another person. In customer service, empathy is an important skill for employees to possess as it allows them to relate to and address the concerns of customers in a compassionate and understanding way.

Feedback: Information provided by customers about their experience with a product or service. Feedback can be positive or negative, and it is used by businesses to improve their offerings and customer service.

Gamification: Gamification is the process of applying game mechanics and design techniques to engage and motivate people to achieve their goals. In the context of customer service, gamification can be used to motivate employees to provide better customer service by turning it into a game with rewards and recognition for achieving specific goals.

Inbound marketing: Inbound marketing is a marketing strategy that focuses on attracting customers by providing them with valuable content and information that helps solve their problems or meet their needs. This can include blog posts, social media content, videos, and other forms of content that are designed to educate and inform customers.

Key driver analysis: Key driver analysis is a statistical technique used to identify the most important factors that influence a particular outcome or behavior. In the context of customer service, key driver analysis can be used to identify the most important factors that contribute to customer satisfaction or dissatisfaction, and to prioritize efforts to improve the customer experience based on those factors.

Key Performance Indicators (KPIs): A set of measurable values used by businesses to assess their progress toward achieving specific goals. In customer service, KPIs might include metrics such as customer satisfaction ratings, response time to inquiries, and resolution time for customer complaints.

Loyalty: The degree to which a customer continues to do business with a particular company or brand. Loyal customers are more likely to make repeat purchases and recommend the company to others.

Multichannel communication: Multichannel communication refers to a business practice that involves interacting with customers through multiple channels, such as email, phone, chat, social media, and in-person. The goal of multichannel communication is to provide customers with multiple ways to engage with a business, which can improve customer satisfaction and loyalty. This approach allows customers to choose the communication method that is most convenient and effective for them, increasing the chances of successful communication and a positive customer experience. Multichannel communication can also help businesses to expand their reach and improve their brand image by being accessible through a variety of channels.

Net Promoter Score (NPS): A metric used by businesses to measure customer satisfaction and loyalty. Customers are asked to rate the likelihood that they would recommend a company or product to others on a scale of 0-10. The scores are then divided into three categories: Promoters (9-10), Passives (7-8), and Detractors (0-6). The NPS is calculated by subtracting the percentage of Detractors from the percentage of Promoters. A high NPS is generally considered an indicator of customer satisfaction and loyalty.

Root cause analysis: A problem-solving method used to identify the underlying cause or causes of an issue in order to prevent it from recurring. This technique involves asking a series of "why" questions to uncover the root cause of a problem.

Service recovery: The process of resolving a customer's complaint or issue to their satisfaction. Service recovery is important for retaining customers and maintaining their loyalty even when things go wrong.

Social media customer service: The process of providing customer support and resolving issues through social media channels, such as Facebook, Twitter, Instagram, and LinkedIn.

Surveys: A research method used to gather information from a sample of people about their opinions, attitudes, experiences, and satisfaction levels. Surveys can be conducted through various channels such as online, phone, mail, or in-person.

Training: A process of teaching and developing employees' skills, knowledge, and attitudes to improve their job performance and productivity. In customer service, training can help employees develop key skills such as empathy, communication, problem-solving, and conflict resolution.

User experience (UX): The overall experience of a customer while interacting with a company's products or services, including the ease of use, design, functionality, and accessibility.

Virtual assistants: AI-powered chatbots or voice-activated assistants that provide customer support and assistance through digital channels, such as websites, mobile apps, and messaging platforms.

Voice of customer (VOC): A term used to describe the feedback, opinions, and preferences of customers about a product or service. Collecting and analyzing the VOC can help organizations understand their customers' needs and expectations and improve their customer experience accordingly.

Website optimization: The process of improving the performance of a website, including its speed, functionality, user experience, and search engine visibility. It involves techniques such as A/B testing, usability testing, and search engine optimization (SEO).

Additional resources for further learning and development in customer service

Customer Service Training Videos: Many online platforms offer video courses that teach customer service skills, such as communication, problem-solving, and conflict resolution. Some popular platforms include LinkedIn Learning, Udemy, and Skillshare.

Customer Service Books: There are numerous books on customer service that can help you improve your skills and knowledge. Some popular titles include "Delivering Happiness" by Tony Hsieh, "The Effortless Experience" by Matthew Dixon, and "Be Our Guest" by the Disney Institute.

Customer Service Conferences: Attending customer service conferences is a great way to learn from industry experts, network with other professionals, and stay up-to-date on the latest trends and best practices. Some popular conferences include the Customer Service Summit, ICMI Contact Center Expo, and Customer Contact Week.

Industry Associations: Joining industry associations such as the International Customer Service Association (ICSA) and the Customer Experience Professionals Association (CXPA) can provide you with access to resources, training, and networking opportunities.

Online Communities: Joining online customer service communities can provide you with access to valuable information and insights from other professionals in the field. Some popular communities include the Customer Service Group on LinkedIn and the Customer Service subreddit on Reddit.

Customer Service Certifications: Earning a customer service certification can demonstrate your expertise and dedication to the field. Some popular certifications include the Certified Customer Service Professional (CCSP) from the National Customer Service Association (NCSA) and the Certified Customer Experience Professional (CCXP) from the CXPA.